Testimon

What Tim has pulled together is a workbook for young players, coaches and parents, meant to be used as a collaborative effort. If you want to help your son or daughter improve in the game and come to understand the requirements for excellence, here is your road map. You will find that these lessons apply in all areas of your lives.

~ **Dom Starsia**, Former head coach of the University of Virginia men's lacrosse program, with whom he won four NCAA national championships. Previously, he served as the head coach of the Brown University lacrosse team where he was twice awarded the F. Morris Touchstone Award as the NCAA Division I lacrosse coach of the year. Starsia was inducted into the National Lacrosse Hall of Fame in 2008. Author of *I Hope You Will Be Very Happy: Leadership Lessons From a Lifetime in Lacrosse*

Coach McDermott helped guide my son and his teammates on the University of Utah Club lacrosse team into a top 20 Division 1 national contender. He seemed to develop a personal relationship with each player and hold them accountable to a high standard while encouraging them with constant enthusiasm and energy to be the best they can be. I would recommend him to mentor anyone who is focused on becoming their very best!

~ **David Neeleman**, Founder of five commercial airlines: JetBlue Airways, Breeze Airways, Azul Brazilian Airlines, Morris Air, and WestJet, as well as a co-owner of the European airline, TAP Air Portugal

Coach McDermott's book, ***The Dojo Decision****, is a must-read for sports coaches, athletes, and their families who want to raise their stakes and become Unstoppable. Through his approach, you will learn how to enhance your discipline, develop grit and resilience, and foster unstoppable leadership for yourself and others. Tim's dedication to mentoring young athletes is truly inspiring.*

~ **Alden Mills**, Keynote Speaker and Author of *Be Unstoppable, Unstoppable Teams,* and *Unstoppable Mindset*

Few books achieve the balance of engaging a younger audience while delivering hard-hitting, best-in-world practitioner and research-backed performance concepts like ***The Dojo Decision*** *by Coach Tim McDermott. This book hits the mark perfectly. As a parent and a performance leader, I was impressed with the content. However, reading it with my 8th-grade lacrosse goalie, who has big aspirations, truly highlighted the power of* ***The Dojo Decision****. Our daughter was captivated by how the book was written, making her feel like the main character. It was incredible to have father-daughter athlete time to learn and reflect together. The content is exceptional, and the time spent with my daughter, watching her enjoy and implement the ideas, was a game-changer. She now does her 15 pushups every morning, inspired by the book's practical advice.* ***The Dojo Decision*** *is not just a book; it's a shared journey toward excellence.*

~ **Hoby Darling**, Co-Founder of Liminal Collective,
Human Performance Leader, former Nike Executive,
former CEO Skullcandy, former Head of Logitech
Sports and Human Performance, and Parent Lacrosse Coach

Parents always ask me, "What does my son need to do to get recruited?" My answer is always obvious... "Your son needs to improve his athleticism, stick skills, and lacrosse IQ... AND to do this he needs to show up to practice each day with more confidence, resilience, and focus." Coach McDermott's ***Dojo Decision*** *shares an easy to implement, actionable plan to reinforce these principles that your son needs to practice on the field (life-lesson that you're already preaching).* ***The Dojo Decision*** *is the answer for athletes who want to practice and improve their mental game on and off the field.*

~ **Chris Rotelli**, Founder/Director of ADVNC Lacrosse.
3X NCAA All American, 2X First team All American,
USILA Midfielder of the Year, 4X MLL All Star, 3X ALL ACC,
ACC Player of the Year, and a 3X High School All American.
Chris led the University of Virginia to the 2003 Championship,
and was honored as the ACC Male Athlete of the Year, and winner
of the Tewaaraton Award, given to the nations most outstanding player

I wish I could go back in time and read this book when I was younger! The lessons and work ethic inside these pages make it invaluable for any young player, and I'll be recommending it to every single player I coach in the future. Many of us have big goals in life, but few of us know what it takes to actually achieve them. This book will provide you with the process you need!

~ **Matt Bocklet**, 3x MLL Champion with Denver Outlaws,
NCAA Champion at Johns Hopkins,
Colorado State Champion Head Coach
at Cherry Creek High School, Director Team 91 Colorado

This book can serve as an incredible guideline for pursuing and achieving your life goals. I would have personally benefited greatly from understanding these messages as a student-athlete, but I now put these teachings into practice as a college coach. It is a must read and can be applied to any type of work!

~ **Drew McMinn**, Head Coach,
University of Utah Lacrosse (2022-present),
2x Atlantic Sun Coach of the Year,
3x Atlantic Sun Regular Season Champion,
Robert Morris University Lacrosse Coach (2005-2021)

I've had the privilege to witness Coach McDermott's work firsthand. Tim's commitment to helping the athletes we coached together find their best versions was unmatched. ***The Dojo Decision*** *is a great tool for all athletes. If they want success/ excellence on the lacrosse field, they must strive for it in all facets of life—classrooms, relationships, weight room, etc.*

This peak performance program provides the secret playbook to help players at any level create a daily process and follow through. I've shared these lessons with my own kids and athletes, ranging from youth leagues to professionals. The Dojo Decision will inspire you to step out of your comfort zones and into excellence. I highly recommend this book to everyone who wants to train and become the best version they can be!"

~ **Brian Holman**, Head Coach, Boston Cannons,
2023 PLL Coach of the Year,
Former University of Utah Head Coach (2017-2021),
University of North Carolina Assistant Coach (2009-2016),
3x All American at Johns Hopkins

I don't know what you said to my son last night, but you lit a FIRE! The kid was up early this morning, drank water with lemon, took a cold shower, did wall ball and a 15-minute stretch session. Incredible! I love that you're reading this with the team. He's so pumped for the season!

~ **Parent** (After her son read a chapter of *The Dojo Decision* with his team over Zoom)

This book is truly amazing. It reminds me of what the most inspiring coaches preach. ***The Dojo Decision*** *will definitely help kids (and even adults) who are looking to improve themselves.*

Journaling and committing to an identity with my accountability buddy has shaped who I am and what I have achieved. I still journal every night, a habit that has affected my life more than I can express.

~ **Junior in High School** (Originally attended the course as a 7th grader, now reading it as an accomplished mentor to his own 7th graders seeking to achieve what he's achieved)

THE DOJO DECISION

LESSONS IN LACROSSE AND LIFE

By Tim McDermott

ISBN (hardcover): 979-8-9905685-0-1
ISBN (paperback): 979-8-9905685-1-8

Journal illustrations by Nada Mamdouh (dew).

Publisher of Record: Riveting Dreams Publishing, BookLayoutPro.com

Do·jo (dōjō), *n.* "The place of the way," It is an honored place where students and masters come together for deliberate practice to develop their skills. *Origins*: Japanese martial arts.

Your Dojo Decision is your decision to train with the focus, confidence, grit, and joy necessary to unleash your potential and master your craft. It's choosing a positive attitude when you're tired, overwhelmed, or overmatched. You have the opportunity to recommit to this decision daily, performing as the best version of yourself, every single moment!

This book will help you learn how to commit to excellence, improve your skills, and enjoy the journey as you strive to achieve your goals. You will learn the habits and routines necessary to win in your athletic pursuits, relationships, and life!

Dedication

To all the coaches, mentors, family, and friends I've been blessed to have in my life. This book is designed to provide similar support to those finding their way through their transformative years.

In particular I'd like to recognize Coach Richie Moran, who selflessly volunteered his time to help me—a total stranger, a young insecure kid—learn the importance of prioritizing the development of my confidence, resilience, focus, and sheer love of training.

In addition, the following coaches have also provided ample opportunities for me to learn many important lessons while playing on their team or coaching beside them:

Tom Cottrell, Nick Patriarco, Steve Hoffman, Matt Cutia, Dan Zech, Rich Cecconi, Dave Basile, Jake Coon, Jake Plunket, Jim Luchsinger, Rich Barnes, Geoff Sorenson, Mark Ferritto, Troy Humphrey, Jim Lyons, Charley Toomey, Steve Vaikness, Matt Dwan, Dan Chemotti, Steve Beville, Dom Starsia, Marc Van Arsdale, John Walker, Joe Starsia, Brian Holman, Adam Ghitelman, Marcus Holman, Will Manny, Parker Teagle, Drew McMinn, Sean Doyle and Jimmy Perkins.

Also, my Park City morning workout crew challenges me to recommit and strive to be my best every day. Thank you Hoby, Jeff, ES, Mike, Luke, PD, Huff, Brian, Josh, Mac, Doug and everyone else who wakes up each morning eager to attack the day!

And of course ... Jen.

Special Thanks

Shout out to **Brian Johnson** and the **Heroic Community** for helping me learn more wisdom in less time. Brian's work inspired me to create this training program, and will help you make your *Dojo Decision* and build your *Black Belt* Mentality.

Please check out his book, ***Areté***, and be sure to download his ***Heroic App*** to practice the lessons you will learn in this book!

You can visit DojoDecision.com or use his *Heroic App* to search any keyword within this text to view his +1 videos that explain the origins of the referenced idea. Brian will help you become a warrior of your mind, not just a librarian of the wisdom we will teach you on your *Hero's Journey!*[1] *(Explore his content now! Scan the QR code below or use the Heroic app to search: 'Librarian,' 'Warrior,' or 'Hero's Journey').*

Also, special thanks to **Alden Mills**, and his framework shared in his books, *Unstoppable Teams, Be Unstoppable, and Unstoppable Mindset*. The second half of this book is based on Alden's team-building C.A.R.E. principles. You can learn more about Alden's services and purchase his books at www.alden-mills.com.

Lastly, I would like to thank all the authors and coaches I reference in this book. I'm truly standing on the shoulders of experts here. Through this peak-performance program, I have attempted to arrange and remix their wisdom in an entertaining story to introduce you to their life-changing ideas. Please consider buying their original texts to gain an even greater understanding of their ideas (and support their work!).

1 +1: Warriors vs. Librarians | The Philosophy of Cognitive Behavioral Therapy by Donald Robertson

Contents

Introduction

Why Should You Read This Book?

Why do you play your sport?

(Why do you do *anything*?)

It's shocking, but most athletes never ask themselves questions like these. Asking and understanding *why* you do something is potentially the most critical question you can ask yourself, because it directly impacts your most valuable resource – your time![2]

You see, the thing about time is:

- You spend it daily–all 1,440 minutes.
- You possess infinite choices about how and where to spend it.
- Once you spend it, it's gone. *Forever.*
- You should spend it wisely!

Therefore, if you choose to spend your time playing a sport, it's vitally important to ask yourself why you play. In doing so, you will appreciate and relish every moment you spend training, recognizing the value it offers you in return.

Listed below are the top two reasons athletes have for playing their sport:

1. To get recruited to play their sport in college.
2. To have fun and enjoy time practicing with their friends.

2 +1: Time Management Drucker Style | The Effective Executive by Peter F. Drucker

Regardless of your WHY, this book is designed for *you*!

Shared within each chapter is an actionable, step-by-step game plan which will help you enjoy the process of achieving your athletic goals. You will learn the following skills to make you feel as if you have *superpowers* on the field:

- How to have more fun playing the sport you love.
- How to develop your ability to summon your confidence—in the exact moment you need it most.
- How to improve your focus. (*Your ability to put your mind where you want, when you want, for as long as you want!)*
- How to build your inner grit (*stick-to-it-ness!*)
- How to both lead and improve your relationships with your teammates.

Elite athletes, Hall of Fame coaches, and great books throughout history all agree on how to win and develop these skills. The key remains consistent: it's all in your hands. *You* must do the work! There are no shortcuts, and nobody can do it for you! The work is rewarding, and it begins with training your mind.

You heard me. Your *mind* is the ultimate key to your athletic success. If you want to be an elite athlete, you must learn to train your mind just as hard as you train your body. (Sometimes harder!) We all know what it's like to operate with an untrained mind. An untrained mind floods you with self-doubt, distracts you from your goals, and tempts you to throw in the towel when you know you should fight on. It's also what ultimately prevents you from being happy, even when things seem almost as good as they can get.[3]

The Dojo Decision packages the lessons taught by sports psychology experts alongside the wisdom gained from reading classic books into a series of fun, inspiring conversations between Jordan, an aspiring athlete, and his sensei-mentor, Coach Brian, teaching him lessons on how to win in lacrosse—*and in life.*

3 PN: +1: Cultivating Your Choice | Waking Up by Sam Harris

Each chapter begins in the present day with Jordan practicing the lessons he has learned from Coach Brian to lead his team in the NCAA National Championship Game. The chapter then jumps back to a time in Jordan's lacrosse journey where Coach Brian originally teaches Jordan the habits and routines necessary to:

1. Get recruited to his dream school
2. Use these same lessons to lead his team to a National Championship
3. Use his Black Belt Mentality to *turn pro* and achieve his goals in his relationships and in his work. *(Turn pro, meaning stop training like an amateur!)*

How to Read This Book

Begin with the End in Mind

Want to see the big picture and start practicing your Black Belt Mentality **now**? Stephen Covey, in *The 7 Habits of Highly Effective People*, tells us that successful people, "Begin with the end in mind." They know *exactly* what they want to create well before they manifest it in reality. Consider jumping to the appendix where I share an overview of how to quickly remind yourself of all the lessons you've learned in this book!

How to Read This Book and Put Everything You Learn into Action

1. **Choose a mentor** or a friend to read this book with (*someone who cares about your success*). The two of you will hold each other accountable in practicing the principles you'll learn in this book. We all need a teammate or a coach if we want to reach our full potential!

2. **Read with the intention to train your focus muscles** (Just like training your muscles at the gym!). When reading, it may help to mentally replace Jordan's name with your own, and Coach Brian's with the name of your own mentor. Read this book like you're training to be a Black Belt at learning! Exert the same enthusiasm you bring when you train to improve your lacrosse skills. You'll learn all about the mindset of a Black Belt in the coming chapters!

   Don't allow yourself to just go through the motions. Invest in the experience. Take notes, engage with the author, and write down any questions that pop up. Speak up often and write your thoughts, even when you disagree. (Especially if you disagree!) Question and test everything!

3. **Read one chapter at a time and prepare to take action.** Don't move forward to the next chapter until you have brainstormed the habits you plan to practice. This will ensure you're actively living out the lessons you learn.

   After each chapter, take some time to journal. Believe it or not, magic happens when you put pen to paper! It's truly powerful.

4. **Practice! Practice! Practice!** Look for opportunities to apply what you learn in your daily routines. You won't see results unless you practice these new habits. We need to be warriors within our minds, not lazy librarians gathering wisdom we'll never use.

    After you read each chapter, take a few minutes to scan the QR codes and learn the origins of each lesson. When you scan the QR code, you will receive **a FREE trial to the <u>Heroic</u> <u>App</u>** *that will help you dive deep into the lessons learned in this program. You can use the journal function in the app to take the first step today to become the person* **you** *want to be tomorrow!*

    You may not be aware, but every single second of every single day you are training your Black Belt Mentality. With every decision you make, you are deciding how you will respond to your current thoughts, emotions and physical sensations. These decision points present themselves thousands of times a day! Every moment is an opportunity for you to practice what you're learning. (The following prompts will remind you to practice what you've learned throughout this book):

    a. The moment you catch yourself lost in thought, recall your best-self identity. This will cue you to practice your best-self habits.

    b. For the rest of your life, follow this process:

        - Delete your bad habits
        - Double down on the habits that are serving you
        - Insert new micro habits that will remind you to act like the ideal version of yourself

    c. Look for opportunities to step outside your comfort zone and live your best life!

Decide to Commit

In the Dojo with Coach Brian

The Summer Before Jordan's Freshman Year in High School

Eight Years Before He Played in the NCAA National Championship Game

"You can approach this day like a martial artist training to become a White Belt," the man said as he walked across the stage. "Or a martial artist training for mastery. A Black Belt." He paused, making eye contact with every attendee before continuing. "But make no mistake, *you* make this choice whenever you step into a karate dojo, onto a lacrosse field, or into any training arena for the rest of your life. In truth, there are thousands of moments every day when you are faced with this choice; it is up to *you* to make this impactful decision."[4] He stood taller, crossed his arms, and took in a deep breath. "So I ask you now, on this day, what do you want?"

"I want to be a Black Belt!" The room erupted in unison.

The response was overwhelming. Jordan stood in stunned silence, amazed at the scene. This was a lacrosse camp, *not* a karate class! What's more, no one in the room knew where the speaker was going with his cryptic message. Jordan was surrounded by 300 of the best 8th-grade lacrosse players in the country, and all of them were smart enough to decide that a Black Belt was clearly better than a White Belt any day.

Each player packed into the tiny auditorium had been invited to this camp because they were the best lacrosse players in their class. They all eagerly sat on the edge of their seats, waiting for the guest speaker to end his dramatic pause and continue. His confident demeanor seemed to promise he possessed the elusive answer

4 +1: +1 or -1= Destiny Math | Motivation and Personality by Abraham Maslow

to the unspoken, burning question these highly driven players were seeking: *How do I get recruited to play lacrosse at the university of my dreams?*

After all, that was why they were all attending this elite recruiting camp in the first place—to get recruited. Weren't they?

"Well, then," the man continued, "if you want to be a Black Belt in your life, then you must decide to approach your training like a Black Belt!"

Jordan smiled. He had never heard someone speak with such confidence or boldness before. Other people might be offended by such an approach, but Jordan found it inexplicably refreshing to witness such unhindered authenticity in someone else.

"If you practice each moment with the confidence, focus, grit, and willingness to learn as a karate master training to become a Black Belt, you will soon put yourself in a position to get recruited to your dream school. It's that simple. In fact, that's how you will enjoy the process of achieving any goal that you choose to pursue."

The man continued, captivating his audience.

"You all have this decision to make at each moment within every drill, for the rest of your lacrosse career. Throughout your life, these Dojo Decision points will show up hundreds or thousands of times each day. After every thought, every emotion, and every sensation you experience, you will have to take action. What mindset will you choose? Black Belt or White Belt? Do you take a step toward growth and success, or a step back, toward fear? Each decision throughout your day impacts the person you become next. Will you move one step forward toward what you want? Or take one step back?"

Jordan, along with every other young lacrosse player in the room, was intrigued. They were all highly motivated to be great. However, to commit every moment of every day to this Black Belt mindset seemed a bit extreme. Was playing college lacrosse *really* worth this kind of "all day, every day" commitment? What kind of person would choose to play this kind of mind game?

As if almost on cue, the speaker answered Jordan's unspoken concerns. "You're breathing, aren't you?"

The audience exchanged awkward looks with each other, some chuckling. He continued. "It's a rhetorical question. You are breathing, which means you're alive. And that means none of you have a choice whether you're going to play this game or not. You're already playing!

"Take this moment for instance. Will you listen to my words with 100 percent presence, trying to absorb the message? Or will you tune me out, scroll through your social media feeds and distract yourself from 100 percent commitment to the present moment?"[5]

Was it really so simple? Jordan thought about the speaker's comment and agreed with the conclusion. He had never truly considered how many choices he made in a day, or their cumulative effect on his life. But regardless of what he knew or didn't know, he was playing the game, in the moment. He smiled, recognizing how even in this moment he could choose to go all in and lean into the present moment ... or he could let his mind wander.

"Make no mistake," the man said, shaking his head. "Being kind of, sort of, all in is essentially a decision to train like a White Belt. This is what most people choose. It's a negative decision that is acceptable for most, but one must also accept it is a decision that will take you off your path, whether your goal is to play college lacrosse, be your best, or fully enjoy each moment of your life.

"In the world of martial arts, a White Belt simply shows up, happy to 'get through' his training. The White Belt may have the talent to excel, yet he is content to go through the motions, to never fully develop his gift.

"However, the opposite mindset is the Black Belt. The Black Belt shows up with the intention to master his craft. He approaches his training with enthusiasm and passion to not just identify his limitations, but how to overcome them. He trains with the understanding

5 +1: The Master | Mastery by George Leonard

that he will never achieve mastery or perfection. Perfection is a pipe dream, a mirage in the desert. No, he happily accepts he is and will always be a work-in-progress, yet he relishes every opportunity to improve in each moment of each training session, for the rest of his life."[6]

He paused again, taking stock of the room, silently identifying those who were engaged and those who had begun to wander within their minds. "So I ask you today: what will it be for you? A White Belt, or a Black Belt?[7] I hear you all saying Black Belt, but I see in your eyes that not all of you are ready to make such a decision. And it is a decision.

"I urge you to not make it lightly. With your mouth I hear you say you want to be a D1 lacrosse player on game day when your fancy gear is shining in the sun, when your families and friends are cheering you on, and the TV cameras are rolling. But the decision cannot be made with your mouth. It must first be made within your *mind.*

"Do you *really* want to be a D1 lacrosse player? Will you want it on the hard days? On days when you have to wake up at 4:30 in the morning and leave the comfy confines of your bed, only to run until you puke? To practice until your hands are covered with blisters? *That* is the life of the Black Belt.

"You see, success on the lacrosse field is easy for those few who are willing to do the work. You just need to follow these three simple steps. First, you must decide "who" you want to *be, not* just what you want to accomplish."[8]

Jordan nodded his head, taking it in.

"Secondly, you must calculate "the price" you will need to pay to become that person, as well as devise a plan. And finally, you must do the work."

---

6 +1: Practice: When Can I Stop | Spiritual Economics by Eric Butterworth

7 +1: Going Through the Motions | How Bad Do You Want It? by Matt Fitzgerald

8 +1: "Want Better Habits, Start with Who!" | Atomic Habits by James Clear

Of course, Jordan thought, smiling.

"You must get busy paying that price with hard work, constant intention, and persistent action. Your current habits are already running your life. Once you identify them, you need to choose to first uninstall the habits that are sabotaging your success and then install the micro, too-small-to-fail habits that will help you improve.[9]

"I've had the privilege of evaluating you all day at camp, and as I look around this room, I see 300 excellent lacrosse players. You are the best in your class. The *best.* Truthfully speaking, I believe you all have the talent to play for your dream school." He watched as their faces lit up and heads nodded in agreement. "However, talent is not enough. Talent, even your talent, is common. The world is *littered* with talented players—players who have decided to squander their potential by approaching their training like a White Belt."

He smiled and pointed at the group. "Ah, but those of you who choose to approach their lives as Black Belts, *you* are the players who will innovate the game. *You* are the ones who will reach your unknowable potential. *You* are the few I am speaking to today!"[10]

Jordan felt like the man was speaking directly to him. He was so inspired by the Dojo Decision speech, right then and there he mentally committed to a life of striving to be his best self—on and off the field.

As the speech concluded, Jordan was filled with an excitement that energized him. He decided to use that energy to thank the speaker and share his desire to become a lacrosse-training Black Belt.

As he fought through the crowd to the auditorium stage, Jordan found a line of people waiting to meet with the speaker. Clearly, he wasn't the only one fired up by the words they just heard.

While waiting in line, Jordan noticed a handful of legendary coaches and current professional players mixed in with his peers who had

---

9 +1: The First Lesson of Navy SEAL Training | 101 Class: Unstoppable Teams by Alden Mills

10 PN: +1: Your Greatness | The Fountainhead by Ayn Rand

been working the camp. Each lacrosse legend waited patiently in line before eventually greeting the speaker with a hug and sincere, joyful conversation. Who was this man to command such respect from all the players and coaches Jordan had always idolized?

He slowly crept to the front of the line. He had determined exactly what he wanted to say. But as he made eye contact and moved to shake the speaker's hand, Jordan found himself at a loss for words.

The speaker stared directly at Jordan with a kind expression. As he extended his hand, the man lit up with such genuine enthusiasm that Jordan felt like the most important person in the world. It was an amazing first impression, and the speaker had yet to say a word!

Jordan was still speechless, but was able to take the man's hand. "Hi, my name is Jordan," he stammered nervously. "I just wanted to let you know how much I enjoyed your speech. And I want you to know, I plan to be a Black Belt!"

"Nice to meet you, Jordan. My name is Coach Brian, and I can't express how grateful I am that you took the time to listen to me speak!"

"Of course! I appreciate you taking the time to speak to us." Jordan continued, unable to contain his enthusiasm. "I want to become a Black Belt. I'm ready to commit! How do I start?"

Coach Brian paused for a long moment before responding to Jordan's question. "You've already started. You've taken the first step, Jordan. You took action and 'went first.'"

"Really?" Jordan asked, his face flushing a bright red.

"You see, many people seek out inspiration. They listen to speeches, read a few books, and they catch enthusiasm from all sorts of sources. Yet, many motivated people don't see the improvements in their lives because they don't transform their motivational energy into taking action.

"Do you see these professional players and coaches I have been greeting?"

"I have! Yes!"

"Once, they were all in your shoes. In fact, many of them were at a camp just like this when they first made their Dojo Decision."

Jordan looked at the Team USA members and elite college coaches in line. "Did they hear the same Dojo Decision speech?"

"They did! And just like you, they didn't wait for good luck to show up at their doorstep. Instead, they 'went first' and took the initiative to ask for help."[11] The man shook his head as his smile faltered a bit. "Jordan, I don't have all the answers in life, but I do know that if you don't ask for help, you won't get it. But when you ask for help, you will be surprised to find that those with the ability to help are itching for the opportunity to do just that. I have mentored many of the players and coaches you see waiting in this line, but even the most talented individuals need someone to challenge and hold them accountable. That being said, how can I help you, Jordan?"

Jordan was blown away by Coach Brian's offer to help. With all the courage he could muster, he asked, "Will you mentor me to transform into a Black Belt?"

Coach Brian didn't hesitate, "Of course I will, Jordan. If that is what you really want."

"Of course that's what I want!" Jordan said, not knowing what Coach Brian was implying.

"Then I will teach you to train like a Black Belt and reach your lacrosse goals."

"Yes!" Jordan pumped his fist in the air and grinned.

---

11 +1: Be Proactive (aka Response- Ability) | The Seven Habits of Effective People by Stephen Covey

The man mirrored his grin. “I love your enthusiasm! However, I have seen many people respond like you just did after hearing an inspiring speech. That speech you just heard is where my motivation stops.”

Jordan frowned. “Oh. Uh...”

“In fact, I can’t truly motivate you. I may be able to fire you up for a brief moment, but *you* must be driven from within, or ‘intrinsically motivated’ as the fancy professors like to say.[12] Only you can motivate yourself, Jordan. And if you can’t find a way to wake up each morning with a genuine excitement to attack your goals, your commitment will dwindle, and you will fall back to your White Belt habits.”

Jordan became nervous. He was excited to commit to the training, but he also recognized what Coach Brian just said was true; Jordan *had* felt this same excitement many times before. When his charismatic coaches and teachers delivered motivational speeches, his spirit soared and he felt ready to run through a wall.

But this felt different. Jordan knew if he didn’t take instant action, time would pass, his enthusiasm would wane, and eventually, he’d lose his motivation. He took a moment to assess his doubts and fears, then nodded again. “I’m in!”

“Great! Oh, I forgot to mention, you must agree to one condition before we start.”

Jordan felt nervous. His eyebrows knit together as he asked, “What’s that?”

“You must tell me what you are willing to give up.”[13]

Jordan’s eyes grew wider.

---

12 +1: The Growth Mindset | Relentless by Tim Grover

13 PN: Be Unstoppable by Alden Mills

Coach Brian continued without giving him a chance to reply. "Let me elaborate. It's lonely when you decide to step into the arena and begin to train as a Black Belt."

"Lonely? I don't understand..."

"You will be separating yourself from many of your peers when you make such a decision, close friends who will be perfectly content to train as White Belts. This is their choice, and it's fine—the world is filled with White Belts."

"Sure."

"But you, Jordan, will need to distance yourself from them. They will be sitting in the figurative stands, staring down as you sweat and strive for mastery on the arena floor.[14] They may say they support you and admire you, but they will nonetheless judge you, criticize you and, most painfully of all, attempt to persuade you to quit." He paused to lock his eyes with Jordan's, now filled with concern and a growing sense of dread. "It is true they will encourage you, but what they will encourage you to do is dial down your enthusiasm and join them in the bleachers. But make no mistake: just as joining a gritty culture is the easiest way to get gritty, hanging out with lazy people is the fastest and easiest way to become lazy."[15]

"Makes sense," Jordan said, nodding.

"So, are you ready to limit the time you spend hanging out with negative people, engaging in counter-productive activities that hold you back? This means cutting out playing hours of video games, mindlessly scrolling Instagram or Tik-Tok, even eating junk food. Jordan, what I'm asking is this: are you ready to accept the tradeoffs that go with a Black-Belt commitment?" He held up his hand before Jordan could speak. "I don't need an answer now. Like I said to the group, this decision is not to be taken lightly."

Jordan now grasped the gravity of his decision. Coach Brian didn't have the time to train those who weren't motivated to succeed. If

14 +1: The Peanut Gallery | Daring Greatly by Brene Brown

15 +1: The Audience Effect | How Bad Do You Want it by Matt Fitzgerald

Jordan wanted to be the best, to reach his full potential, he knew his life would have to change. And he had to admit, not many of his current friends were willing to walk this kind of path. It would be difficult and likely painful, but Jordan was ready to give up caring what they thought of him. He was even ready to give up the junk in his life, the food, and media inputs. He didn't see this as a sacrifice. Instead, it was a decision to be great.[16] He was on a path to greatness, determined not to let anything or anyone knock him off his path.

"I'm in, Coach," he answered. "I'm ready to give up the distractions that will keep me from becoming the best I can be!"

16 +1: Sacrifices vs. Decisions | The Way of the Fight by Georges St-Pierre

TAKE ACTION: COMMIT

(Use your Journal page or your *Heroic App*)

1. Download the **FREE trial of the Heroic App** to access:

    - The +1 wisdom expanding on the big ideas referenced within each chapter, Along with the full library of 1,400 *(and growing*) +1s, 600+ Philosophers Notes, 50+ 101 Master Classes.

    - The Heroic journal function, to remind yourself of your identity and habits for the *big three* areas of your life: energy, work, and relationships.

    - Heroic Social! Join a social network of like-minded people who encourage you to pursue your goals.

2. Use the journal page in this book and your Heroic App to:

    - Decide what mountain you want to climb (the #1 goal you want to pursue).

        - Find a mentor or accountability partner to read this book with.

    - Assess where you're at on your *Dojo Decision* journey.

        - *Quantify* each on a 1-10 subjective scale.

    - Assess how motivated you are to improve.

        - *Quantify* each on a 1-10 subjective scale.

    - Decide what you're willing to 'give up' in order to reach your goals.

Commit

- I REALIZE MY TIME IS MY MOST PRECIOUS RESOURCE. THEREFORE, WHATEVER I COMMIT TO, I WILL COMMIT TO IT WITH 100% FOCUS AND EFFORT. ONCE I COMMIT, THERE IS NO TURNING BACK. I WILL CUT OFF ALL OTHER OPTIONS AND MAKE WHATEVER I DECIDE TO PURSUE THE RIGHT DECISION.
- I WILL WAKE UP EACH MORNING EXCITED TO MAKE PROGRESS TOWARDS MY GOAL.
- TO FUEL MY PASSION. I WILL CONSTANTLY FEED MYSELF POSITIVITY AND LOOK FOR INSPIRATION THROUGH ROLE MODELS, SPEECHES, MOVIES, BOOKS... EVERYWHERE! I ALSO RECOGNIZE MOTIVATION MUST COME FROM WITHIN. I KNOW MY PATH, AND CHOOSE TO WALK IT! I WILL RISE ABOVE THE POSITIVE PRAISE OR NEGATIVE CRITICISM OF OTHERS, AND COMPETE FIRST AND FOREMOST TO MAKE MYSELF PROUD.
- I AM WILLING TO GIVE UP THE DISTRACTIONS THAT GET IN THE WAY OF MY GOALS. I MUST MAKE A CHOICE: CONSUME ENTERTAINMENT OR CREATE AN INSPIRING LIFE. IF I WANT TO SUCCEED I MUST INVEST MORE TIME PRACTICING MY CRAFT THAN I SPEND IN FRONT OF SCREENS (WATCHING TV, SCROLLING SOCIAL MEDIA, OR PLAYING VIDEO GAMES).
- I WILL LEAN ON MY TEAMMATES, COACHES, FRIENDS AND FAMILY FOR SUPPORT. I AM COMMITTED TO EMPOWERING A MENTOR OR TEAMMATE TO SUPPORT ME, ALONG WITH A TEAMMATE TO TEACH MY BLACK BELT MENTALITY.

I, _ _ _ _ _ _ _ _ _ _ _ _ pledge to recommit to this every morning to start my day!

Signature: Date:

name _

Go to dojodecision.com for inspiration!

Have many pathways past your obstacles on your journey towards your goals! Plan for setbacks!

0. COMMIT

What Is Your Goal?

(Your mountain to climb and your arena to apply the lessons you learn in this book?)

____

____

For that goal, (1) being just starting, (10) being arrived, Where are you now on your road of success? (1-10)

Just Getting Started!!	1	2	3	4	5	6	7	8	9	10	Arrived!

How bad do you want it? Will you quit after the first obstacle or distraction? What is your level of commitment to improve? (1-10)

I will quit at the first obstacle!	1	2	3	4	5	6	7	8	9	10	I will never quit!

What are some obstacles or distractions that could get in the way of achieving that goal? What unproductive habits will you give up?

____

____

____

What is your plan to address each obstacle?

____

____

____

My Teacher/ Accountability Partner:

____

____

Everyone needs a coach, mentor, accountability partner to help them commit. Who will hold you accountable?

My Student

____

____

When learning a new skill, the easiest way to hold yourself accountable is to teach it to someone else. Who will you teach?

How To Use This Journal

Congratulations on committing to your Dojo Decision!

Many people seek out inspiration. They listen to speeches, read a few books, and they catch enthusiasm from all sorts of sources. Yet, many motivated people don't see the improvements in their lives because they don't transform their motivational energy into taking action.

Taking action is what this journal is designed to do!

That's the secret to success in lacrosse and in life. Long-term success is rarely solved by adding more technology or magic bullets. Instead, It's always solved when you simplify your process and take action toward your goals. All you need to do is these three things:

Science has proven that when you reflect on your ideal identity, you increase your probability of success by 42 percent and your happiness by 10 percent. That's why you must journal, reflect, and meditate to remind yourself of WHO you need to be, to make yourself proud and be worthy of accomplishing the goals you set for yourself.

1. Decide what you want, and more importantly, who you need to be to accomplish it.
2. Identify and plan the habits and routines of that person.
3. Practice those habits every day."

This journal will help you do all three!

The first and second steps are highly introspective. They are personal processes that may take hours to complete. Take your time; don't rush. But don't obsess over making it perfect, because you will always be a work in progress. However, once you know what you want, and you have a plan to achieve it, you can begin the third step, which must be repeated multiple times each day!

You must REMIND yourself to be that person every single day! Life will distract you. Obstacles will get in your way. You must plan for these setbacks!

10% Happier
Gratitude Works!
By Robert A. Emmons

42% Increase in Probability of Success
Everything is Figureoutable
By Marie Forleo

Journaling is a tiny action that will move you closer to being the person you want to be. It's a micro decision that will help you build momentum to start each day. It's a decision that is easy to make, it only has to take a moment, but it's also just as easy to ignore. DO IT! You can't be the person you want to be if it's not front-of-mind. I don't care how you journal. You can write in ink, use an App, or simply rehearse your intentions in your mind. Experiment to find what works best for you.

I prefer doing it, 'old-school', in a notebook, magic happens when you put pen to paper! It's truly powerful.

No time? No problem! In the appendix, I have shared instructions on how to draw the Dojo Decision logo, which you can draw in twenty seconds to remind yourself of all the lessons you have learned in the book.

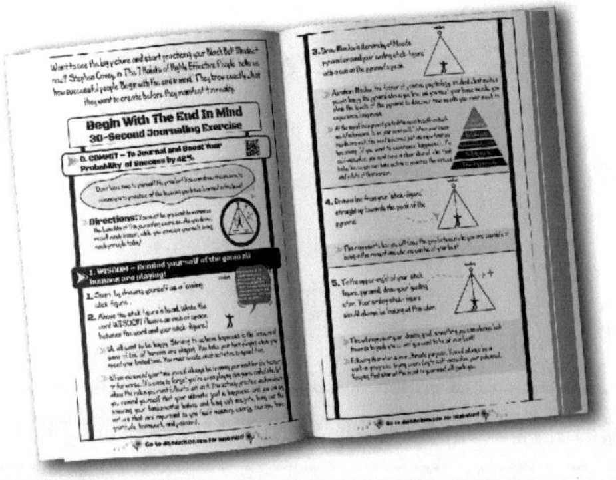
Begin With The End In Mind
30-Second Journaling Exercise

Not into writing or drawing? , That's also fine! Sign up for a FREE trial to the Heroic app that makes it easy to recommit to your Dojo Decision.

The point is to do something. Take action. The more you remind yourself of who you want to be, the more apt you're to practice the necessary habits to become that person more often!

Good luck and enjoy the process of committing to be the best you can be TODAY!

Coach McDermott

Decide to Commit (+1's)

Visit DojoDecision.com, scan the QR code below, or search the keywords in the *Heroic App* to learn the origins of the lessons introduced in this chapter!

4. **+1: +1 or -1= Destiny Math | Motivation and Personality by Abraham Maslow**
5. **+1: The Master | Mastery by George Leonard**
6. **+1: Practice: When Can I Stop | Spiritual Economics by Eric Butterworth**
7. **+1: Going Through the Motions | How Bad Do You Want It? by Matt Fitzgerald**
8. **+1: "Want Better Habits, Start With Who!" | Atomic Habits by James Clear**
9. **+1: The First Lesson of Navy SEAL Training | 101 Class: Unstoppable Teams by Alden Mills**
10. **PN: +1: Your Greatness | The Fountainhead by Ayn Rand**
11. **+1: Be Proactive (aka Response- Ability) | The Seven Habits Of Effective People by Stephen Covey**
12. **+1: The Growth Mindset | Relentless by Tim Grover**
13. **PN: Be Unstoppable by Alden Mills**
14. **+1: The Peanut Gallery | Daring Greatly by Brene Brown**
15. **+1: The Audience Effect | How Bad Do You Want It? by Matt Fitzgerald**
16. **+1: Sacrifices vs. Decisions | The Way of the Fight by Georges St-Pierre**

PART I

LEADING YOURSELF

1

Wisdom

Black Belt Mentality Athletes know what they want, and who they need to become to achieve it. They remind each other of the ultimate game we're all playing—to create more moments of joy and to share them with our teammates, friends, and family.

This is why we play lacrosse ... this is why we do anything!

***This chapter is dedicated to Todd Herman for his wisdom shared in* The Alter Ego Effect.**

Jordan's Championship Season - Present Day

Day of the NCAA National Championship Game

It had been eight years, two months, and three days since Jordan first heard Coach's initial speech and made his *Dojo Decision* to approach his lacrosse training as a Black Belt rather than a White Belt. He knew the exact date because he knew his current streak, 2,985 days to be exact, when he had hit his *floor goals*, his too-small-to-fail habits he had committed to all those years ago.[17] Coach Brian, the legendary speaker from his fateful eighth-grade lacrosse camp, had given Jordan a lifetime of great advice over the years, but the Dojo-Decision speech he had delivered on that critical night was undoubtedly the decision point that launched Jordan onto his new trajectory in life. Today he was playing on the biggest stage, in the biggest game, in the specific arena he had chosen to pursue.[18]

It was overtime in the National Championship game. Jordan's team had won the opening face-off, settled the ball, and called time out. With only ten seconds left on the clock, they had a chance to score a goal and win the game. Jordan had the ball in his stick and over 50,000 fans watching him from the stands. He paced his opponent's goal-line, waiting for the ref to blow the whistle to resume play. He was exhausted, yet excited about the opportunity laid out before him.

This was it. Jordan's chance to win the National Championship for his team! He knew the nerves he felt were just his body preparing him for success.[19] He also knew if he lost his focus, even for a moment, he could easily be overwhelmed by the internal and external distractions constantly pleading with him to quit, abandon his dreams, and settle for a mediocre career.[18]

Fortunately, Jordan had prepared for these distractions well ahead of time. He had psychological blinders on to counteract the thousands of fans screaming for his attention from the stands. On the

17 +1: 'Floors and Ceilings' | How to be an Imperfectionist by Stephen Guise

18 +1: 'The Optimizer in the Arena' | Daring Greatly by Brene Brown

19 +1: I'm Excited! | The Upside of Stress by Kelly McGonigal

field, he wasted no energy responding to his opponent's poor attempt at trash talk. On top of that, Jordan was exhausted from a full sixty minutes of sprinting in the 95-degree heat. He relished the physical discomfort.

"Bring it on!"[20] Jordan whispered quietly to himself. He had programmed this mantra to rehearse in moments just like this, silencing his lower-self whiner voice, flipping his script, and reminding himself of the truth that this heat would be affecting his opponents much worse if they hadn't trained for moments like this.

The external distractions were nothing when compared to the constant negative, nagging voice, forever echoing in the back of his mind. It repeatedly whispered lies that he was no good, too tired, too overwhelmed, that he should quit now, before he embarrassed himself.

Fortunately, Jordan had prepared for these internal distractions as well. He'd practiced and planned for this moment,[21] and he refused to be distracted today.

The referee blew the whistle.

Jordan took a deep breath and smiled confidently. Then, just as he had practiced countless times before, he rehearsed his best-self identity. *"Tasmanian Devil-Connor Shellenberger."*[22] Rehearsing this mantra gave Jordan the confidence he needed to block out the distractions, stay present, and instantly transform and re-commit to *who* he had chosen to be all those years ago.[23]

20 +1: 'Your Infinite Potential and Where to Find it' | The Tools by Phil Stutz and Barry Michels

21 +1: 'Name it to Tame it' | Mindsight by Dan Siegel

22 +1: 'Identity-->Behaviors--> Feelings' | Resilience by Eric Grietens

23 +1: Recommitment | Willpower by Roy Baumeister & John Tierney

Back in the Dojo with Coach Brian

Jordan's Freshman Year in High School

Eight Years Before Playing in the NCAA National Championship Game

"Tasmanian Devil-Connor Shellenberger," Jordan said, rehearsing the words with complete conviction.

"That is who you want to be?" Coach Brian asked. *"At your best?"*

It was 5:30 AM, Monday morning before school began, exactly one week after Jordan had returned from his lacrosse camp. He met Coach Brian on the practice field to begin his Black Belt Mentality training. It was dark, and a thin layer of frost still covered the field. It felt like they were the only two people awake in the world, let alone practicing lacrosse.

Jordan didn't know what to expect when he walked onto the field to meet Coach Brian. He had little doubt the man was an expert coach. He had already mentored dozens of elite professional athletes along with musicians, actors, and business titans who all praised Coach Brian's system for their success. So Jordan was curious. What could this Coach have taught these elite performers that made them stand out so drastically from their competition?

At this point, Jordan could only guess. He looked back through the years and could only think of a handful of coaches he considered amazing mentors. Some motivated him with inspiring pre-game speeches that would have Jordan and his teammates ready to run through a wall. Others dazzled Jordan with their tactical knowledge of the game as they drew up plays that left their opponents' heads spinning.

However, back in the lacrosse camp's auditorium, Coach Brian specifically told Jordan he couldn't motivate him, that he didn't have any magic drills to transform him into an all-star. Motivation came from within, he said, and if Jordan wasn't 100 percent committed, they would simply be wasting their time.[24]

As Jordan approached him on the field, lost in thought, he tried to anticipate the direction Coach Brian's legendary training would lead him in.

Coach Brian broke the silence, walking up to greet Jordan with a smile. "Jordan! Congratulations on showing up!"

Jordan frowned. "What's that supposed to mean?"

Coach shrugged. "Some people talk the talk but never walk the walk, telling me what they think I want to hear in the moment, even though they have no intention of changing. But you ... you have made it to the starting line, which is closer than the vast majority of athletes get to reaching their goals. Getting started is half the battle."[25]

"Thanks," Jordan said, nodding. "Happy to have exceeded your expectations so far."

Coach smiled wider. "My expectations are rising with every passing second." He held up a finger. "But before we begin, I'd like you to tell me your goal."

"My goal?"

"Yes. That, and what it is you're willing to give up to achieve it."

Jordan didn't hesitate, "Easy. I want to play lacrosse in college and help my team win a National Championship."

Coach nodded. "And?"

"And I'm willing to give up wasting my time playing video games, mindlessly watching Netflix, and scrolling social media."

---

24 PN: +1: Intro | The Alter Ego Effect by Todd Herman

25 +1: Get to the Starting Line | The Most Challenging Part of a Race | Spartan Fit by Joe De Sena

"Excellent! You are motivated! This is crucial, because as I told you last week, this is something one can never coach. No one can. *You* need to determine what it is you truly want in life. I can't make you want to wake up at 5:00 AM to run drills and sprints. I can't make you want your goal so badly you'll be driven to overcome any obstacle, no matter how high the cost."

"Well, I'm not so sure about that!" Jordan remarked, laughing.

Coach's smile faltered for a moment. "Oh?"

"Look," Jordan continued. "Your Dojo Decision speech really motivated me last week in the camp auditorium. It did. You practically had all 300 of us ready to storm the field!"

Coach Brian laughed. "Sure, I shared my energy with you, but *you* are the one who channeled it to feed your personal goal. If you aren't already motivated, any energy you happen to gain from a charismatic leader will be short-lived. This short-term energy injection is powerful, no question about that. It may even help you accomplish your short-term tasks. But make no mistake; this is not what impresses me as a coach."

"It's not?" Jordan shook his head. "Then what—"

"Jordan," Coach Brian said, leaning in closer. "I don't want you to accomplish *my* goals in life. I want you to accomplish *your* goals!"

Jordan nodded. "Oh. Well, yeah. That makes sense."

"Let me ask you a question, Jordan. Why did you agree to give up the activities you mentioned, potential moments with your friends that your lazy self enjoyed?"

Jordan shrugged. "First off, I know you don't know me that well, but I've never been lazy. Ever. You look up 'lazy' in the dictionary? You're not gonna find my photo."

Coach laughed. "Well said."

"And second, I just like who I am when I'm training to be my best. I mean, sure, I enjoy vegging out on the couch just as much as the next kid, but I always feel kinda worse afterwards and end up regretting it."

"Fantastic!" Coach Brian declared. "You just described your *why*. If you can describe *why* you want to give up your lower-self habits, you will be even more inspired to succeed."

"I'm totally inspired to succeed," Jordan said with a nod.

"Having a strong enough *why* allows you to lean on that reason in the future when times get tough."

"I hear ya."

"And times *will* get tough, Jordan. In the moments when you're ready to quit, you will need to be able to remind yourself of your *why* to push through your discomfort.[26] When an energetic coach believes in you, he can share his passion, but it's up to *you* to channel that energy and feed your *why*. You do this by taking action and reminding yourself of the person you want to be!"

Jordan nodded his head but said nothing, listening patiently as Coach Brian took a deep breath and continued preaching what seemed to be one of his pivotal ideas.

"That's what I try to teach my students. I help them turn their 'big why' into their 'big who.' This gives them a simple command to rehearse in the exact moment they need it, to remind them to practice the habits that will help transform them into *who* they are capable of being when they're at their best.

"When you rearrange your 'what you want' goal into your 'who you want to be' goal, you create an actionable mantra that prompts you to show up as your best you, your ideal self, every minute of every day."

"And it's that simple? Just knowing your *who*?"

---

26 +1: The Right Why | No Sweat by Michelle Segar Ph.D.

"It is!" Coach Brian continued, enthused with Jordan's question. "Knowing *who* you want to be allows you to invoke all your goals with a single identity descriptor. Then, with a single word and a power pose,[27] you can *flip the switch.*"

"Flip the what? What does that even mean?"

"Picture your mindset as a light switch," Coach Brian said. "In the same amount of time it takes to bring light to a dark room, you can instantly transform yourself from who you are currently into the person you are *capable* of being – your *best* Jordan."

Jordan grinned. "I like how that sounds."

"In every moment you have the opportunity to close this gap,[28] and the best part is it doesn't matter how long your room has been dark!"[29]

"I guess that makes sense," Jordan said. "So, you're saying if I can think of and focus on *who* I want to be, my best-self identity thing, I will have a simple identity to rehearse that will remind me of all the traits, goals, and habits of that person. I can then start practicing those habits to show up at my best!"

"Yes! You've got it! It's important to know exactly who you want to be at your best. If you can vividly picture what that looks like, then you have the ability to transform and express that person's superpower."

"Like Superman?"

"Exactly. He wasn't always Superman, right? He would first run into a phone booth as Clark Kent, a dorky, unconfident reporter. But when he emerged, he had transformed into a superhero with the strength to save the world."[30]

---

27 +1: Expanding into Your Best-Self | Presence by Amy Cuddy

28 +1: Close the Gap! | Ego Is the Enemy by Ryan Holiday

29 +1: The Time Between Light And Darkness | An Inspired Life by Ernest Holmes

30 +1: Clark Kent's Changing Room | The Rise of Superman by Steven Kotler

"I always loved that scene."

"I'm glad you've seen it. I was thinking you'd be too young to know what a phone booth was! It's wild to think people had to share public phones because cell phones didn't exist back when that movie was made! Phone booths aside, we all have this same ability to transform into our own superhero selves. You, Jordan, can summon your best self by rehearsing what I like to call your Identity Goal."

"My Identity Goal?" Jordan asked, unaware of this term. "Wouldn't my identity goal simply be, 'to be the best version of myself?' I'm happy with who I am. Sure, I'd like to be in a better mood more often, but I've never wanted to be someone else."

"I understand completely, but we all need a guide to show us what our best could look like. Your identity goal is a term I use to emphasize what you just described—you, in your best mood, performing your best habits that will make you most proud of who you are. I understand we're all unique, and I don't want to encourage you to be anyone else. However, imagine yourself learning a new skill. Would you say it's easier to practice after you see a good player perform it?"

"Well, yeah. Obviously."

"Right. So how about when you learn a new idea in a book? Do you remember it better if the book includes an example of how the idea is used in the real world?"

"I guess," Jordan admitted. "I can't say I've ever really given it that much thought."

"Point is, it's great to have a unique identity, but the admirable traits you see in others also provides a unique vision of what your best could look like. Superheroes from comics, everyday heroes from real life, even characters in movies — each one has the potential of providing you with a role model you can identify with. Before you can *flip the switch* and transform into your best self, you need to know with the utmost clarity what the superhero version of yourself looks like. Let's figure out who that is for you!"

"Sounds like a plan," Jordan said. He had always had role models, but he'd never taken much time to think about their heroic traits—traits he would want to possess if he was a superhero.

Coach Brian, sensing Jordan was deep in thought, suggested a prompt to guide his brainstorming. "Let me ask you a question; is there a player who you look up to as a role model? Someone you would want to transform into if you could, someone who would enable you to perform at your best?"

Jordan quietly reviewed his mental list of the characteristics he most wanted to possess. Strong, fast, confident. Definitely a competitor. Better yet, someone who could score at will!

Coach Brian continued to encourage Jordan's thought process. "If you can't think of an exact person, then think of the characteristics your best self would possess. If that doesn't work, think of a fictional character from a movie, or a legend from the NFL or NBA who may possess the characteristics you would like to invoke.

"Would you want to lead like quarterback Tom Brady? Shoot and communicate on the field like Marcus Holman? How about preparing for a game with the confidence of Batman? Or maybe—"

"I know!" Jordan exclaimed, interrupting Coach Brian. "Tasmanian Devil-Connor Shellenberger!"

Coach Brian leaned back. "Excuse me?"

"Tasmanian Devil-Connor Shellenberger!" Jordan repeated. "That's who I'm gonna be!"

Coach looked at him, somewhat amused. "Tasmanian Devil..."

"...Connor Shellenberger," Jordan finished, his eyes lighting up. "Yeah. I want to bring the characteristics of those two identities together."

"That's who you want to be at your best?"

"Absolutely!" Jordan said enthusiastically. "Here's the thing: when I think of transforming into Connor Shellenberger, the legendary Virginia attackman, I picture myself playing with unshakable confidence, grit, and focus. You know, protected from all distractions."

"Okay," Coach Brian said, nodding slowly.

"I'd be constantly communicating on the field and in our huddles to best coach and encourage my teammates, helping us execute our game plan with precision. As for the Tasmanian Devil..."

"The ... Tasmanian Devil?" Coach interrupted. "From those Looney Tunes cartoons?"

"Exactly!" Jordan said. "When I picture myself as Taz, I think of playing with an unmatched sense of urgency, tearing through any opponent in my path! There'd be no stopping me! Seriously, I would love to hunt down ground balls with that kind of intensity! Putting those two identities together? *Kapow!* It would make me unstoppable on the lacrosse field!"

"Wow," Coach Brian exclaimed, genuinely excited to hear Jordan's answer and train of thought. "Just when I thought I'd heard it all..."

"You like it?"

"I do. But it doesn't matter what I think. It only has to be meaningful to you. Can you feel the hair stand up on the back of your neck when you rehearse that identity? Do you get filled with a sense of confidence?"

"Definitely," Jordan said grinning. "If I'm Tasmanian Devil-Connor Shellenberger, or 'Taz-Shelley', as his teammates have nicknamed him, I'm gonna be instantly poised, confident, and ready to dominate on the field!"

"Alright, then! I think you're ready to begin your training this morning!"

"Finally! Let's go!!"

"We want to groove in that sensation of readiness within every rep of each drill you'll practice today. Focus on your physical reaction, whatever it may look like."

Jordan frowned. "I don't get it."

"For example, the hair on the back of your neck might stand up, or you might feel a chill down your spine, a wave of warm confidence flooding through your consciousness."

"Oh. Yeah, sure."

"Or perhaps something specific to you. When you feel that physical change, you can be confident you're transforming into the best version of yourself. You will then train with more focus, confidence, grit, and presence. You will undoubtedly groove in the habits of your chosen role model, the ... Tasmanian Devil-Connor Shellenberger." He smirked. "Am I saying that right?"

Jordan smiled and gave him a thumbs up. "Nailed it." He pictured himself on the field, transforming into that absolute beast of a player. He could actually envision himself burning a hole in the net with his powerful shot, dominating every ground ball with tenacity, and pushing through exhaustion and discomfort to lead his team to victory. "This is gonna be awesome," he whispered, eyes alight with excitement.

Coach Brian couldn't hide his smile. "Then let's get started, Taz-Shelley!"

He dumped a bucket of balls in front of the goal and started to explain the drill. "You need to focus on three things. Understood?"

"Three things. Got it," Jordan said, nodding in agreement.

"First, you must rehearse your best-self identity immediately before each shot."

"Check."

"Second," Coach Brian continued, "If you are proud of your shot, shout out loud, "That's like me!"[31] and grin like you've just scored a winning goal in the National Championship."

Jordan nodded, "Alright. Got it."

"And conversely, if you are not content with your shot, you say, "Needs work."

"Needs work?"

Coach nodded. "Needs work," he repeated. "Acknowledge it needs to be improved, but feed it little attention."[32]

"Oh. Yeah, I guess that makes sense. Don't feed the bear, right?"

"Indeed. Now ... *Practice*!"

Over the next twenty minutes Jordan took shot after shot, diligently practicing the mental exercises Coach had impressed on him. After a few bad shots, Jordan was visibly shaken, standing on the field, glaring at the goal.

"'Needs work' isn't working," he muttered. "Sorry, Coach." He felt the negativity blossoming up inside him, threatening to take him down the rabbit hole of despair.

"Name him," Coach said.

Jordan glanced over at him, frowning "What?"

"Name him."

"Name who?" Jordan said, shaking his head. "What are you *talking* about?"

---

31 +1: That's Like Me! | With Winning in Mind by Lanny Bassham

32 +1: Needs Work! | With Winning in Mind by Lanny Bassham

"That voice in your head," Coach Brian continued. "The one telling you you're not good enough and never will be. The one saying you need to stop kidding yourself, to stop wasting your time..."

Jordan's face fell. "How did you—?"

"Name. Him." Coach looked into Jordan's eyes intently. "That inner whiner needs a name. Then you need to manifest him in your mind as realistically as possible. That voice is like the most annoying friend you've ever had to spend time with."

Jordan looked away, thinking of his annoying friend who was always incredibly negative, bringing up worse case scenarios. He was still part of his crew, however, so they always allowed him to tag along. Jordan started smiling.

"There it is," Coach said. "You have it, don't you? The name?"

He nodded. "I do."

"Good. And always remember you need distance. You are not your thoughts, Jordan. They are thoughts, merely thoughts, and you are the observer. Acknowledge them, but do not accept them."

Jordan resumed his training and found he honestly enjoyed training alongside his annoying, pessimistic friend, Dopey, as he had named him. It only took a handful of attempts to silence Dopey and put him in the corner of his mind, making space for Taz-Shelley to step forward and lead the show.[33]

Although the training was similar to the shooting drills Jordan had experienced in the past, the results felt significantly different. He could feel confidence welling up within him like a physical force, slowly becoming deeper and deeper ingrained into his shooting process with each passing second. He still acknowledged his failures, but chose to feed those unsatisfying missteps as little energy as possible. It wasn't magic. The secret to Coach Brian's training method was to build micro habits on top of his preexisting shooting protocols. The result? Jordan was filling up the goal with well-

33 +1: Name It to Tame It | Harry Potter & The Sorcerer's Stone by J. K. Rowling

placed shots. By the end of the practice session a small hole began to wear through each corner of the net where Jordan had been aiming his shots.

"That!" Jordan exclaimed, looking back at Coach Brian and pointing to the worn net. "*That's* like me!" He didn't wait for a response, but walked off the field to where Coach had a bottle of water ready for him. Exhausted and drenched in sweat,[34] he felt as if he had just discovered the secret sauce of a champion recipe. He couldn't wait for his next practice session. He believed Coach's simple process would take him to places he had never imagined.

TAKE ACTION: WISDOM

(Use your Journal page or your *Heroic App*)

- Brainstorm who you want to be at your best. Your *Best-Self Identity!*
- What are the traits, characteristics and 'self-talk' of that Identity?
- What is the #1 habit you need to adopt to transform into that Identity, and what's the #1 habit that is blocking your success that you need to eliminate?
- What's the name of your lower self, 'whiner' voice? "Name it to Tame it!"

34 +1: Channeling Mia Hamm | The Champion's Mind by Jim Afremow

1. Wisdom

Who Do You Want to Be?

1. Goal: What is your current goal that you are committed to achive?

2. identity: Great! Now let's turn your goal into an Identity Goal! 'WHO' is a Superhero, a role model, or a star athlete you can channel who would have no problem accomplishing that goal? Use the framework below to brainstorm that hero!

3. Traits: Associated with that identity

What are his/her traits. Why did you pick this role model?

	Energy/Your Sport	Work/School	Relationships
1. Goal	feel great		
2. Identity	I am...	I am...	I am...
3. Traits Associated with that identity			
4. Behaviors (one habit to start doing, one habit to stop doing that will help you be more like this person)	+ –		

What's the name of your lower self, inner, 'whiner' voice? The voice that you need to ignore! "Name it to Tame it!").

Go to dojodecision.com for inspiration!

To improve at anything, it's helpful to have a goal. Lacrosse is our passion, so let's start there! In the upcoming chapters you'll learn about setting an identity goal for each area of your life. Go through this same process to set a goal for work or school and in your relationships!

Wisdom (+1's)

Visit DojoDecision.com, scan the QR code below, or search the keywords in the *Heroic App* to learn the origins of the lessons introduced in this chapter!

17. **+1: 'Floors and Ceilings' | How to be an Imperfectionist by Stephen Guise**
18. **+1: 'The Optimizer in the Arena' | Daring Greatly by Brene Brown**
19. **+1: I'm Excited! | The Upside of Stress by Kelly McGonigal**
20. **+1: 'Your Infinite Potential and Where to Find it' | The Tools by Phil Stutz and Barry Michels**
21. **+1: 'Name it to Tame it' | Mindsight by Dan Siegel**
22. **+1: 'Identity-->Behaviors--> Feelings' | Resilience by Eric Grietens**
23. **+1: Recommitment | Willpower by Roy Baumeister & John Tierney**
24. **PN: Intro: The Alter Ego Effect by Todd Herman**
25. **+1: Get to the Starting Line | The Most Challenging Part of a Race | Spartan Fit by Joe De Sena**
26. **+1:The Right Why | No Sweat by Michelle Segar Ph.D.**
27. **+1: Expanding Into Your Best-Self: Presence by Amy Cuddy**
28. **+1: Close the Gap! | Ego Is The Enemy by Ryan Holiday**
29. **+1: The Time Between Light And Darkness | An Inspired Life by Ernest Holmes**
30. **+1: Clark Kent's Changing Room | The Rise Of Superman by Steven Kotler**
31. **+1: That's Like Me! | With Winning in Mind by Lanny Bassham**
32. **+1: Needs Work! | With Winning in Mind by Lanny Bassham**
33. **+1: Name It To Tame It | Harry Potter & The Sorcerer's Stone by J. K. Rowling**
34. **+1: Channeling Mia Hamm | The Champion's Mind by Jim Afremow**

2

Self-Mastery I (Habits & Routines)

Black Belt Athletes help each other build & practice the daily habits that will inevitably run their lives. Focusing on your habits is how you will silence your internal and external distractions to 'win the ultimate game that we're all playing.' The ultimate game is to experience more moments of joy and to share those moments with the people we care about.

***This chapter is dedicated to James Clear and BJ Fogg for the wisdom shared in their books* Atomic Habits *and* Tiny Habits.**

Jordan's Championship Season - Present Day

10 Minutes Before Taking the Field: Day of the NCAA National Championship Game

Jordan finished the last segment in his pre-game routine. He had been out on the field visualizing the plays he needed to make to help his team win the National Championship. He took his time, envisioning every play, every shot and every goal to first score in his mind before manifesting it in the game to come. After he finished his warm-up and his mind and body were primed with invigoration and renewed confidence, he walked back into the locker room where his forty teammates were winding down the final minutes of their individual routines, before their coach delivered one last pep-talk to unite them as a team.

He knew exactly what he'd see when he opened the locker room door. His goalie, Avery, was lying down with a towel over his face as he envisioned each shot he expected to see in the game. Jordan scanned the room. Their shut-down defenseman, Alex, had his headphones on, head-bobbing, jamming out to the same playlist he'd been listening to before every game since high school. Jaime, their sharp-shooting midfielder, was re-taping his stick with the focus of a master craftsman as he did before every game.

Jordan's own pre-game routine had actually begun the previous night when he closed his hotel room door and told his teammates he was going to bed.[35] He'd been taught that if he wanted to wake up ready to dominate the day, he had to practice the PM habits that would put him in a position to do so. This led to him waking up this morning excited and energized to attack the day! Throughout the morning, Jordan completed numerous morning rituals to maintain his energizing momentum.[36] When his team arrived at the stadium, Jordan channeled his excitement through a predetermined routine, allowing him to show up at game time with the calm confidence he needed to succeed. The routine ended with his 15-minute on-field visualization where he spent the first five minutes envisioning him-

35 +1: PM Counts Twice | Why We Sleep by Matthew Walker

36 +1: Carpe Momentum | Coaching the Mental Game by H. A. Dorfman

self as a kid, just having fun and playing lacrosse. For the next five minutes, he visualized his past successes, and in the final five minutes, he envisioned himself making pivotal plays in the upcoming game.

Exactly two minutes before they were set to take the field, their coach came in to give his final motivational and tactical instruction. He had a pulse on the team's attitude and knew they were as ready as they would ever be.

After exiting the locker room, Jordan and his teammates jogged onto the field in unison, two-by-two, to begin their final warm-up before facing off in the biggest lacrosse game of their lives.

Jordan felt as if he had already lived this moment. In fact, he had. In his mind, he'd visualized and dreamt about this moment every night for as long as he could remember. Today, that moment was finally becoming reality. He had visualized every aspect of the entire experience of this championship game, including the warm-up. However, there was one distracting variable he couldn't have possibly foreseen—the inescapable heat.

It was noon, an hour before the opening face-off, and so hot. Ninety-five degrees and rising, with heat also radiating up from the surface of the artificial turf. They were only half a lap into their pre-game warm-up lap and sweat was already dripping off Jordan's forehead and burning his eyes. Alex, one of his teammates, was complaining about the discomfort.

Jordan frowned. This was not the chatter of a team on the verge of winning the National Championship. He turned to Alex. "Come on, Rocky," he playfully jabbed. "You gonna let a little heat get in the way of you dominating today?" Rocky, the name of the Philadelphia boxing brawler played by Sylvester Stallone, was the alter-ego identity Alex had chosen. Calling Alex "Rocky" was intentional, their pre-planned gentle reminder to push on. It wasn't designed to embarrass Alex, but remind him of who he was capable of being at his best. Alex received the message loud and clear and grinned. "Copy, brother. *Flipping the switch* now. Let's go!"

Just like that, as quickly as turning a light switch from *off* to *on*, they were back on track.

This simple teammate communication was just one of the precautions Jordan's team had built into their warm-up routine, preparing them to recognize and respond to the distractions they knew would come their way.

Jordan knew there would be distractions, but he hadn't anticipated how they would manifest today. Right now, it was his teammate Alex complaining about the heat; the next moment, it would be something entirely unrelated. Jordan learned early on how there was a chaotic force in this world, constantly testing us all to make sure we are worthy of success.

His mentor had taught him to name this negative force in an effort to tame its destructive power. Jordan had named it *Part-X.* Some called it their *demon.* Others referred to it as an *inner whiner.* Whatever the name, the one thing Jordan could count on in a stressful moment was *Part-X* would be hard at work alongside him, trying to distract him and his teammates from their goals.[37]

Never one to leave this to chance, his team included predetermined actions in their warm-up routine designed to battle *Part-X,* address distractions, and remind each other of the team they were capable of being at their best. In moments like this, Jordan could hear Coach Brian's voice say, *"The worse you feel, the more you need to commit to your protocol."*[38]

To recommit to his protocol, Jordan rehearsed the predetermined mantra he had been using to simplify the battlefield,[39] *"I'm only a lightbulb, and it's my job to stay screwed in."*[40] It was one of his favorite mantras, one he used to guard himself against distraction and plug into the positive, divine, creative force in the universe.

37 +1: Whineysaurus Part-X | Coming Alive by Phil Stutz and Barry Michels

38 +1: Emotional Stamina - What to do when you're having a rough day? | The Tools by Phil Stutz and Barry Michels

39 +1: Simplify the Battlefield | The Way of the Seal by Mark Divine

40 +1: We're Only the Lightbulbs - Our job is to Remain Screwed In | Falling Upwards by Richard Rohr

This same eternal voice was equally at play, urging him to get out of his own way and allow God's enthusiasm to flow through him.[41]

His team's pre-game routine had been orchestrated down to the smallest detail, with nothing left to chance. Being part of this gritty, championship culture made it easy for Jordan and his teammates to create a replicable mindset. Before every game, they followed a consistent protocol:

- Stretch to warm up their bodies.
- Partner pass to warm up their sticks, maximizing their touches and emphasizing simplicity.
- Practice their reads in an odd man situation to warm up their lacrosse IQ.
- Match the level of intensity they'd shortly be playing at in a ground ball drill to warm up their competitive muscles.

Today would be no different. After Jordan's team completed their pre-game rituals their bodies and minds were primed for the game, they lined up on the sidelines and stood proud, facing the flag as they listened to the National Anthem, paying homage to all those who had sacrificed to give them an opportunity to play a game they loved.

Jordan and his teammates then took the field to start the game. He looked to the stands and whispered a quiet, "Thank You," the last habit in his routine.[42] This reminded him how simply being here, able to play the game he loved, made all his sweat and sacrifice worthwhile. He had defied the odds. Of the millions of kids that grew up playing lacrosse, only 100,000 play in college, only 4,000 play Division 1, and only 84 kids get to play in this Championship game. He was humbled when he zoomed out and took a telescope look at his accomplishment. However, Jordan knew he was only able to get here by putting his routines under the microscope.[43]

---

41 +1: Attack Each Day with Joy and Enthusiasm | Think Like a Warrior by Darrin Donnelly

42 +1: Thank You. Thank You. Thank You. | Words to Live by Eknath Easwaran

43 +1: Microscopes & Telescopes | An Astronauts Guide to Life On Earth by Chris Hadfield

Back in the Dojo with Coach Brian

10:00 AM, Freshman Year of High School

8 Years Before Jordan's NCAA Championship Game

"Whether you like it or not," Coach Brian said, looking over the field, "you have already programmed thousands of habits that currently run your life. Some good, some bad. To be fair, most of them are so small you probably won't even recognize them as habits."[44]

It was mid-morning, and Jordan and Coach stood on the field dissecting Jordan's subconscious process of resuming play after a ball's been shot out of bounds. Jordan admitted this was a process he had never put much thought into until this moment.

"What do you mean I wouldn't recognize them?" Jordan asked. "You don't think I'm smart enough?"

Coach smiled. "Oh, you're smart Jordan, but even intelligent people often fail to grasp the importance of tiny habits. For instance, have you ever deliberately thought about how you would pick up the ball off the end-line during a stoppage of play?"

Jordan shook his head. "I ... no ... I guess I haven't."

Sensing Jordan needed a more obvious example of the importance of micro habits, Coach Brian changed gears. "What is the first thing you do when you wake up?"

Jordan frowned, trying to decipher how his morning routine had anything to do with dissecting a defense. "I don't know," he said, shaking his head. "Brush my teeth, I guess."

Coach Brian looked at Jordan, nodding slowly. "Is that really the first thing you do? The very first thing?"

"Uhhhh..."

---

44 +1: You: Athlete + Scientist + Director | Atomic Habits by James Clear

Urging Jordan to dive deeper, he continued, “Think smaller. Before you even leave your bed, what is the very first thing you do?”

Jordan fell silent, lost in the question and trying to anticipate what Coach wanted to hear.

“Here’s a hint; before we begin our work together, many of my new students share the very first habit they practice when they wake up is to pick up their phone from the nightstand.”

“Oh. Sure,” Jordan said.

“They then check their texts, emails, and Instagram feed.”

Jordan nodded. “Yeah. Okay, so I guess I yawn and stretch when I first wake up ... and then ... you’re right. I check my phone to see what’s new on my Instagram feed and scroll through the texts friends sent me overnight.” He blushed as the realization of his answer settled into his mind. “Oh, man, I wasn’t even aware that I do all that before I brush my teeth!”

“Amazing, right?” Coach responded.

“‘Embarrassing’ is more like it...”

“Without your conscious knowledge, I bet you’d agree that you most likely practice this sequence of habits the majority of your mornings. If you think about it, I mean really stop to give it some thought, you’d discover a handful of additional habits you practice before you even brush your teeth.”

Jordan closed his eyes. He reflected on what Coach Brian had said, running through his typical routine in his imagination. “You’re right, every morning I always do the same things: yawn and stretch, sit up in bed, check my phone for messages, roll outta bed, and walk to the bathroom to brush my teeth.”

"Do you make your bed?"[45] Coach Brian asked, sensing Jordan was still unaware of the many habits he was practicing, or in this case, *not* practicing in his morning routine.

"Maybe? Sometimes? I ... don't really know," Jordan answered honestly. "Sorry."

Coach Brian waved off his apology with a smile. "My point is that, we all unknowingly practice dozens of habits, all within the first moments of waking up. Now, if you are unaware of all these habits within a two-minute span, can you imagine how many micro habits you're practicing throughout a 60-minute lacrosse game?" He paused to let this nugget of wisdom sink in. "And if you are unaware you're practicing a habit, how can you even begin to improve it?"[46]

Jordan's eyes lit up as he followed Coach Brian's thought process. "I think I get it! You're saying if I'm clueless about the many habits running my life, I can't possibly devise a plan to improve."

Jordan paused to take mental inventory of all the routines he practiced every day.

- Waking up
- Eating breakfast
- Driving to school
- Going to class
- Walking to the next class
- Eating lunch
- Driving to practice
- Preparing for practice
- Practicing lacrosse
- Driving home
- Eating dinner
- Doing his homework

45 +1: Make Your Bed | Make Your Bed by Admiral William H. McRaven

46 +1: Want to Improve: Measure! | Eat, Sleep, Move by Tom Rath

- Hanging out with his friends and family
- Preparing for bed

He was only scratching the surface, and Jordan was already overwhelmed: "Holy cow! There must be hundreds—no, thousands—of these micro habits within my routines! Stuff I'm not even aware of!"

"You got that right!" Coach Brian said enthusiastically. "The exciting thing is you can train yourself to use each habit to improve your routines and achieve the results you want. As they say, we become our habits. Our identity is ultimately composed of what we repeatedly do. We can choose to install the habits which serve us best by following these three simple steps:

1. Identify them.
2. Once you recognize your routine, eliminate any micro habits getting in the way of your success.
3. Begin adding and practicing only habits that will help you become the best version of yourself!"[47]

"That..." Jordan said, his smile widening. "Is really, really cool. I totally get it now!"

Coach Brian was excited to see how quickly Jordan was catching on. "Very well, then let's see if you can apply what you just discovered to your lacrosse routine!"

"Oh. Uhhh ... yeah. Sure! Let's do it!"

"So, if you're on the end-line with the ball in your stick, waiting for the ref to blow the whistle and begin play, what is the first thing you do?"

Jordan thought deeply. He frowned, recognizing he wasn't proud of the first habit that came to mind, but in the spirit of getting better, and with his trust in Coach Brian's mentorship, he went through his current process:

47 +1: How to 100,000x Your Performance! | Principles by Ray Dalio

1	**IF:** I have the ball on the end-line:
	THEN: I usually look in the stands before the play to see if my friends are watching.

2	**IF:** I hear the ref blow the whistle:
	THEN: I read the defense and start dodging toward the goal to beat my man and draw a slide.

3	**IF:** the opponent guarding me overplays me:
	THEN: I will switch directions and attack the other side of the goal.

4	**IF:** I attack the other side of the goal **AND** no one slides:
	THEN: I shoot and score.
OR:	
	IF: I attack the other side of the goal **AND** The defenseman guarding my teammate slides to stop my dodge:
	THEN: I pass to my open teammate who shoots and scores.

"That's a great start! Now, are there any habits in that sequence you would like to delete? Are there any habits getting in the way of your success?"

"I don't have to look into the stands. It's certainly distracting me from my success."

"Excellent! Let's delete that habit from your process since it is not serving you. Now, let's see if we can identify a micro-habit we can add to improve your routine. To help you brainstorm, think of your best-self identity, 'Taz–Shelley.' How would he approach each micro habit in your sequence?"

"Hmmm," Jordan took a minute to think. "At the beginning of the routine, instead of looking into the stands, I think he would remind himself to transform into the best version of himself. In my case, this would be 'Tasmanian Devil–Connor Shellenberger.' I think that would help me to reset from the chaos of the game and be more apt to practice the habits in my routine with more confidence, grit, and focus."

"Awesome, Jordan! That's what I'm talking about—you're onto something! One of the best coaches I've worked with shared that the most important thing he asks of his players is to look for opportunities throughout the game to reset and re-commit to being the players they can be at their best. These moments could come after every face-off, every time the referee blows the whistle, or after any transition point you can brainstorm throughout a game. You see, most players have an idea *who* they want to be and they have the skill to be that player, but the trick is to actually *be* that person for more moments throughout a game. The team that has a system in place to accomplish this is the team that usually wins. We don't rise to the occasion; we fall to the level of our training!"[48]

Jordan nodded in agreement.

"And how about your other habits within this lacrosse routine? Can you undertake them with more intention? Can you expand on each habit with a routine of how your 'best self' would attack each habit?"

Jordan thought long and hard and came up with this new list of habits to practice from now on:

1	**IF:** I have the ball on the end-line:
	~~**THEN:** I usually look in the stands before the play to see if my friends are watching.~~
	THEN: [I will take a deep breath, smile, and survey the field. I will rehearse my best-self identity to remind myself of the player I am capable of being at my best!]

48 +1: Raise the Basement | The Art Of Learning by Josh Waitzken

2	**IF:** I hear the ref blow the whistle:
	~~**THEN:** I usually look in the stands before the play to see if my friends are watching.~~
	THEN: [I will read the defense and dodge full speed to initiate contact with my defensemen] as I dodge toward the cage to beat my man and draw a slide **[I will always do so with my head up surveying the field]**.

3	**IF:** my opponent overplays me:
	THEN: I will switch directions and attack the other side of the cage **[and drive upfield to a spot 5 yards above the goal to give me the room I need to roll under and still have a great shooting angle].**

4	**IF:** I attack the other side of the goal **AND** no one slides:
	THEN: I shoot the ball **[looking at the white of the net and changing shooting planes].**
OR:	
	IF: I attack the other side of the cage **AND** The defenseman guarding my teammate slides to stop my dodge:
	THEN: I will pass the ball to my open teammate and communicate "shoot" so he knows he should shoot the ball.

5	**IF:** We score:
	THEN: I immediately celebrate with my teammates and encourage them to keep doing what's working!
OR:	
	IF: We don't score AND we turn the ball over:
	THEN: I will see how fast I can win the game of reacting before my opponent and begin the ride, always being proactive, thinking one step ahead.

Jordan was proud of his new list. He had identified new micro habits to practice, and he could see himself grooving in this process at every upcoming practice, gradually improving day-by-day.[49] He would no longer just go through the motions in his training. Coach Brian had given him a plan for continuous, never-ending improvement,[50] and he could always delete, add, and improve his micro habits to better his routines later on.

He was excited to start implementing this habit discovery process into every aspect of his lacrosse game. Coach Brian instructed him to go through each mini-sequence throughout a game, and he now recognized how he already had a base sequence of habits installed for many of his tactical lacrosse routines:

- When he caught a pass from a teammate
- When he was getting ready to shoot
- When he missed a shot and had to turn and hustle back to play defense

He could even plan his best-self habits based upon how he, as Tasmanian Devil-Connor Shellenberger, would react to defining moments throughout the game. These moments included the inevitable times when:

- A teammate dropped a pass
- He was exhausted at the end of a game
- He was overwhelmed after an opponent went on a scoring run
- An opponent talked trash or fouled him
- His team lost a tough game

Jordan felt more in control of his success than ever before. He now realized if he could identify an act that had already occurred, he could create his best-self response to that act. He was excited to evaluate and apply this system to each of his tactical lacrosse

49 +1: The Gift of Greatness | Peak by Anders Ericsson & Robert Pool

50 +1: CANI! + Kaizen! | Legacy by James Kerr

routines as well as the emotional responses he often experienced throughout a game.

As Jordan mentally built his lists of habits, he kept asking himself, *"How would Tasmanian Devil-Connor Shellenberger respond in this scenario?"* He knew in the future he could always tweak each process and break down additional micro habits, but for now he was pleased with the list of routines he was constructing.

As he continued to build his habit routines, Coach Brian encouraged Jordan to share each list with his coaches and teammates. By making his best-self goals public, his teammates could hold him accountable. Jordan was excited to see just how good he could become if he kept perfecting all aspects of his lacrosse game!

TAKE ACTION: SELF-MASTERY I (HABITS & ROUTINES)

(Use your Journal page or your *Heroic App*)

- Brainstorm the micro habits/routines that are currently running your lacrosse life:
  - Pre-game routine
  - In-game performance routines
  - Post-game routine
- Identify any additional routines that will directly impact your athletic performance.
  - Brainstorm the micro habits for that routine!
- What current routines are working? (Circle them!)
- What micro habits do you want to eliminate? (Cross them out!)
- Finally, what micro habits do you want to insert into each routine?

Don't overwhelm yourself!
+1: 100% on ONE Keystone Daily Micro Habit:
Mini Habits by Steven Guise
Scan QR code below or visit
https://www.heroic.us/optimize/plus-one/quick-how-to-on-habits

Need Inspiration?
Go to DojoDecision.com
and explore habits used by elite performers!

2.

In our 'Wisdom' chapter, you identified 'Who' you want to be at your best.

1. Remind Yourself Here:

_ _

There is only one way to actually transform into this 'best—self: you must practice the habits of that ideal identity... and to practice, you must have a plan.

2. Brainstorm Your Habits:

This is a personal process. Think of yourself as that Superhero. What behaviors would that version of you practice to perform at your best? Lacrosse is our passion, so let's start with those habits and routines.

1. Brainstorm the sequence of habits that are currently determining your success.

   IF: this happens: THEN: I do that

2. Circle the ones that serve you.
3. Cross-out the ones that are getting in the way of your success.
4. Add additional micro habits within your routines that the best version of yourself would practice.

As you brainstorm, consider your micro-habits (the habits that are too small to fail, that this identity would practice to become that person), These could be mantras (things you say to yourself) or power poses (physical gestures) that you can hang on other habits to remind yourself of 'Who' you want to be.

i.e.	Routine	If:	Then:
1.	Pre-game routine.	IF: I am preparing for a game or practice:	Then: I visualize myself succeeding.
2.	Tactical lacrosse routines.	IF: I want to pass to a teammate:	Then: I make sure I have a clear passing lane.
3.	Post-game routine.	IF: The game ends:	Then: I reflect on what I did well.

Pre-Game Habits or Routines (Sequence of Habits)

1.	IF: _ _ _ _ _ _ _ _ _ _	Then: _ _ _ _ _ _ _ _ _ _
2.	IF: _ _ _ _ _ _ _ _ _ _	Then: _ _ _ _ _ _ _ _ _ _
3.	IF: _ _ _ _ _ _ _ _ _ _	Then: _ _ _ _ _ _ _ _ _ _
4.	IF: _ _ _ _ _ _ _ _ _ _	Then: _ _ _ _ _ _ _ _ _ _
5.	IF: _ _ _ _ _ _ _ _ _ _	Then: _ _ _ _ _ _ _ _ _ _

Tactical Lacrosse Routines (Sequence of Habits)

1.	IF:	Then:
2.	IF:	Then:
3.	IF:	Then:
4.	IF:	Then:
5.	IF:	Then:
6.	IF:	Then:
7.	IF:	Then:
8.	IF:	Then:
9.	IF:	Then:
10.	IF:	Then:
11.	IF:	Then:
12.	IF:	Then:
13.	IF:	Then:
14.	IF:	Then:
15.	IF:	Then:

Post-Game Habits or Routines (Sequence of Habits)

1.	IF:	Then:
2.	IF:	Then:
3.	IF:	Then:
4.	IF:	Then:
5.	IF:	Then:

Go to dojodecision.com for inspiration!

Self Mastery I (+1's)

Visit DojoDecision.com, scan the QR code below, or search the keywords in the *Heroic App* to learn the origins of the lessons introduced in this chapter!

35. **+1: PM Counts Twice | Why We Sleep by Matthew Walker**
36. **+1: Carpe Momentum | Coaching The Mental Game by H. A. Dorfman**
37. **+1: Whineysaurus Part-X | Coming Alive by Phil Stutz and Barry Michels**
38. **+1: Emotional Stamina - What to do when you're having a rough day? | The Tools by Phil Stutz and Barry Michels**
39. **+1: Simplify the Battlefield | The Way of the Seal by Mark Divine**
40. **+1: We're Only the Lightbulbs - Our job is to stay plugged in. | Falling Upwards by Richard Rohr**
41. **+1: Attack Each Day with Joy and Enthusiasm | Think Like a Warrior by Darrin Donnelly**
42. **+1: Thank You. Thank You. Thank You. | Words to Live by Eknath Easwaran**
43. **+1: Microscopes and Telescopes | An Astronauts Guide To Life On Earth by Chris Hadfield**
44. **+1: You: Athlete + Scientist + Director | Atomic Habits by James Clear**
45. **+1: Make Your Bed | Make Your Bed by Admiral William H. McRaven**
46. **+1: Want to Improve: Measure! | Eat, Sleep, Move by Tom Rath**
47. **+1: How to 100,000x Your Performance! | Principles by Ray Dalio**
48. **+1: Raise The Basement | The Art Of Learning by Josh Waitzken**
49. **+1: The Gift of Greatness | Peak by Anders Ericsson & Robert Pool**
50. **+1: CANI! + Kaizen! | Legacy by James Kerr**

— Self-Mastery II — (Create Time to Choose Your Best Response)

Back in the Dojo with Coach Brian

After Jordan's Morning Workout. Freshman Year of High School

Eight Years Before the NCAA National Championship Game

After practice, Coach Brian invited Jordan to lunch to continue their conversation about how Jordan could master his mind and take better ownership of his success.

"I'd say we made a lot of progress today, wouldn't you?" Coach asked.

"Definitely," Jordan said, "No question."

"I'd usually stop to allow your mind time to digest what you've learned, but we're on such a roll I believe we should continue to build our focus muscles and continue the conversation. Are you up for it?"[51]

"Bring it on!"[52] Jordan exclaimed, excited to lean into the challenge. "But I don't really get what you mean by my 'focus muscles.'"

"Tell me this, Jordan, why do you go to the gym?"

"Build muscles, mostly. Hone my body so I can run faster, jump higher, and shoot harder!" Jordan replied.

---

51 +1: Extreme Ownership | Extreme Ownership by Jocko Willink and Leif Babin

52 +1: "Bring It On!" | The Tools by Phil Stutz and Barry Michels

"Excellent. And just like you lift weights to improve your physical performance, you must also train your mental performance. It's like having a rare superpower when you possess the ability to put your mind *where* you want, *when* you want, and for *as long as* you want."

"That sounds awesome."

"It is awesome. It is also exceedingly rare in people these days.[53] If you want to be successful in anything, you first need to learn how to train your mind, to harness this superpower."

Jordan had never thought of training in this way. "How do I start?" he asked.

"Well, there are many professional, focus-training activities you can choose from, but the activity you are practicing at this moment is learning to sit still and listen to an old man ramble for much longer than the average teenager's attention span!"

Jordan smiled. "You know? For an old man, you're still pretty funny."

"So I've been told."

"And just for the record, I'd like to think I'm not your average teenager," he said. "At least, that's not how I see myself. Not anymore."

"Well said, and yes, I am impressed." Coach Brian looked down at his phone and continued. "Also for the record, Google tells me that attention span is typically an average of eight seconds."

"That's ... just depressing."

"Yet it makes sense, since that's about how long you'll watch an Instagram video before you get bored and move on to the next one. Compare this to the attention span of a teenager growing up *before* the invention of television or the cell phone. Back in the 1800s, teenagers were considered adults on their 16th birthday."

---

53 +1: Hit the Focus Gym - Heroic Coach Program

"No way."

"It's true. What's more, they were regularly expected to sit still for hours while attending church or watching a play in the theater. They would actually choose to do this for fun!"

Jordan cringed, thinking of what his life would look like without screens before thinking of how stir-crazy he'd become if someone asked him to sit quietly for four hours *without* his phone.

"My point," Coach Brian said, "is that everyone is born with this innate ability to focus. However, humanity has lost this skill we once performed mindlessly. As a baby, you were able to focus and learn new skills every moment you were awake. Then, somewhere along the line you were introduced to technology which replaced your drive to problem solve. It only makes sense you would lose a skill you didn't practice, right? So I ask you this: do you think you might be a little rusty if you hadn't played lacrosse for the past ten years?"

Jordan frowned. "Oh yeah. 'Rusty' is an understatement."

"Which is exactly why you must learn to train your focus. Can you imagine how good you would be at lacrosse if you had the patience to throw a ball against a wall for hours? And I'm not talking about just robotically going through the motions. I'm talking about envisioning yourself making a play in a National Championship game with each and every repetition."

Jordan closed his eyes and tried to imagine the scene. He currently struggled to stay focused throughout a twenty-minute wall-ball training session, so he had a hard time comprehending how difficult it would be to maintain that level of intensity for hours. However, he also recognized that this exact discipline was the price all the best players paid for their extraordinary stick skills.

"When you practice with that kind of focus, that level of intensity," Coach Brian continued, "you are training your attention. Some call it meditation. However, if that word makes you think of a monk wearing robes and rehearsing the mantra *ohmmm* on top of a mountain, then simply call it 'focus training.'"

"Kinda reminds me of Kung Fu Panda," Jordan said, smiling. "If I'm Po, can I call you Shifu?"

"You may not."

"That's fair."

"Whatever you decide to call it, Po, practicing this skill every day is important."

"Wait, you just said I can't—"

"Call me Shifu. Yes. But that doesn't mean I cannot call you 'Po'."

Jordan laughed. "Alright, then." He clasped his hands together and bowed slightly. "Continue, Master."

Coach laughed. "You need to carve out a few moments each day to stay present, totally focused on the task at hand. That is how you will enter your flow state."[54]

"My flow state?" Jordan cocked his head to the side "You lost me there."

"Your *flow state* is your mind's optimal state when it's completely present, free from regrets of the past or anxious thoughts about the future. Many people refer to this as 'being in the zone.' Have you ever experienced that phenomenon? When time slows down and everything just seems to click?"

"Oh yeah! It's the best feeling in the world! Experiencing that flow state is one of the reasons I love playing lacrosse."

"And the amazing part is one can enter a flow state at will, whenever they practice a challenging activity with enough focus. This is why playing in a game is more fun than practice. On game day the

54 +1: Flow and How to Get it | Flow by Mihaly Csikszentmihalyi

stakes are higher, so you are more focused and in flow. Now, do you think you can experience this feeling in practice?"

"I ... think so? I guess I kinda have to find a way to raise the stakes in my mind, first, because practice rarely feels like a game. I'd say it definitely helps when our coach adds competitions to practice and all my teammates are fully engaged."

"Good answer. Have you ever heard the expression, 'You get out what you put in?'"

Jordan chuckled. "Yeah. My parents tell me that all the time."

"Are they right?"

He laughed. "Yeah, they are..."

"Putting effort into an activity is how you train your attention. But we don't need to be playing a sport to train our focus. It's even more powerful to train your focus in moments when you are bored or uninterested in a topic. For instance, what if you could snap your fingers and be completely immersed in a boring topic at school?"

"School? Boring topics?" Jordan said, faking confusion. "Do tell."

"The more boring, the better."

"Ugh. Please share your secret. I need it."

"Think of it as training with weights. When you hit the lacrosse field, it'll feel like you took those training weights off. You'll be dialed in, thinking one, even two plays ahead of your opponent!"

Jordan nodded, taking a sip of his water before he glanced at Coach and smirked. "Did my parents put you up to this?

Coach Brian frowned. "I don't understand."

"The whole 'getting out what you put in' thing? Did they tell you to say that?"

"I'm afraid I haven't spoken with your parents yet, but I'd be happy to meet them. They sound like delightful people."

Jordan chuckled. "They are. I'm just messing with you, 'cause it just sounds so much like what they'd say. But it does make sense. Just like I see more gains in the weight room when I use heavier weights, I get it, how putting more energy into a difficult task is gonna help me improve. I can't wait to practice with that mindset in school tomorrow."

"Why wait? We can start practicing right now by doing the seemingly simplest activity possible. You have time? It'll only take a moment."

"Let's do it!"

Coach Brian took a deep breath, gathering his thoughts. "I want you to sit silently and stare at the blank wall in front of you. Your only task, your one job, is to focus on your breath, noticing your thoughts coming and going, all without judgment or being carried away into a daydream. How's that sound?"

Jordan laughed, thinking Coach Brian was joking. "Um ... I'd say that sounds pretty easy! Stare at a wall? Thought you said I'd have to challenge myself if I wanted to enter my flow state."

Coach Brian chuckled again. "If you think sitting still while attending church for four hours would be difficult, think about how challenging it would be to stay present with absolutely zero entertainment! You will find this is one of the most challenging activities you will ever practice.[55] Trust me, your thoughts will take you for a ride! Each time you get wrapped up in a thought, you will have to catch yourself, refocus on your breath, and start again. Give it a try now."

"Now?"

Coach nodded. "Thirty seconds. You're on the clock!" Coach looked down at his watch and nodded to Jordan. "Begin!"

---

55 +1: Start Again | As a Man Thinketh by James Allen

Jordan faced the wall and selected a specific spot. He lowered his eyes and began to think about ... nothing. Five seconds passed and he found himself already hopelessly lost in thought, distracted by the savory smells coming from the kitchen. His mind began to wander.

When will the food come out?

I hope the eggs I ordered come with bacon...

If so, will it be crispy? Or soft?

And will they have—

"Time's up!" Coach Brian's voice shocked Jordan back from his day-dream of aimless thoughts.

"Whew! Alright, I see what you mean, now. That ... was a heckuva lot harder than I thought it'd be!"

"I can't say I didn't warn you! Staying present takes constant effort. However, the superpower you gain is worth every second of practice."

"I'll get out whatever I put into it." Jordan said, before pausing. "No, I'll get out *more* than I put into it."

"Exactly! This training results in more time and space to step between the stimulus you're currently experiencing and your response to it. In that moment, you will have the opportunity to ask: how would Tasmanian Devil-Connor Shellenberger respond?"

"I like that!"

"Trust me, Jordan. You'll need this superpower when you are overwhelmed in the chaos of a lacrosse game with your head spinning so fast you don't know which way is up! In those moments, an untrained mind will feel like it's swimming in quicksand. The more you struggle to focus your thoughts, the faster you will sink. *That* is when you will need to step out from under the waterfall of your thoughts and choose your best response! The benefits of your practiced meditation will help you here. It will be like taking an all-natural, magic pill, one that will reduce your anxiety and increase your performance.[56]

Jordan could already envision catching himself distracted in a big game and then using his superpower of focus to *flip the switch* and resume his best-self identity.

ACADEMICS

The two finished breakfast, making small talk about the other areas of their lives outside of lacrosse.

"Listen, Jordan, I know we have shared a lot today, but there is one more thing we need to revisit if you have another 15 minutes of focus left in you."

Jordan laughed, still high on comparing his focus training to weight training. "For sure. I'm ready to pump and focus my mental muscles like Arnold Schwarzenegger." He shook his head. "You know you can't put me to sleep, right? Coach, I'm gonna remember every word so well I can teach it to my teammates!"

"Alright, we'll have to test that theory!" Coach laughed. "When you pursue a Black Belt Mentality, the way in which you approach every task matters. Every micro-decision—from the moment you wake up in the morning to when you go to bed—will move you closer or further from greatness. Therefore, I need to emphasize how important training in the classroom is to your athletic success. You see, many athletes fail to see the classroom for what it is—a dojo—just like the lacrosse field."

"Oh, wow," Jordan said, nodding. "That makes sense."

"The Black Belt Mentality is about approaching everything you do with excellence. Plus, I would hate to see you fall short of your lacrosse goals simply because you didn't handle your business in the classroom. College coaches won't recruit a player who excels in athletics but neglects their academic or relationship goals." He

56 +1: The Magic Pill of Meditation | The Happiness Hypothesis by Jonathan Haidt

stopped and waited for this realization to sink in before he continued. "Jordan, imagine what would be possible, what you could accomplish, if you chose to apply your Black Belt Mentality to your scholarly pursuits?"

Jordan grew silent and thought about it, none too excited that the challenge had subtly moved the conversation back to his academic performance. Still, he knew Coach Brian was telling him the truth. "Honestly, I think ... I think I'd be earning straight A's."

"Really?"

He nodded. "Yeah. And ... I'd probably have a better chance to play lacrosse at an elite academic school."

"That's right! You would! So let's shift from 'what if' to 'what's next.' What would you say is your first step to bringing your Black Belt Mentality to the classroom?"

Jordan paused, picturing how he could best apply this lesson to bring the Tasmanian Devil-Connor Shellenberger version of himself to the academic environment. He didn't think the same urgency and competitiveness necessary on the field would serve him in the classroom. No, he would have to adopt an entirely original outlook. "Well, for starters, I guess I'd need to start brainstorming a new identity."

Coach Brian sat back in the booth and grinned. "Continue."

"I don't know," Jordan said. "Something that's more fitting to the classroom, but a best-self identity would remind me to bring more energy and enthusiasm."

Coach Brian smiled in agreement. "It wouldn't hurt to rehearse World's Best Student and choose a seat in the front row of your class. The strategy will work in your academic dojo the same way it works on the lacrosse field. Is it safe to assume you remember how *that* works?"

"Of course," Jordan shrugged. "Once I decide who I want to be in a situation—any situation—I need to remind myself to act like that person."

"You got it!" Coach Brian said. "And the more often you do this, the deeper you program yourself to behave like that individual. The habits you practice as that person will eventually become your core identity."[57]

Jordan smiled. "My core identity. I like that."

"The goal is to upgrade your routines in each area of your life. To understand this idea, it may be helpful to think of yourself as a cell phone."

"Huh?" Jordan scowled. "Did you just say I should think of myself as ... a phone?"

"No," Coach Brian corrected. "A cell phone."

"Oh. Well, now it makes perfect sense. Thank you for clarifying that..."

"Do you get those periodic reminders from cell phone companies reminding you to upgrade your OS to the latest version?" Coach asked.

"Sure." Jordan secretly looked forward to those notifications because they meant his phone would be less buggy, have longer battery life, and sometimes have a handful of cool new features to explore.

"When you install your new habits, you will upgrade yourself—just like your phone—to the latest version of your new operating system. Your upgrades will include:

- Being less irritated by inevitable setbacks and difficult people.

57 +1: Your Identity = ? | Atomic Habits by James Clear

- Having more battery life to fuel the pursuit of your goals and build stronger relationships.
- Having new skills and tools to help you accomplish your goals.

You upgrade your programming when you choose to start deleting your bad habits, installing your new habits, and doubling down on each of your current awesome habits!"

Jordan nodded. "I can already see how my micro habits off the lacrosse field will take my game to the next level."

"Yes. The secret to success—in lacrosse and in life—is surprisingly simple. Long-term success is never solved by adding more technology or magic bullets. Instead, It's always solved when you simplify your process and take action toward your goals.[58] I've said it before, and I will say it again, all you need to do are these three things: decide who you want to be, determine the habits and routines of that person, and practice those habits every day."

"To any habit you currently have programmed, you can always add self-talk and assume a power pose that will remind you to transform into the highest version of yourself."

GOALS

Jordan was happy to hear Coach Brian summarize the simplicity of mental toughness training. He was committed to this transformational process, yet he had one lingering question to reconcile about goals he had been taught in school.

"Coach, I love your idea of Identity Goals. I've seen it work on the lacrosse field, and I'm sure it'll work in a classroom, too. When I rehearse 'Tasmanian Devil-Connor Shellenberger,' I'm able to instantly recommit to practicing the routines I imagine he would engage in. However, many of my teachers have told me I need S.M.A.R.T. goals." He paused, looking across the table. "You know what those are, right?"

58 +1: Simplify the Battlefield | The Way of the SEAL by Mark Divine

Coach nodded. "Goals that are specific, measurable, achievable, realistic, and timely. I'm impressed. Your teachers are smart!" Coach chuckled at his lame play on words.

"Ow. That was actually painful to hear..." Jordan teased. "So, yeah, my Identity Goal is specific, but I don't think it meets any of the other S.M.A.R.T. parameters."

"S.M.A.R.T. goals are good tools. I refer to these as 'benchmark' goals, necessary to keep you on track as you look up and follow your big, pie-in-the-sky 'identity target.' Jordan, you are ahead of 99 percent of other people in the world."

"Wait, what? What are you talking about?"

"I'm talking about the 99 percent of the world's population who haven't brainstormed who they want to be at their best. You will need that guiding star; your big, audacious goal that will help you wake up every morning full of enthusiasm and zest and excited to make progress toward achieving it. Along the way, you will reach your S.M.A.R.T. milestones, achievements that will help you measure and manage the process.

"A fun way to look at how these goals work together is to imagine yourself as a sea boat captain trying to sail across the ocean from New York to Paris."

Jordan grinned. "I can't wait to see where this one goes... Lay it on me!"

"Before technology came along to help a captain plot his course, sailors followed the stars. Your guiding star is your Identity Goal. Now, as you travel, navigating by your star, you will inevitably get knocked off course by tumultuous seas and strong headwinds. In your case, these are the internal and external distractions you face each day."

"Like someone who hasn't decided what he wants in life, blown and tossed by the wind," Jordan said.

"Indeed. I believe studies have shown the average person has 10,000 automatic negative thoughts reeling through their minds each day."

"Each *day*?!?" Jordan exclaimed a little too loudly. He blushed and lowered his voice. "That's a whole lotta negativity going on."

"All is not lost," Coach Brian said, lowering his voice to match Jordan's. "If one can identify them, they can learn to see each one as an opportunity to practice transforming into their best self. This is where your S.M.A.R.T. benchmarks come into play. They let you know if you're on track or if you need to realign your course. As you sail through life, you will have many benchmarks that will allow you to stay on track. Eventually, you will reach your destination. But it is the process of following your guiding star that will keep you enthused throughout your journey. Although you may never reach that star, it will constantly remind you of your 'why' and encourage you to continue on your chosen path—even when things get tough. *Especially* when things get tough. Does that make sense?"

"I think so," Jordan said. "So ... without my guiding star, I may get discouraged, lose heart, and decide it's not worth the effort to continue on to Paris."

"Exactly! And what would happen when you finally arrived in Paris? Would you stop following your guiding star?"

Jordan shook his head. "Nah. No way. I'd keep following it and plot my next benchmark city to see how far I can go towards my final destination."

Coach Brian was impressed once again. "That is wise. Many top performers have realized their success by dreaming big and following their star. Think of the incredibly successful entrepreneur, Elon Musk."

"Modern Tony Stark," Jordan said.

Coach laughed. "Yes. So, Elon's current guiding star is becoming the first man to colonize Mars. As he strives for this seemingly impossible goal, he has accomplished amazing feats, creating Tesla, SpaceX and resurrecting Twitter..."

"Some people don't like him," Jordan interrupted. "But, others love him. What do you think?"

Coach Brian laughed again. "It doesn't matter what I think. Elon certainly wouldn't care what I think. He's so busy creating cool stuff he doesn't have time to worry about his critics. The fact is, he's given the world many new inventions. That is a prime example of the benefits you will also experience when you follow your unbelievably big goal. You, too, will enjoy the process and create an amazing life along the way."

Jordan looked down at his watch and frowned. "Oh, I really gotta go. But let me try to recap your lesson. Do you have a sec?"

"I have time," Coach said. He lifted his hand and motioned toward the table. "Proceed."

Jordan took a deep breath and focused his thoughts. "First, I start by asking myself who I want to be in any given moment. Second, I nail down why I chose that identity and the traits I need to develop. Third, set S.M.A.R.T. goals and benchmarks to provide me with feedback and encouragement."

"Excellent," Coach said, nodding. "And...?"

"Finally, I have to commit to the habits I'll need to delete, tweak, and install to reach my identity goal, my guiding star." He sat back and looked across the table at Coach. "I miss anything?"

"Not a one!" Coach replied. "You named them all! Now that you know the game you're playing and the price you need to pay to win, it's time to get busy paying for it!"

Jordan frowned. "You don't mean paying for breakfast, do you?" He reached into his pocket and pulled out a ten-dollar bill. "'Cause this is all I have, and I didn't know you were gonna order the steak and eggs..."

Coach laughed. "Put your money away," he said. "This one's on me."

TAKE ACTION: SELF MASTERY II

(CREATE TIME BETWEEN STIMULUS AND RESPONSE)

- Download a meditation app and commit to a daily *floor goal*,[59] a too-small-to-fail mindfulness habit.
  - Calm (https://www.calm.com/), Headspace (https://www.headspace.com/), Waking Up (https://www.wakingup.com/), etc. (Search 'meditation' on your phone's App store). Most apps offer a FREE trial!
- Extra: Record your personal meditation script!
  1. Record yourself rehearsing your previous journal exercises:
     - Your best-self identity.
     - The virtues important to that identity.
     - The self-talk that identity would use to encourage themselves.
     - The habit you will practice to live as that identity.
  2. Put peaceful music behind your inspirational mantra.

59 +1: Floors and Ceilings | How to be an Imperfectionist by Stephen Guise

Self-Mastery

Tips

100% Commitment!

Pick an anchor: your breath, a mantra, a sound, etc.

Build in micro-focus reset sessions throughout the day!

Start with Why! Remind yourself of how it will help you before you start!

Do it everyday! That's how you build a habit and see results!

Why should you have a daily mindfulness practice?

- ◆ Have more patience for my teammates, family, and friends.
- ◇ Practice staying calm, focused, and energized in a high pressure situation.
- ◆ Put my attention where I want, when I want, for as long as I want!
- ◇ Create more time and space to choose my response!
- ◆ Build my willpower.
- ◇ Connect with something bigger than myself.
- ◆ **Write your own statement here:** _

Use Technology! Don't let it use you.

Download a meditation app and commit to practice a 'floor goal', a too small to fail breath or mindfulness habit. (Most apps offer a FREE Trial) Here are a few we like Waking Up, Calm, Headspace, Insight Timer

Reduce your variability!

Practice the same time everyday to build a routine! When will you meditate, focus and breath each day? What activities will you use?

_ _ _ _ _ _ _ _ _ _ _ _
_ _ _ _ _ _ _ _ _ _ _ _

Mastery: Consider using the meditation scipt on the following page to record your personal script meditation of your best-self identity. what's your identity? what are the characteristics of that identity? what is your self-talk? What are your ideal habits? Need help? Go to Dojodecision.com and work with a Black Belt Mentality Coach!

Create Your Own 5-Minute Meditation Script

How to create your own meditation.

It's as easy as 1-2-3.

1. Download your favorite meditation background music on your phone.

2. Download Soundlab from the App Store

1. Click Audio Editor
2. Click plus sign in the title bar --> Select from i cloud drive Library --> select your downloaded background music.
3. Click the plus sign again --> select "Instant Recording" --> Done! Generate file and share!

3. Record yourself reading this script (Insert your identity, the traits, values, and habits of that identity). Focus on just your lacrosse identity, or expand to your school, work, and relationship identities as well (Or you can create separate meditations for each identity!)

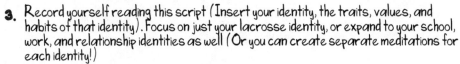

Bring attention to my breath...
slow inhale...
slow exhale...
...
Straighten my spine.
Center myself. Relax my body.
Start from the top of my head, and relax every muscle in my body down to my toes.
.....
Focus on my inhale and my exhale.
Inhale for 5 seconds.....
Hold for five seconds......
Exhale for 5 seconds.....
Hold for 5 seconds.....

Go to dojodecision.com for inspiration!

Science has proven when I reflect on my ideal identity, I increase my probability of success by 42 percent, and my happiness by 10 percent. That's why I journal and meditate, To remind myself of WHO I need to be, to make myself proud and to be worthy of accomplishing the goals I set for myself.

Now, I will bring my best self. I am: (Rehearse your IDENTITY) (Use your Wisdom journal page)

In my mind's eye, I see myself transforming into this identity right NOW. I feel my body reacting to the transformation. I'm confident, determined, and excited to perform at my best.

As this identity, I am: (Your Characteristics, Traits, and Virtues)

As this identity what do I do?: (Your ideal positive habits)

What don't I do?: (The negative habits holding you back from your potential)

Now I will visualize myself going through my day as this person. I see it in my mind before manifesting it in my life.

I know what I want – To (REHEARSE YOUR WISH) (Use you 6. Hope Journal entry)

I know how I will feel when I achieve it: (REHEARSE YOUR OUTCOME)

I know what obstacles could get in the way of my success (REHEARSE YOUR OBSTACLES)

I have a plan to respond to each obstacle. (REHEARSE YOUR PLANS)

If everything went perfect in my life, I worked hard to embody the ideals I wanted to possess, what would my life look like in ten years? What will I accomplish? Who will I be?

Feel into that best-self vision now...

Now, i will bring my awareness back to the space i'am in.
Focusing on my inhale and my exhale.
inhale 5.
hold for 5.
exhale for 5.
hold for 5 seconds.

Feeling empowered and inspired. Feeling this best-self vision calling me to dominate today.
See myself consistently showing up and making myself proud.
Planting seeds of success with every action I take.
Living with integrity with my best-self vision.

What will I do to step more fully into my best-self vision today?

Enjoy one more deep breath. Slow inhale and slow exhale.
Let's make today the best day of my life.

And Voilà! You have a 5-minute recording that you can listen to before games, at halftime, whenever you need it to remind yourself of who you're capable of being at your best!

Go to dojodecision.com for inspiration!

Self Mastery II (+1's)

Visit DojoDecision.com, scan the QR code below, or search the keywords in the *Heroic App* to learn the origins of the lessons introduced in this chapter!

51. **+1: Extreme Ownership | Extreme Ownership by Jocko Willink and Leif Babin**
52. **+1: "Bring It On!" | The Tools by Phil Stutz and Barry Michels**
53. **+1: Hit the Focus Gym - Heroic Coach Program**
54. **+1: Flow and How to Get it | Flow by Mihaly Csikszentmihalyi**
55. **+1: Start Again | As a Man Thinketh by James Allen**
56. **+1: The Magic Pill Of Meditation | The Happiness Hypothesis by Jonathan Haidt**
57. **+1: Your Identity = ? | Atomic Habits by James Clear**
58. **+1: Simplify The Battlefield | The Way of the SEAL by Mark Divine**
59. **+1: Floors and Ceilings | How to be an Imperfectionist by Stephen Guise**

3

Energy

Black Belt Mentality Athletes honor their fundamental habits to show up each day with energy and enthusiasm to play the ultimate game of life–to create more moments of joy.

***This chapter is dedicated to Jon Gordon and Brian Cain for the wisdom shared in their books* The Energy Bus *and* The 10 Pillars of Mental Performance.**

Jordan's Championship Season - Present Day

The Morning of Jordan's NCAA National Championship Game

Jordan's alarm was about to buzz. It was set to make sure he didn't oversleep, but after years of conditioning his process, he was now a well-oiled machine, habitually waking up seconds before his alarm. As it went off, he smiled and stretched, rehearsing his morning mantra to greet the day like clockwork. "Today is going to be a great day!"

Without wasting a second, he immediately rolled out of bed, dropped to the floor, and began to rep out ten burpees.[60] As he executed each burpee, he chanted a different mantra:[61]

1. **Wisdom:** 'I know the game I'm playing—to share more moments of joy with people I care about.'
2. **Self-Mastery:** 'I know how to win that game—by practicing my habits!'
3. **Energy:** 'I dominate my fundamental habits and live one day at a time!'
4. **Courage:** 'I act in the presence of fear!'
5. **Hope:** 'I have an inspiring goal, the confidence to achieve it, and a plan to push past the obstacles in my path!'
6. **Gratitude:** 'I appreciate all the blessings in my life!'
7. **Teamwork:** 'I am present, connected, and encouraging!'
8. **Passion:** 'I pay attention to what's working and what needs improvement!'
9. **Lacrosse Identity:** 'Tasmanian Devil-Connor Shellenberger!'
10. **Relationship Identity:** 'World's Best Teammate!'
11. **School/Work Identity:** 'World's Best Student!'

---

60 +1: Meet Mr. Royal H. Burpee | Spartan Up! by Joe De Sena

61 Review - Jump to the Appendix to review all the lessons you learn in this book!

He always surpassed his goal with an extra rep to remind himself how champions do more than the minimum.[62] With each burpee, Jordan felt himself becoming more energized, more focused on his goals, and less groggy from the eight hours of sleep he had just accumulated.

It was a special day. In less than six hours Jordan would be competing for a National Championship. He had been repeating his burpee ritual at 5:30 AM every morning for the last several years. Today would be no different.

After his brief wake-up exercise, Jordan rose to his feet and quietly moved to the bathroom, careful not to wake his sleeping teammate in the hotel bed a few feet away. Jordan respected that everyone has their own idiosyncratic process,[63] and he knew his teammate's game-day preparation called for more sleep. However, after years of experimenting with different morning routines, Jordan knew he was at his energetic best on the days he woke before the sun.[64]

In truth, Jordan cherished this early morning time block between 5:30 AM - 7:00 AM when he could almost guarantee he would not be interrupted. No calls, no texts, no distractions. It was pure solitude from the world, his time to energize and focus his mind to prepare for the obstacles the day would inevitably bring.

Once Jordan successfully navigated his way to the hotel bathroom, he retrieved his phone from the counter, which he had purposely placed outside of his bedroom the night before.[65]

Jordan scrolled through his apps to find the audiobook inspiration he had queued up so it was ready to play this morning.[66] His phone was intentionally toggled to airplane mode, which made it easier for him to bypass the dozens of *"good luck!"* notifications and the overnight media stories. Yet, even with his precautions in place, Jordan still noticed his fingers slowly creeping toward the button to

---

62 +1: Champions Do More | The Success System That Never Fails by W. Clement Stone

63 +1: Idiosyncratic Optimizing | Manage Your Day-to-Day by Jocelyn K. Glei

64 +1 Ready. Fire. Aim | 10-Minute Toughness by Jason Selk

65 +1: Precommitment | Willpower by Roy Baumeister and John Tierney

66 +1: PM Counts Twice! | Why We Sleep by Matthew Walker Ph.D.

disable airplane mode so he could check these notifications now.[67] He celebrated the act of catching himself almost deviating from his process, placed his phone back on the counter with a smile, and immediately recommitted to the next task in his morning routine.

With his audiobook now playing, Jordan gulped down the glass of water he had conveniently placed on the counter next to his phone. Immediately after, he dropped to the floor and began to stretch. In a quasi-meditative state, Jordan worked every muscle as he visualized successfully navigating each moment of the upcoming day.

Once his body felt limber and flexible, he jumped up, grabbed his toothbrush, and began intentionally brushing his teeth. As he brushed, he gained momentum, reading each sticky note affirmation he had taped to his bathroom mirror. Each note affirmed Jordan of the man he wanted to become today—on and off the field. These constant reminders were the purpose of his regimented AM routine. Jordan had been taught to live one day at a time.[68] Coach Brian had once told him it was hard to have a bad day when you have had a great morning and he was right.

Within fifteen minutes of waking, Jordan was feeling great! He had re-hydrated, his body was moving, and he had fed his mind positivity. His AM process was complete. As he headed to breakfast and saw his teammates, he was excited to share his abundant energy. He would use this to fire up his teammates and pursue his longtime goal of winning a National Championship. He felt ready for what lay ahead. Today he would be an energy giver, not an energy vampire!

---

67 +1: How to Add 11 Years to Your Life | Irresistible by Adam Alter

68 +1: Day Tight Compartments | How To Stop Worrying and Start Living by Dale Carnegie

Back in the Dojo with Coach Brian

Jordan's Junior Year of High School

Six Years Before the NCAA National Championship Game.

"We need more Energy! Energy! *Energy!*" Jordan's Coach's words fell empty upon a deflated locker room. He continued, "Without energy, gentlemen, you are no good to this lacrosse team!"

It was halftime, and Jordan's team was losing by six goals. The game wasn't over, but it was on the verge of getting out of hand. Coach was in the midst of trying to breathe some life into Jordan and his teammates, and although it seemed to be too little, too late, he continued his speech.

"We have all the talent in the world to win this game, but we're not controlling the few things which remain completely within our control—our energy, attitude, and where we focus our attention."

Jordan surveyed the room before returning his gaze to the mirror in front of him. He couldn't help but agree. His team was defeated. The room was quiet, heads were down, and many of his teammates even began to bicker and blame each other. There was no enthusiasm in this locker room, absolutely no juice.

His coach could feel the negative energy in the room and sadly realized his words were in vain. Frustrated, he laid down a challenge. "Fellas, you always have a choice. Control what is within your control, or admit defeat. At any moment in life you can choose your attitude. I hope you will talk amongst yourselves and make the necessary changes to turn this game around. I know you can if you want to."

He took a deep breath and sighed. "Right now, as I look around this room, I see a lot of energy vampires. Energy and attitude is contagious. If you wonder what that term means, ask yourself if your energy is worth catching.[69] If you can't answer with an emphatic yes, then you're an energy *vampire*; your energy is not contributing to the success of this team. Your attitude is taking us in the opposite direction of our goals, and you're sucking this team dry of the enthusiasm we need to win this game. Captains, this is *your* team, step up and fix it!"

With that, His coach stormed out of the locker room and back onto the field with his assistants in tow.

The locker room fell silent. Each team member stared at the floor, waiting for someone else to speak. As captain, Jordan tried to deliver an encouraging speech, but he could quickly tell it was useless. After all, he had also become caught up in his teammates' negativity and couldn't muster the optimism necessary to turn the tide. As he and his teammates trudged back onto the field, he knew what was in store, and sure enough, his team continued to get pummeled throughout the second half.

The game was an absolute disaster.

THE NEXT MORNING:

When Jordan woke up the next morning he felt like he had been hit by a truck. He was utterly devastated by the loss. On paper his team was much better than their opponent. The game should have resulted in a landslide victory. As he went through his morning routine he tried to sort out what went wrong. *Why didn't his team show up? Why did the lack of energy, excitement, and hustle play such an important role in their success?* Jordan decided to turn to the man he knew would have the answers he needed.

He headed to the field where he knew Coach Brian would be volunteering his time on a Saturday morning. As he approached, he could hear his mentor encouraging a group of young players to bring their best to the current moment.

---

69 PN: +1: Is Your Energy Worth Catching? | The 10 Pillars of Mental Performance by Brian Cain

"Let's go, boys! Bring the juice! How good do you want to be today? Show me how far you want to go on your lacrosse journey!"

The boys immediately ramped up their effort. They were hooting and hollering, and their enthusiasm was bouncing around the field like a beachball at a rock concert.

Jordan could not help but think if he and his teammates had shown up with the energy that Coach Brian and these kids possessed, they would have dominated their opponent last night. Unfortunately, his teammates' negative energy had been contagious, and he had caught the negativity bug. He had been so lost in thought throughout the game he had completely forgotten to practice his best-self habits.

However, he reasoned there was no time like the present to get back on track.[70] With that, Jordan put on his equipment, grabbed his stick, and picked a specific brick on the training wall to start playing catch with. With each rep, he rehearsed his best-self identity, the traits he wanted to embody, and the mantras that fired him up. As his blood started flowing, he immediately felt his mood elevate as he entered his flow state.

He was jolted out of his training meditation when he heard Coach Brian jokingly ask, "Are you trying to hurt that wall? I bet it would be begging you to ease up if it could talk!"

He had finished coaching his youth team and had followed the familiar, repetitive "thud" of a lacrosse ball being thrown against a wall. He found Jordan practicing with the intensity of a man on fire who was desperately seeking a pond.[71] Coach Brian had been watching silently for some time, not wanting to interrupt Jordan's therapeutic practice.

Jordan looked back and smiled. "Hey, Coach."

"Must be something on your mind. Care to share?"

---

70 +1: Never Waste a Mis-Take | Spiritual Liberation by Michael Beckwith

71 +1: Simmer Vs. Boil | The 10X Advantage by Grant Cardone

Jordan took a break, "Guess you heard about the results of last night's game?"

Coach nodded. "I assumed half of your team didn't bother to show up. What happened?"

Jordan filled Coach Brian in on his team's energy woes and the coach's halftime speech. "You ever heard the term *energy vampire*?"[72]

Coach Brian shuddered at the mere mention of the word. "Indeed I have. I try to avoid those parasites at all costs! Unfortunately, this is an unrealistic approach. So I take proper precautions to ensure I don't transform into one myself."

Jordan couldn't imagine Coach Brian transforming into an energy vampire. "No way *you* could turn into an energy vampire. Please."

"Even me!" Coach answered. "You'd be surprised. Energy is a powerful thing you can feel. It's extremely contagious, and it only takes a moment of ignoring your self-care habits to catch someone else's negativity and seep into your own pessimistic mood."

"So, there are two ways to become an energy vampire?" Jordan asked.

Coach Brian nodded. "You can catch it like a virus, or you can become one if you starve yourself of energy by ignoring your fundamental habits."[73]

"Fundamental habits?"

"Habits essential for a human to survive. Every human must sleep, eat, move, and breathe. If you neglect any of these, even for a day, your cognitive abilities will decline. Neglect these, and you can forget about having the necessary energy to show up at your best to pursue your goals.[74] And if you don't have your own energy, where do you think you'll turn to get it?"

---

72 Book: The Energy Bus by Jon Gordon

73 +1: The Fundies | Wooden by John Wooden

74 +1: Get to the Starting Line | Spartan Fit by Joe De Sena and John Durant

"I suppose I'd have to feed off others, becoming an energy vampire."

"Bingo!"

Jordan internalized this. He saw how starving himself of energy early in the day may have affected his performance in last night's game. He had woken up with such high hopes. But as he reflected, Jordan thought of how yesterday's events unfolded. His downward spiral started when he slept through his alarm. This caused him to skip his pre-planned AM routine along with his breakfast. His original mistake soon snowballed into missing the bus and arriving late for school. When he finally ate, he realized he'd made a poor decision to join his friends for lunch at the fast-food buffet.

When Jordan accounted for yesterday's performance from the standpoint of energy deposits and withdrawals, he could clearly see he had not honored his fundamental habits.[75] It was no wonder he ended up feeling lethargic, irritated, and exhausted before his game. In this state, he realized he never had a prayer to show up at his best and serve his team.

"Wow! Upon reviewing my day, it's easy to see how my habits yesterday morning impacted not only the rest of my day, but my performance during the game," Jordan admitted.

"True but your performance will always be influenced by the habits you choose much further upstream, and not just those you practiced that morning. In my household we like to say, 'The day begins the night before.' We know we can best manage our energy by segmenting our lives into day-tight compartments.[76] I believe we start building our positive energy reserves well before the previous 24 hours; but for our purpose, let's assume the day starts with our PM ritual the night before—"[77]

"Wait," Jordan interrupted. "Your day starts the night *before*? Seriously?"

---

75 +1: +1 or -1 Destiny Math | Motivation & Personality by Abraham Maslow

76 +1: Day-Tight Compartments | How to Stop Worrying and Start Living by Dale Carnegie

77 +1: PM Counts Twice | Why We Sleep by Matthew Walker PhD

"Think about it; if you want to wake up feeling great, then you must practice the habits that will help you sleep better. Studies vary, but most experts agree you need seven to nine hours.[78] However, for most people to accumulate eight hours of actual sleep, they need to be lying in bed for nine or even ten hours![79] You must allow your body and mind this time to recover. If you want to take it to the extreme, consider modeling the sleep habits of some of the greatest athletes of all time. Tom Brady is arguably the best quarterback in NFL history. He goes to bed at 8:30 PM. How about NBA superstar Lebron James and tennis great Roger Federer? Their sole job is to operate at their very best, so they prioritize getting 11 to 12 hours of sleep each night!"[80]

"Wow," Jordan said. "That's impressive."

"Jordan, what was your PM routine last night?"

Jordan grimaced. He could see where this was going, and was embarrassed to share his negative habits. "Uhhh..."

"Don't be embarrassed by your habits.[81] An important part of the process of developing a Black Belt Mentality is building up your self-compassion.[82] We often fall short of reaching our best-self identity—that's a given. Just like when you take a shot on the field you're not proud of, you should take notice when you practice a habit you're not happy with. But there is no need to beat yourself up over it."[83]

"Okay."

"You must talk to yourself like you would a close friend, or a child."

"Are you serious? A child?"

78 +1: Sleep Efficiency | Why We Sleep by Matthew Walker PhD

79 +1: Think You Can Get By On Little Sleep? | Why We Sleep by Matthew Walker PhD

80 +1: Sleeping with Tom Brady | Sleep Smarter by Shawn Stevenson

81 +1: There Are No Perfect People | Motivation and Personality by Abraham Maslow

82 +1: The Science of Self-Compassion | Self-Compassion by Kristen Neff

83 +1: Good Bad Days | The Champion's Mind by Jim Afremow

"Would you ridicule a child over an unintended mistake?"

"Of course not!"

"Exactly! So in the same way, you need to be kind to yourself—don't treat yourself worse than you'd treat another person. Simply note when your behavior needs work,[84] and reaffirm your intention to do better next time. Feeling regret is only a useful emotion if it encourages you to make a change in the future. For us lucky ones who choose to live our lives one day at a time, we have a whole new life to start again and improve tomorrow!"

With that encouragement, Jordan shared the previous night's sequence of events. "Well, at:

- 7:00 PM My practice ended.
- 7:30 PM My mom and I picked up pizza on our way home (I ate in the car).
- 8:00 PM I arrived home and took a shower.
- 8:15 PM I began my homework.
- 9:00 PM I finished my homework.
- 9:15 PM I said 'goodnight' to my family and went to my bedroom.
- 9:15 PM - 1:00 AM I watched TV before dozing off with the TV still on."

Coach Brian didn't have to say a word. He simply looked at Jordan and nodded slowly.

Jordan sighed. "I can clearly see where my night went wrong and why I slept through my alarm."

"Good. I can't tell you what habits to practice within your nighttime ritual. You must experiment to determine what works best for you.[85] However, I can tell you that the habits you choose will lead to the current outcomes you're experiencing. It's inevitable—we be-

---

84 +1: Needs Work! | With Winning In Mind by Lanny Bassham

85 +1: How to Throw Away Your Alarm Clock | The 5 Second Rule by Mel Robbins

come our habits.[86] So, if you want to perform at your best the next day, you need to define your habits before they define you."

"I'll work on it," Jordan said, and made a promise to himself. He desperately wanted to perform better throughout the day. He knew if he wanted to wake up feeling energized, he needed to start building his reserves the night before.

However, as Jordan took a deeper look at his previous routine, he couldn't see where to find time to build in new habits. "But Coach, here's the problem: by the time I finish practice, I'm already rushing to eat dinner and shower and then I still have to complete my homework. When I finally finish, I'm too exhausted to do anything but head to bed! I just don't see where I can find time to add any new habits."

Coach Brian had heard this before. In fact, 'not having enough time' was the most common objection he heard. Nevertheless, the elite performers he worked with always had time for what they prioritized. When someone told him they didn't have time, he was really being told it wasn't their priority.

"You're right," he said.

"Wait, what?" Jordan exclaimed. "*I am?!*"

"From your account of last night, it appears you don't have room for new habits. However, you always have more time than you think you do. When it comes to building your energy deposits, you must find time."

"Let's dig deeper into your schedule," Coach continued. "To discover more time we need to identify the micro habits you are currently practicing in your transition routines."

"My transition routines? Care to elaborate?"

"Transition routines are the sequence of habits we practice when we transition from one activity to another. Your goal is to identify

86 +1: Identity = "Repeated Beingness" | Atomic Habits by James Clear

your existing habits, and then hang new micro habits on them to improve your results. Let's review. Start at the time you transition from lacrosse practice to your PM routine. I believe you said:

- At 7:00 PM your practice ended.
    - This is the start of your PM routine—when you transition from school, work, or practice and begin to wind down your day.
- Then, at 7:30 PM you picked up pizza on your way home (you ate in the car).
- 8:00 PM You arrived home and took a shower.
- 8:15 PM You began your homework.
- 9:00 PM You finished your homework.
- 9:15 PM You said 'goodnight' to your family and went to your bedroom.
- 9:15 PM -1:00 AM—You fell asleep with the TV on."

"Right," Jordan said. He shrugged. "But I still don't get where I can find free time."

Coach Brian beamed. "Here's where the magic happens. The first thing we need to do is identify some time when you can practice your new habits. Let's go through your routine again, but this time, ask yourself the following questions, and remember we're looking for times to practice tiny habits.

"When practice ended, did you magically arrive at the pizza store?"

"No, we drove in the car for about fifteen minutes."

"Did you snap your fingers and magically arrive home after the pizza shop?"

Jordan laughed. "Uh, no, we got back in the car and drove for another ten minutes."

"Then, when you arrived home, did you teleport up to the shower?"

"No, I'm afraid my teleporter is broken. I walked upstairs instead."

"Do you see where I'm going with this?"

"I ... think so?"

"We are only scratching the surface, and we've already discovered plenty of moments when you can install micro habits to feed your energy."

Jordan now saw he had failed to account for the time *between* activities, but he was still perplexed. "I see what you're saying, Coach, but what exactly are these tiny habits you're talking about? And where do I fit them in my schedule? I actually thought taking a short nap was my best bet to regain energy on my short ride home from practice. And walking up the stairs to shower? What could I possibly do differently than simply putting one foot in front of the other, taking the steps one at a time?"

"You are right," Coach Brian admitted.

"I am?! That's two for two!"

"There will be times when taking a nap may be the best way to recharge. However, you'd be surprised what your body is capable of. Many times we become *mentally* exhausted well before physical exhaustion sets in. In those instances, you can use a tool to recharge."

"A tool?" asked Jordan. "Like, a power up in a game?"

"Yes! Well, kind of. A tool is a tactic you have ready at hand, at the moment you need it, to help you *flip the switch* and show up as your energetic best. The tools I'm talking about often take the form of a mantra—something you say to yourself. Or a power pose—a physical gesture, or perhaps another micro-habit that will only take a second to perform, but reminds you to relax and reset."

"For example...?"

"The trick is to identify a habit you're already doing, and then add an additional tiny habit on top of it. The tiny habit will change your mindset, and therefore change the way you feel while performing the same activity. Your goal is to feel a bit more relaxed, productive, or grateful. For example, let's look at an opportunity you clearly overlooked; wedged between the time you finish your practice and when you ate dinner."

7:00 PM Your routine starts:

IF: practice ends:
THEN: You thank your coach for his time on your way off the field.

IF: You thank your coach on your way off the field:
THEN: You encourage a teammate for his effort and attitude as you walk off the field together.

IF: You walk off the field:
THEN: You rehearse a gratitude mantra as you intentionally put your equipment neatly in your bag.

IF: You intentionally put your equipment neatly in your bag:
THEN: You think of three things you did well, one thing that needs work, and one thing you plan to improve upon during your next practice. (Keep a journal in your bag for bonus points!)

IF: You complete your post-practice review:
THEN: You walk to your car and connect with a teammate.

IF: You arrive to your car:
THEN: You neatly place your bag in your car.

IF: You open your car door:
THEN: You rehearse a productivity, relaxation, or gratitude mantra as you buckle your seatbelt.

IF: Someone is driving you:
THEN: You thank them, ask them about their day, and commit to staying 25 percent more engaged.

IF: You pass predictable landmarks on your way to a destination:
THEN: You rehearse a mantra that fires you up and reminds you to practice excellence in the moment.

7:30 PM You picked up pizza on your way home (you ate in the car).

"Wow." Jordan was stunned at how much Coach Brian had packed in between leaving practice and arriving at the restaurant to pick up food. "I'm impressed. That's a lot!"

"Do you see all the moments you may have overlooked? Now you give it a try! Do you see any moments in your evening routine where you might have time to build in micro-routines that would optimize your time? Choose one of your activities to expand upon by adding micro-moments before transitioning to the next task.

- 8:00 PM You arrived home and took a shower.
- 8:15 PM You began your homework.
- 9:00 PM You finished your homework.
- 9:15 PM You said 'goodnight' to your family and went to your bedroom.
- 9:15 PM -1:00 AM - You fell asleep with the TV on.

"At first glance, it doesn't appear you have much control over your schedule—at least, not until you tell your family you're going to bed. However, is there anything you could do differently to feel more energized throughout the night and the next morning?"

"Turning my TV off before I go to bed would be an easy place to start," Jordan admitted. "But, let's begin with how I can feel more refreshed before I start my homework. For example, I think I'll start adding a mantra and a power pose before I transition to my next activity."

"Like what?"

"Uhhh ... perhaps, I'll stand up taller? Stretch my arms over my head and shout, 'Let's do this!' to convince myself that I'm excited to get started. Also, I'm going to take more cold showers!"

Coach Brian looked at him and raised an eyebrow. "Oh, really?"

"Sure! They always leave me feeling more alert and energized."[87]

"Excellent!" Coach Brian exclaimed. "I love it! You're a brave man for willfully *choosing* to endure the cold—there is also a ton of research that supports the benefits. And taking up more space will always leave you feeling more powerful; just look at the involuntary celebrations of athletes after they score a crucial goal; their arms always shoot straight up to the sky! These ideas are great ways to maintain your energy when you're tired. When you practice these habits you will build an excess energy supply. You'll be feeling great and can share your energy with others! Imagine how adhering to these habits will help you show up at night with your parents and siblings. And when you're encouraging and appreciating others, you become the opposite of an energy vampire; you become an energy bank! A hero! You use your superhuman strength to shield others from becoming energy vampires.[88] When you choose to be enthusiastic, you protect yourself and your teammates from catching negativity. Now, do you remember the second way to become an energy vampire?"

"You catch it!" said Jordan, with all the zest he could summon.

"Yes! Energy vampires prey on those bitter people who are just existing, those who choose to go through life without enthusiasm. You see, in any interaction, there is always competing positive and negative energy. When they mix, who do you think wins?"[89]

"The one that's stronger!"

---

87 +1: A Cold Shower A Day Keeps The Doctors Away | Wim Hoff Method by Wim Hoff

88 +1: Heroes | Natural Born Heroes by Christopher McDougall

89 +1: The Battle Within | Why Your Life Sucks by Alan Cohen

"That's right. Think of this as two people painting a picture. One has white paint, the other has black. As they mix, what color will they create?"

"Gray."

"Sure. But if the person painting white paints *faster*, using *more* paint, then the canvas will slowly but surely become lighter."

"And if I'm painting with black paint ... same thing?"

"Exactly. The same is true when energies mix! A real-life example was your locker room at halftime last night. If there was more positive energy than negative, your teammates would have been jumping up and down, raring to go, thinking about the process of winning, not the distraction on the scoreboard."[90]

Jordan knew Coach was right. The score completely distracted his team from focusing on the process of getting back in the game. Instead of thinking about what actions they could take to get back into a winning mindset, they wasted their precious time feeling sorry for themselves. "You're right, we *were* distracted. We had no enthusiasm or energy left."

Coach Brian then challenged Jordan with a rhetorical question. "Jordan, what's the point of doing anything without energy? After all, nothing great was ever accomplished without enthusiasm.[91] When you find yourself unwilling to put your heart into an activity, that's the time to remind yourself of the *why*. Why do you choose to play in the first place? If that *why* doesn't fire you up, well, then I'm afraid it's time you found another activity that does." He shrugged, letting the gravity of his words settle into Jordan's mind.

"As my mentor once said, 'If you're juiceless, then you're useless.' Without energy, it's impossible to approach life with a Black Belt Mentality. You won't improve. He'd say, 'If you aren't getting better, then you're getting bitter.' And you know what we call people who

90 +1: Did I Win? | With Winning In Mind by Lanny Bassham

91 +1: How To Live With Radiant Enthusiasm | The Selective Writings of Ralph Waldo Emerson

are content to go through their life bitter, feeding off everyone else's enthusiasm?"[92]

"Energy vampires!" Jordan chimed in.

"You got it!" Coach continued. "We need to guard against catching their bitterness. Even if you have passion, and you're aware of the energy vampire threat, you still need to be aware of where negativity lurks. It often hides in plain sight, disguising itself. By the time you notice, it may be too late to fight the storm that's coming."

"Can you give me an example?"

"Sure. Some behaviors are easy to recognize and avoid, like criticizing, whining, or complaining.[93] But often, these behaviors are masked, which is why they slowly deplete you. Energy vampires don't want to be discovered. They thrive in the dark. For example, an energy vampire may infect teammates with negativity through seemingly harmless behavior, such as:

- Making a *sarcastic* joke. Even if it's at their own expense. It can't help but undermine their authenticity.
- Acting *passive aggressive.* How do you feel when interacting with someone who doesn't have the courage to openly address their feelings? You can feel the tension but can't make progress towards a resolution.
- *Gossiping.* I'm sure you have a teammate who is kind and caring. Perhaps that's why you put up with their gloominess, but I'm sure you feel exhausted after listening to them talk negatively about others.
- *Complaining* about how their situation is not fair. This is a waste of time. We all know life's not fair.

"These micro-aggressions will steal your energy," Coach Brian continued. "We tolerate them because we justify that these behaviors aren't *that* bad. Yet, these constant, micro paper cuts may mount

92 +1: Are You Getting Better Or Bitter? | 1% Better by Brian Cain

93 +1: Principle #1: Stop Criticizing! | How to Win Friends and Influence People by Dale Carnegie

and become worse than a swift, lethal blow. When your life force is slowly drained, it may take years to see the need to change your situation before you realize it's too late."

"Yikes," Jordan said, shaking his head.

"Therefore, anyone who plays a victim is a disguised energy vampire, and one you must guard against. Remember, we all want to be the hero of our story, never the victim, and certainly not the villain, who is often just a victim who has built up so much resentment they want others to join them in their unhappiness."[94]

Jordan understood. "Got it, Coach. I'll make sure to dominate the energy in any room. I know this is in my control. I will feed myself optimism and commit to sharing it with my teammates so last night's fiasco never happens again!"

TAKE ACTION: ENERGY

(Use your Journal page or your *Heroic App*)

- Brainstorm the habits in each of your energy routines:
  - AM Routine[95]
  - PM Routine[96]
  - Transitioning to Your Next Activity Routine
  - Fundamental Habit Routines: Eat Routine, Move Routine, Sleep Routine, Focus/ Breath Routine
- Download the Habit Share App (https://habitshareapp.com/)
  - Enter and share the sequential habits you want to be held accountable to each day.
  - Share each habit with your accountability partner.

---

94 +1: Hero On a Mission, What Role Are You Playing? | Hero On a Mission By Donald Robertson

95 +1: Morning Routines | Rest by Alex Soojung-Kim Pang

96 +1: AM + PM Bookends | The Compound Effect by Darren Hardy

3.

Q: What is the game all athletes are playing?

A: To enjoy our lives by being the person we're capable of being at our best, on and off the field.

Q: How do you win that game?

A: When you practice the habits your best self would practice on and off the field.

Now, to even be in that game, you must wake up excited, with the energy and focus necessary to give your all to your lacrosse, school, work, and relationships! Without energy, you won't have a prayer to reach your goals! As Ralph Waldo Emerson said, "Nothing great was ever built without energy and enthusiasm!"

To make sure you show up with energy tomorrow, you must plan today.

Book-End Your Days!

Remember, You have 100% control over your AM (before you tell people you're awake) and your PM (after you tell people you're going to bed and shut off your screens). You control your inputs. Choose energizing habits!

Plan our 'Masterpiece Day'

Use your IF/THEN framework to plan your AM, Transition, and PM routines. From the second moment when you wake up to the moment when you go to bed, what tiny, micro habits can you practice? Micro habits that will help you wake up excited to attack your goals and maintain that energy through the day, months, and years it will take to reach your goals.

AM Time Block

How many hours of sleep do you usually get?
What time does your AM routine start?

Sleep is a necessity, not a luxury! Put yourself in a position to show up at your best today!

How much time do you usually give yourself before you begin to respond to inputs?

Use this time when your mind is fresh wisely! Be productive! Create your ideal life before you react to what others want from you! What habits can you perform to start your day?

i.e.	IF:	THEN:
1.	IF: I wake up:	Then: I recite my Wake-up Mantra i.e. "Today's going to be a great day!"
2.	IF: I recite my Wake-up Mantra:	Then: I roll out of bed as fast as possible and rep 10 burpees.
3.	IF: I rep my burpees:	Then: I hydrate with a glass of water.

1.	IF:	Then:
2.	IF:	Then:
3.	IF:	Then:
4.	IF:	Then:
5.	IF:	Then:

Transition Routines:

(Tiny habits you can sprinkle in throughout your day to stay: focused, energized, confident, hopeful, present, connected, and passionate)

Build Rhythms Throughout Your Day:
I will get up and move every 'x' minutes.

Moving several times an hour will keep you more alert than a cup of coffee!!

Build intense focus time blocks throughout your day, planning your breaks
I will only work 'x' minutes before taking a break

Plan blocks when you're 100% focused on your activity. But also plan for breaks to recharge! These breaks are a good time for a transition habit!

i.e.	IF:	THEN:
1.	IF: I walk through a door:	Then: I stand tall and smile.
2.	IF: I am transitioning to my next activity:	Then: I rehearse my best-self identity.
3.	IF: I am walking to my next activity:	Then: I visualize how I can be successful.

1.	IF:	Then:
2.	IF:	Then:
3.	IF:	Then:
4.	IF:	Then:
5.	IF:	Then:
6.	IF:	Then:
7.	IF:	Then:
8.	IF:	Then:
9.	IF:	Then:
10.	IF:	Then:
11.	IF:	Then:

PM Time Block

What time does your PM Routine start? (When do you start shutting down from practice, school, or work?)

What time do you usually tell people you're going to bed?

Remember, this is your time. THE #1 obstacle to getting a good night of sleep is using your technology way too late.

Go to dojodecision.com for inspiration!

i.e.	IF:	THEN:
1.	IF: I end my day at school, practice, or work:	Then: I transition to focus my attention on my relationships, hobbies, and well-being. I am fully present!
2.	IF: I tell people I'm going to bed:	Then: I shut off my screens and practice the habits that will prepare me to wake up feeling energized.

1.	IF:	Then:
2.	IF:	Then:
3.	IF:	Then:
4.	IF:	Then:
5.	IF:	Then:

What Are Your Fundamental Energy Routines?

Eat | Move | Sleep | Breath/Focus

To complete your masterpiece day, you must address your fundamental habits. These are the habits everyone, especially athletes needs to practice each day. We all must eat, move, sleep, and breathe. You already know you will practice these habits each day, so if you want to be your best on and off the field, you need to know how your best self would approach these habits!

Dialing in your fundamental habits is a unique process for everyone. We tried to start your brainstorming with a few habits that most experts would agree on. However, if one of them doesn't work for you, simply cross it out and write something that does!

EATING

i.e.	IF:	THEN:
1.	IF: I'm eating:	Then: I will limit my sugar.
		Then: I will eat more greens.
		Then: I won't overeat, so i don't feel worse, leaving the meal with less energy than before!
		Then: I will drink ___ ml of water each day.
		Then: I will experiment to figure out what foods make me feel my best, and then eat them at the times that make me feel good.
		Then: I will have self-discipline!

1.	IF: ________	Then: ____________
2.	IF: ________	Then: ____________
3.	IF: ________	Then: ____________
4.	IF: ________	Then: ____________
5.	IF: ________	Then: ____________

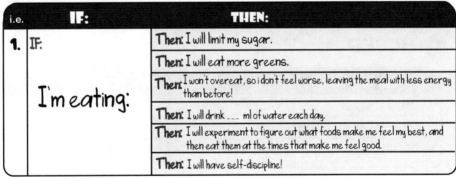

MOVEMENT

i.e.	IF:	THEN:
1.	IF: I wake up:	Then: I get moving as soon as possible to get my body feeling good.
2.	IF: I am going throughout my day:	Then: I will get at least ___ (i.e. 10,000) steps in a day. Walking is essential.
		Then: I will get ___ minutes of high heart rate (over 140 BPM) exercise.
3.	IF: I am sitting for 20 minutes:	Then: I move! Exercise is always more energizing than a cup of coffee. Simply stand up, stretch, rep one push-up, ten burpees, etc. (Scale as you see fit.) Just move! when you do so you will stay energized and focused.
4.	IF: I park in my car:	Then: I will choose the farthest spot away from the entrance to get more steps. I will look for opportunities to move throughout the day.
5.	IF: I get out of the car:	Then: I will do one burpee (scale as you see fit).

1.	IF:	Then:
2.	IF:	Then:
3.	IF:	Then:
4.	IF:	Then:
5.	IF:	Then:
6.	IF:	Then:
7.	IF:	Then:

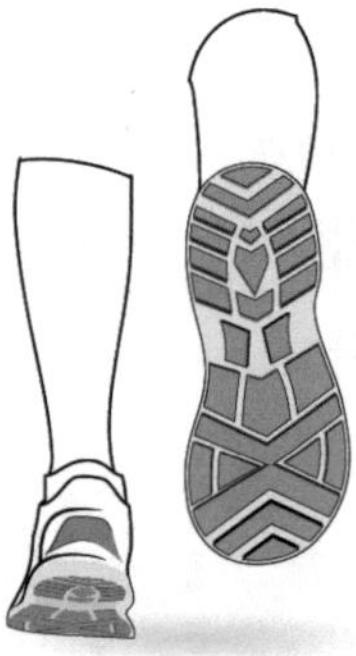

SLEEP

i.e.	IF:	THEN:
1.	IF: It's 2 hours before bed:	Then: I stop eating.
2.	IF: It's 1 hours before bed:	Then: I turn off my screen. I put away my cell phone, and turn off the TV.
3.	IF: It's 1 hours before bed:	Then: I read 5 pages of a book, meditate, or engage in some other relaxing habit.

1.	IF:	Then:
2.	IF:	Then:
3.	IF:	Then:
4.	IF:	Then:
5.	IF:	Then:

BREATH/ FOCUS/ MEDITATE

i.e.	IF:	THEN:
1.	IF: It's a scheduled time of day:	Then: I will meditate, breathe, or focus for __ minutes (one breath, 5 minutes, 20 minutes, etc., scale as you see fit!)
2.	IF: I'm conscious of my breathing:	Then: I will breathe through my nose rather than my mouth.
3.	IF: I'm stressed or feel anxious:	Then: I will box breathe. Inhale for 5 seconds. Hold for 5. Exhale for 5. Hold empty for 5 seconds.
4.	IF: I'm warming up to play lacrosse:	Then: I will breathe through my nose for as long as possible.
5.	IF: I'm working out:	Then: I will practice gear-up breathing... Gear (1) in/out through nose (2) in through nose, out through mouth (3) in through mouth, out through mouth.

1.	IF:	Then:
2.	IF:	Then:
3.	IF:	Then:
4.	IF:	Then:
5.	IF:	Then:
6.	IF:	Then:
7.	IF:	Then:
8.	IF:	Then:
9.	IF:	Then:
10.	IF:	Then:
11.	IF:	Then:
12.	IF:	Then:
13.	IF:	Then:
14.	IF:	Then:
15.	IF:	Then:

If you have extra space, feel free to write down any additional habits that will leave you feeling energized!

Go to dojodecision.com for inspiration!

Energy (+1's)

Visit DojoDecision.com, scan the QR code below, or search the keywords in the *Heroic App* to learn the origins of the lessons introduced in this chapter!

60. +1: Meet Mr. Royal H. Burpee | Spartan Up! by Joe De Sena

61. Review - Jump to the Appendix to review all the lessons you learn in this book!

62. +1: Champions Do More | The Success System That Never Fails by W. Clement Stone

63. +1: Idiosyncratic Optimizing | Manage Your Day-to-Day by Jocelyn K. Glei

64. +1 Ready. Fire. Aim | 10-Minute Toughness by Jason Selk

65. +1: Precommitment | Willpower by Roy Baumeister and John Tierney

66. +1: PM Counts Twice! | Why We Sleep by Matthew Walker Ph.D.

67. +1: How to Add 11 Years to Your Life | Irresistible by Adam Alter

68. +1: Day Tight Compartments | How To Stop Worrying and Start Living by Dale Carnegie

69. PN: +1: Is Your Energy Worth Catching? | The 10 Pillars of Mental Performance by Brian Cain

70. +1: Never Waste a Mis-Take | Spiritual Liberation by Michael Beckwith

71. +1: Simmer Vs. Boil | The 10X Advantage by Grant Cardone

72. Book: The Energy Bus by Jon Gordon

73. +1: The Fundies | Wooden by John Wooden

74. +1: Get to the Starting Line | Spartan Fit by Joe De Sena and John Durant

75. +1: +1 or -1 Destiny Math | Motivation & Personality by Abraham Maslow

76. +1: Day-Tight Compartments | How to Stop Worrying and Start Living by Dale Carnegie

77. +1 PM Counts Twice! | Why We Sleep by Matthew Walker PhD

78. +1: Sleep Efficiency | Why We Sleep by Matthew Walker PhD

79. +1: Think You Can Get By on Little Sleep? | Why We Sleep by Matthew Walker PhD

80. +1: Sleeping with Tom Brady | Sleep Smarter by Shawn Stevenson

81. +1: There Are No Perfect People | Motivation and Personality by Abraham Maslow

82. +1: The Science of Self-Compassion | Self-Compassion by Kristen Neff

83. +1: Good Bad Days | The Champion's Mind by Jim Afremow

84. +1: Needs Work! | With Winning In Mind by Lanny Bassham

85. +1: How to Throw Away Your Alarm Clock | The 5 Second Rule by Mel Robbins

86. +1: Identity = "Repeated Beingness" | Atomic Habits by James Clear

87. +1: A Cold Shower A Day Keeps The Doctors Away | Wim Hoff Method by Wim Hoff

88. +1: Heroes | Natural Born Heroes by Christopher McDougall

89. +1: The Battle Within | Why Your Life Sucks by Alan Cohen

90. +1: Did I Win? | With Winning In Mind by Lanny Bassham

91. +1: How To Live With Radiant Enthusiasm | The Selective Writings of Ralph Waldo Emerson

92. +1: Are You Getting Better Or Bitter? |1% Better by Brian Cain

93. +1: Principle #1: Stop Criticizing! | How to Win Friends and Influence People by Dale Carnegie

94. +1: Hero On A Mission, What Role Are You Playing? | Hero On A Mission By Donald Robertson

95. +1: Morning Routines | Rest by Alex Soojung-Kim Pang

96. +1: AM + PM Bookends | The Compound Effect by Darren Hardy

4

Courage

Every moment you have a choice: you can choose the easy or the hard path. Every decision can be a step forward into growth or a step back into safety. With each decision, Black Belt Athletes decide to step outside of their comfort zone and transform into the best version of themselves.

***This chapter is dedicated to Phil Stutz, Barry Michels, and Ryan Holiday for the wisdom shared in their books* The Tools *and* The Obstacle is the Way.**

Jordan's Championship Season - Present Day

10:00 Minutes Left in the First Quarter of the NCAA Championship Game

"Two-minute non-releasable penalty!"

Jordan cringed as he made his way to the penalty box, confused and frustrated with himself. His team was already down two goals, and now with this penalty, nothing seemed to be going his way. He felt as if the referees were plotting against him. This was *not* how Jordan had envisioned kicking off the first five minutes of the National Championship Game.

"I hit him right in the chest. It was a clean hit! There's *no way* that was a penalty!" Jordan argued to himself, unaware he was becoming lost in thought. His mind was quickly spiraling out of control and downshifting his thoughts into victim mode. This was not where his mindset needed to be if he wanted to be the hero of his championship story.

From the opening whistle, his team was completely dominated. Their opponent swung first, and Jordan felt as if his team had been punched in the face. His opponent was playing much better than he had expected—fast, skilled, and seemingly unfazed by the brutal heat.

Meanwhile, Jordan's legs were growing increasingly heavy, he felt like he was playing in slow motion. He looked to his teammates for encouragement and saw they were equally tired, if not more so. Succumbing to his mounting frustration, Jordan took a lazy approach to his opponent's dodge, arrived too late, and was forced to illegally push him to prevent him from scoring an uncontested goal.

Jordan knew deep down it was a legitimate penalty, but his emotions were running the show now and he directed his frustration at the referee. He was stuck in mental quicksand; the more he struggled to turn things around, the more he struggled to succeed. If he stayed on this path, Jordan feared the game would be over before it even began.

While in the penalty box, Jordan watched as his team attempted to defend his opponent's powerplay. He suddenly realized he was getting lost in his thoughts. It was brief, but that moment of awareness was what he needed to step between his self-sabotaging thoughts, 'flip his mindset,' and refocus on becoming the player he knew he could be at his best.[97]

With that sudden realization, Jordan's well-trained mind quickly took control of the moment and he celebrated the act of catching himself lost in thought.[98] He took a deep breath, smiled, and rehearsed one of his mantras. He asked himself, "How is this good?"[99] The mantra quickly reminded him that there was still a lot of time left in the game, and the level of his opponent's play would actually help to challenge him and bring out the best in him.

"Penalty released!" the ref yelled.

Hearing this, Jordan took another deep breath, smiled, *flipped the switch* in his mind and returned to the field. Physically and mentally, he was back in the game!

Back in the Dojo with Coach Brian

Jordan's Freshman Year of High School

At Practice with Coach Brian

"Jordan, are you a good dancer?" Coach Brian asked with the utmost sincerity.

Jordan laughed out loud. "What does *that* have to do with anything?"

---

97 +1: Stuck in Mental Concrete? | Golden Rules for Everyday Living by Omraam Mikhaël Aïvanhov

98 +1: How to Celebrate. Immediately and Intensely | Tiny Habits by BJ Fogg

99 +1: "Roger That": What to Say To The Heroic Gods | Discipline Equals Freedom by Jocko Willink

"Just ... answer the question, please." The smile on Coach's face told Jordan this wasn't just a random question.

Jordan thought for a few seconds before answering. "Well, I don't think I'm gonna win any breakdancing competitions in the near future, but I will admit I was the first of my friends in our middle school gym class to learn the steps to the Macarena," Jordan joked, unsure if he was answering the question correctly.

Coach Brian laughed. "The Macarena! That's ... not exactly what I was getting at. But what if I told you the best lacrosse players are also the best dancers?"

After considering it for a moment Jordan replied, "Coach, I'm confused. I honestly don't see how those two are connected. I mean, my sister's an excellent dancer, but she's not interested in playing lacrosse at all. I guess what I'm saying is I just don't see how dodging past a defender correlates to learning graceful dance steps."

Coach laughed. "Yes, I imagine your sister wouldn't be a great lacrosse player if she isn't interested in playing, but that's not where I'm going with this. Let me ask you another question: do you think the smoothest or most graceful dancers are always the ones who have the most fun on the dance floor?"

As Jordan thought, he remembered his Dad making a fool of himself at his cousin's wedding last year. The man had absolutely no rhythm, yet he also seemed to be having the time of his life. "Not always," he said, "but I'd at least have a few moves prepared so I didn't embarrass myself."

Coach Brian agreed. "It's always good to be prepared, but let me pose the question another way. Have you ever been the first to cross the room and ask a girl to join you on the dance floor?"

Jordan blushed "Dude! You're describing one of my biggest fears! I mean, what if she said no? I'd be the laughingstock of my friends!"

"I'm not your Dude, Buddy. Please call me Coach. I'm pretty hip, but many coaches don't appreciate their players calling them 'Dude.'"

"Understood, Coach," Jordan said respectfully.

"But yes, that's it!" Coach Brian said, excited Jordan had keyed into the point he was making. "The best lacrosse players are the best dancers because they are the best at taking action in the face of fear. They feel the fear and take action anyway.[100] They recognize how, at its core, fear is the same emotion as excitement."

"What? Are you for real?"

"Jordan, did you know the only difference between fear and excitement is that when you're excited, you expect a positive outcome?"[101]

"I ... I never really thought of it that way, but that kinda makes sense," Jordan said.

"In the game of lacrosse, you can't be afraid to act. You can't be scared of what others will think of you. You need to be above the good or bad opinions of your critics.[102] Does that make sense?"

"Sure."

"Can you think about a time on the lacrosse field when this would apply?"

Jordan laughed and shook his head. "Where do I start? As a freshman on my team, I'm pretty afraid to look like a ball hog, so I tend to pass the ball to my older teammates and let them shoot, even when I know I'm in a better position to score."

"If you want to be your best self, you must stop caring about what people think of you. Luckily, you already have a tool in your arsenal ready to combat this fear."

Jordan thought about the tools he had ready at hand to combat fear; one instantly came to mind. "I could rehearse my identity!

---

100 +1: Courage Tools | The Courage Quotient by Robert Biswas-Diener

101 +1: I'm Excited–What to Say to Yourself When You're Feeling Nerves | The Upside of Stress by Kelly McGonigal

102 +1: The Peanut Gallery vs. Fellow Heroes in the Arena | Daring Greatly by Brene Brown

I'm pretty sure Taz-Shelley wouldn't give two licks about what his teammates, opponents, or fans think of him."

"Exactly!" Coach Brian exclaimed. "Transforming into your ideal identity is an easy way to summon your courage at the exact moment you need it. Now, can you think of some other times on the lacrosse field when you need to practice courage?"

"Definitely," Jordan admitted and began to rattle off a list of scenarios where he felt fear. "When I'm exhausted and can't run anymore, or when I have the ball and the score is tied. Not to mention when our opponent's best midfielder is lining up to test me in a one-on-one matchup."

"Good," Coach Brian said. "Excellent examples. Those are crucial times when you need a plan to combat your growing exhaustion and fears. You need to practice your responses ahead of time so you're ready when you experience it in the heat of a game. I'm sure your coaches constantly put you in a position to experience this type of mindset."

Jordan immediately reflected on the many times his coaches had sent his team to the endline to run sprints until they were exhausted. "Oh, yeah ... no question."

"When your coaches ask you to perform when you're tired, they aren't just conditioning you into peak physical condition; they are also training you to act in the face of adversity. It's their job to start that conversation between your ears where you must choose to take a step forward toward courage, or a step back toward fear. This will prepare you for the same decisions you will have to make within a game."

"That makes perfect sense," Jordan said, envisioning himself rehearsing his Taz-Shelley identity the next time his coach instructed his team to run sprints. He thought it would certainly give him the jolt of energy he needed to embrace being pushed outside of his comfort zone. "So they're not just being jerks when they make us run. They're actually preparing us for the future, to be better players."

"Exactly! Now, aside from rehearsing your identity, what are some additional tools that could help you push through stressful situations and recommit to your Dojo Decision?"

Jordan thought about this along with all the past lessons he had learned from Coach Brian. "Well, I could get outside my head and encourage my teammates, for one. Or, I could visualize my legs as robotic legs that never get tired. And I could focus on enjoying the process. You know, think of the big picture of why I'm running. It's not a punishment. It's doing the necessary work to become a champion."

"Go on," Coach encouraged.

"I could think, 'What if this is the last time I get to run?' and immediately become more present and stop feeling sorry for myself. And when things go sideways, I could ask myself, 'How is this a good thing?' and try to actively come to the conclusion that adversity isn't a bad thing, but always makes me stronger!"

Coach Brian smiled. "Jordan, these are all great tools you can practice when you feel any negative emotion throughout your day. Maybe you're overwhelmed, frustrated, sad, anxious, or angry. The key in these moments is remembering you have a tool, a predetermined response, prepared and ready-at-hand, to combat your emotions. Once you have mastered your Black Belt Mentality, you'll notice any negative feeling, sensation, or thought is really just a signal to practice your tools!"

"Oh, wow. Yeah! I like that!" Jordan knew negative emotions were a fact of life. He couldn't avoid them. But if he could recognize them as cues to take action, he would experience more moments of joy. "To clarify, you're saying I *shouldn't* avoid my negative emotions? That I should, I dunno, *embrace* them?"

"That's correct. More than that, I want you to charge *toward* them."

Jordan's face fell. He felt horrified. "Uhhh ... I don't think—"

"I want you to charge toward them screaming, 'Bring it on!' Because once you begin to recognize how negative emotions and pain are really opportunities for growth, then you can reverse your deep-rooted instinct to avoid them. Having a predetermined plan will make you less likely to dwell on that pain, and far more likely to use it as fuel for growth."

"I think you're right," Jordan said, realizing how his lacrosse routines were really just plans for responding to triggers beyond his control. Without these in place, he would forever be a victim of circumstance. "From now on, whenever I feel an unwanted emotion, I'll have a tool prepped and ready, reminding me to act like my best self."

"Excellent! Now, let's brainstorm a few responses while the idea is fresh in your mind. When you have more time you can always refine your list."

"Sounds good," Jordan said, excited to take instant action.

"To start, think of a few occurrences within a game that trigger you to feel bad."

Jordan began to visualize circumstances that negatively impacted him throughout a game, "I feel overwhelmed when our opponent jumps out to an early lead. Frustrated when I miss a shot. Anxious when the score is tied late in a game. Angry when my opponent talks trash, and pretty darn sad when I lose."

"Good! I love how you identified the underlying emotion. That is the first step to brainstorming your response. Often people can recognize they feel off, but they struggle to pinpoint exactly what it is they're feeling. But once you name the emotion, you can choose your response. Can you think of how you, as Tasmanian Devil-Connor Shellenberger, would respond to each scenario?"

Jordan began to share his thoughts:

IF: I feel overwhelmed when our opponent jumps out to an early lead:
THEN: I take a breath, smile, and realize the game is just getting started!

IF: I feel frustrated when I miss a shot:
THEN: I will say, "Needs work!" I will notice the opportunity to improve, but will focus my energy on the next play.

IF: I feel anxious when the score is tied late in a game:
THEN: I will say to myself, "I'm excited!" and remember the symptoms of anxiety I'm experiencing are just my body preparing me for success.

IF: I feel angry when my opponent talks trash:
THEN: I will feed off their wasted energy! I will remind myself I am the Tasmanian Devil-Connor Shellenberger! I am a superhero and I don't even notice the pettiness of humans! This will help me remember that every moment my opponent is thinking about me is a moment they are not thinking about the next play they need to make to beat me.

IF: I feel sad when I lose:
THEN: I will practice gratitude by thinking of how lucky I am to have just competed in the game I love!

"I'm impressed!" Coach Brian said. "That's a great start."

"Thanks!" Jordan said, proud of his list. Remembering his prior lessons, he added, "And you know I'll have a smile on my face, standing tall with my chest out and chin down, power-posing when I face these challenges!"

Coach Brian grinned. "You took the words right out of my mouth! I'm confident you'll find having these responses prepared will change your perspective on avoiding negative emotions. When you realize each moment of adversity is a chance to grow, you will start searching for obstacles to practice your routines."

"Search for obstacles? Seriously?" Jordan asked. "I'm not so sure about that. I'm not exactly a glutton for punishment, you know..."

"I am very serious," Coach answered. "Jordan, you need to realize life isn't supposed to be easy. If you don't challenge yourself, you won't grow.[103] You, and you alone, are the author of your life, and you have the responsibility to make it meaningful. If you want to live a fulfilling life, you will need to write a compelling story. I mean, would you read a book where the hero of the story never fails or has to deal with hardship?"

Jordan shook his head. "Yeah, I may start it, but you're right, A story without any serious conflict would put me to sleep."

"That's right. When it comes to writing a good story, the more hardships the better! In every great quest, the hero must want something that is difficult to achieve. The more impossible it seems, the better![104] Readers enjoy watching their hero face obstacles with courage; uncertain of the outcome.[105] Think of your favorite story. Did the hero win right from the start?"

Jordan thought of his favorite movies. In *Miracle*, nobody thought the United States hockey team had a prayer against the Russian juggernaut. His favorite movies, *Rudy, Rocky, Invincible,* even *Dodgeball*, followed the same storyline. At first, the heroes looked beaten, but through miraculous courage they squared up, faced their demons head on, and eventually defied the odds to achieve victory.

"You're right," he said. "Those stories were all exciting because the heroes set their sights on lofty goals and overcame the odds. I mean, sure, they always failed at the start of their journey, but they always got back up, learned new skills, developed their superpowers, and ultimately succeeded." He stopped and grinned. "It's like that song, 'I get knocked down, but I get up again, you're never going to keep me down!'" Jordan sang enthusiastically.

"Something like that," Coach answered, enjoying the reference to the obscure hit from the 90s.. "But let's try and stay on track before you start dancing..."

"Which we've already established, I'm great at..."

---

103 +1: Approach vs. Avoidance | Mindfulness by Mark Williams and Danny Penman

104 +1: Really Hard Vs. Impossible | Spartan Up by Joe De Sena

105 +1: YOU are a Hero on a Mission | Hero on a Mission by Donald Robertson

"Of course. But, as both the author and the hero of your life's story, you have an advantage over the fictional heroes you see in the movies."

"Yeah? What's that?"

"You possess the power to determine how your story ends! For instance, I've already written the last sentence in my life's story. It reads, 'Coach Brian reached his goals and lived happily ever after.'"

"I ... never thought of it that way. Do you really believe you'll eventually reach your goals? Even when it looks like everything seems to be going wrong?"

"Darn right I do! Why wouldn't I? We all have this choice to make. In fact, optimism like this is what gives people of faith the unshakable confidence others can't dream of. They know if they live by the principles of whatever religious book they believe in, they will end up in their version of Heaven. As you plan for the obstacles, why not choose to be what others would call relentlessly optimistic?"

Coach Brian continued. "If you already know your story's fairytale ending, there is no reason not to set bold goals and write exciting challenges into your storyline. Your life will be so interesting, if it *were* a book a reader would never think of putting it down! You do this in your life when you seek out obstacles, stand up to bullies, and help people in need. Therefore, I encourage you to join me on my quest to look for at least three opportunities to step outside of your comfort zone, each and every day."[106]

"Can you give me an example?" Jordan asked, unsure of just how far outside his comfort zone Coach Brian wanted him to stretch. "What are we talking about, like ... stopping traffic? Dancing in the street, or ... and this is gonna sound nuts ... doing all my crossword puzzles in pen?"

"In pen?" Coach Brian said, chuckling. "You madman."

"What can I say? I like a challenge."

106 +1: Your Infinite Potential | The Tools by Phil Stutz and Barry Michels

"The goal is simple. You want to 'stretch' yourself a little further each day, but you don't want to 'snap' by stepping so far outside of your comfort zone that you have a panic attack. Therefore, feel free to push a little further than ... ah ... filling out your crossword puzzles in pen, but stop short of stopping traffic.[107] Listen to your thoughts to guide you. When I hear my fearful internal voice tell me *not* to do something, that is my signal to feel the fear and do it anyway.[108] For example, I still hear that voice whenever I begin talking to a stranger, speaking in front of a group, and just before I begin a grueling workout. Your fearful voice may start cautioning you the moment before you decide to take many intimidating actions. Asking a pretty girl to dance, speaking up to protect a teammate or a friend from a bully, committing to trying as hard as you can during practice, taking an important shot in a big game, or standing up to peer pressure.

"There are endless opportunities when you will hear that fearful voice. I'm just asking you to deliberately choose three moments each day where you can intentionally practice courage. That's how you become the hero—rather than the victim—of your life story."

Jordan thought about this for a few seconds. "So, why is this so important? I mean, I'm sure most people live perfectly happy lives staying inside their comfort zones."

Coach grew quiet, then took a deep breath. "Because that's where your growth is—just outside your comfort zone. This is where you'll experience joy throughout your life. If you don't believe me, ask your other coaches or your parents to share an example of when they were happiest. I guarantee they will cite a time when they were on an adventure striving for something great, yet were uncertain of the outcome.

"Competing in lacrosse is *your* adventure right now, and also your opportunity to step outside your comfort zone. That, Jordan, is how you will activate your hidden potential."

---

107 +1: Dynamic Tension | The Power of TED by David Emerald

108 +1: Feeling Fear? Take One Step Forward | The Hero Code by Admiral William H. McRaven

"My hidden potential?"

"Yes. Your hidden potential is the point at which you achieve your Tasmanian Devil-Connor Shellenberger identity. For example, water boils at 212 degrees. Fire burns at 451 degrees. But what do you think happens up to that exact point of transformation?"

"I ... don't know," Jordan said. "I'll be honest, chemistry isn't really my thing."

"Well, then, I'll tell you what happens. Nothing."

"I'm sorry. Did you just say 'nothing'?"

"Absolutely nothing. And until you push yourself outside your comfort zone, nothing of significance will happen in your life, either."[109]

"So, you're saying I need to step into my discomfort?" Jordan asked, still unconvinced if seeking discomfort was necessarily the path that would bring him the most happiness.

"Yes. Each time you step outside your comfort zone, your discomfort will fade. Or to say it another way, your comfort zone will *expand*. Think of your confidence as a boat cruising across the ocean. It starts out the size of a canoe, where even little waves will tip you over. But each time you step outside your comfort zone, you strengthen your confidence. You cast a vote that you are the type of person who becomes stronger when waves crash over your bow, not weaker. You build the capabilities of your boat and your skills as a captain.

"Over time, you will build your confidence into the size of an aircraft carrier. At that point, those little waves that once ruined your day will no longer even register! That's why, when we get better at lacrosse, we look for stronger competitions to challenge us. The more obstacles the better. Agreed?"

"Agreed! Bring it on!" Jordan said.

---

109 +1: Simmer Vs. Boil | The 10x Rule by Grant Cardone

"The point is every moment of every day, you're always building your confidence. If you only plan to practice being confident when you are on the lacrosse field, you will miss out on the majority of time you have available to improve. Whether you like it or not, all life is practice—there are no ordinary moments.[110]

"Another example of a hero who provides courageous inspiration is Hercules. You can channel his strength on the lacrosse field. Are you familiar with his story?"

"Sure. I've seen the movie, both the animated version and the one with The Rock."

"That's correct. But did you know that long before he became a hero saving towns and slaying monsters, young Hercules was walking on a path and came to a fork in the road. He was offered a choice by the Gods; he could have a comfortable life filled with pleasure and luxury with little effort. Or he could choose a great life full of adventure, joy, and meaning; but it wouldn't be easy."

"Ohhh ... that's tough."

"On this path, he would have to embrace discomfort as he challenged himself to grow and be worthy of the life of a hero.[111] The Goddess who advocated for this path told Hercules that if he deliberately planned to be less than his God-given ability, then he would be unhappy for the rest of his life. Sure, he would have pleasure, but like any addiction, the laziness that once brought him pleasure would someday cause him pain. Like Hercules, who chose the path of greatness, we all have to make this choice each day.[112] So Jordan, what will be for you? A life of luxury, or a life of greatness?"

Jordan looked away, lost in thought. He wanted to be great, but he knew everyone feels pain no matter how much they might try to avoid it. Finally, he knew Black Belt Athletes consistently decide to feel their pain in the form of daily discipline. White Belts, on the

110 +1: Maximizing Minutes | Chasing Excellence by Ben Bergeron

111 +1: The Choice of Hercules | How to Think like a Roman Emperor by Donald Robertson

112 +1: How to High Five Your Inner Daimon | Ego is the Enemy by Ryan Holiday

other hand, feel it at the *end* of their careers, and most typically in the form of regret.[113]

He made his choice. "Bring it on!" he shouted, mentally recommitting to his lacrosse training. Without warning, he sprinted the length of the field, leaving Coach Brian standing alone, smiling and nodding with approval that his message had been not only heard, but received.

TAKE ACTION: COURAGE

(Use your Journal page and/or your *Heroic App*)

- Identify the micro-habit, your 'best-self' response, you will use to respond to each negative emotion.
- Identify situations that tend to repeat each day. Plan your 'best-self' response to each.[114]

113 +1: Ty Cobb Playing Baseball at Age 70 | The Ten Pillars of Mental Performance by Brian Cain

114 +1: Fear and Expectations | What to Say When You Talk to Yourself by Shad Helmstetter, Ph.D.

Courage/ Confidence:

Throughout a game, you will experience many emotions, thoughts, and physical sensations. Take a minute to brainstorm a few scenarios that may test your courage or confidence?

SCENARIO	HOW DO YOU FEEL?	HOW DO YOU WANT TO FEEL?
An opponent jumps out to an early lead.	Overwhelmed	Calm
You miss a shot.		
You're down a goal late in the game.		
An opponent talks trash or hits you late.		
A ref misses a call.		
Running sprints and exhausted.		
A teammate you respect yells at you.		

The good news is this:

Although your circumstances may change, your underlying emotions tend to repeat. Therefore, you can use your IF/THEN framework to plan for them.

You feel an emotion

What habit will you practice to perform at your best?

EMOTIONS IF/THEN

1.	IF: exhausted or overwhelmed:	Then:
2.	IF: scared:	Then:
3.	IF: anxious or nervous:	Then:
4.	IF: angry:	Then:
5.	IF: sad:	Then:
6.	IF: in pain:	Then:
7.	IF:	Then:
8.	IF:	Then:
9.	IF:	Then:
10.	IF:	Then:
11.	IF:	Then:
12.	IF:	Then:

Once you decide on the micro-habit responses to each emotion, you can begin the real work: practicing your reactions with intention when you experience these emotions throughout the day.

Q: When can you practice?

A: All day, every day. Moment to moment to moment.

This is how you 'win the game' of life and reach your goals. However, practicing each moment takes courage. You must repeatedly exit your comfort zone and step into this best version of yourself.

This exercise is best done while reflecting or journaling in your AM or PM time block.

Can you think of three times you can step outside your comfort zone today? Perhaps during a game or practice?

1.	
2.	
3.	

Courage (+1's)

Visit DojoDecision.com, scan the QR code below, or search the keywords in the *Heroic App* to learn the origins of the lessons introduced in this chapter!

97. +1: Stuck In Mental Concrete? | Golden Rules For Everyday Living by Omraam Mikhaël Aïvanhov

98. +1: How to Celebrate. Immediately and Intensely | Tiny Habits by BJ Fogg

99. +1: "Roger That": What To Say To The Heroic Gods | Discipline = Freedom by Jocko Willink

100. +1: Courage Tools | The Courage Quotient by Robert Biswas-Diener

101. +1: I'm Excited–What to Say to Yourself When You're Feeling Nerves | The Upside of Stress by Kelly McGonigal

102. +1: The Peanut Gallery vs. Fellow Heroes in the Arena | Daring Greatly by Brene Brown

103. +1: Approach vs. Avoidance | Mindfulness by Mark Williams and Danny Penman

104. +1: Really Hard Vs. Impossible | Spartan Up by Joe De Sena

105. +1: YOU are a Hero on a Mission | Hero on a Mission by Donald Robertson

106. +1: Your Infinite Potential | The Tools by Phil Stutz and Barry Michels

107. +1: Dynamic Tension | The Power of TED by David Emerald

108. +1: Feeling Fear? Take One Step Forward | The Hero Code by Admiral William H. McRaven

109. +1: Simmer Vs. Boil | The 10x Rule by Grant Cardone

110. +1: Maximizing Minutes | Chasing Excellence by Ben Bergeron

111. +1: The Choice of Hercules | How to Think like a Roman Emperor by Donald Robertson

112. +1: How to High Five Your Inner Daimon | Ego is the Enemy by Ryan Holiday

113. +1: Ty Cobb Playing Baseball at Age 70 | The Ten Pillars of Mental Performance by Brian Cain

114. +1: Fear and Expectations | What to Say When You Talk to Yourself by Shad Helmstetter, Ph.D.

5
Hope

Black Belt Athletes have confidence they will achieve the incredibly bold goals they set for themselves. They also have small, can't miss, daily, process goals that keep them focused as they ascend toward their bold goals and navigate the obstacles they will inevitably encounter on their path.

***This chapter is dedicated to Gabrielle Oettingen and Shane Lopez for the wisdom shared in their books* Rethinking Positive Thinking *and* Making Hope Happen.**

Jordan's Championship Season - Present Day

NCAA Award Ceremony – The Night Before the NCAA Semi-Final Game

Four Days Before the NCAA Championship Game

"...and the Player of the Year, the recipient of this year's Tewaaraton Trophy, goes to ... Jordan Johnson!"

The room erupted in applause as Jordan's teammates, coaches, and peers stood in admiration while he made his way up the aisle to accept his award for being recognized as the best lacrosse player in the country.

As he arrived at the podium, Jordan collected his thoughts and prepared to address the crowd. He recalled all the obstacles he had alchemized into fuel to propel him to this very moment.[115] Although he didn't know it at the time, the challenges he overcame had served to sharpen his will and drive, encouraging him to seek a mentor, and forcing him to constantly improve himself. Of course, the media would paint the picture that his success had arrived virtually overnight, that he had been born with talent and had always been destined to be on this stage tonight, the retroactive fairy tale they always told when a star achieved success.[116] Jordan, however, knew better, and was about to set the story straight.

He took a deep breath, glanced out at the crowd of smiling faces, and nodded. "Thank you! I'm not going to lie, I'd always hoped to one day be standing on this very podium, accepting this very award. Even when it felt hopeless, I never lost faith in my goal. But it wasn't just me. So many other people played a part in winning this award alongside me. I'd like to thank my coaches, my family, and my teammates, who all taught me so much. I also want to take a moment to recognize and express my sincere appreciation for my opponents and those of you who challenged me to be my best. With-

115 +1: OMMS–the Hero's Mantra | Spartan Fit by Joe De Sena & John Durant

116 +1: The Oak Sleeps in The Acorn | As a Man Thinketh by James Allen

out your resistance, I would never have trained so hard to improve. So thank you."

He paused to look down at his notes, then his eyes returned to the audience. "Truthfully, I owe my success to many people. So many. But I especially need to thank one man who humbly would not want to be named. He was my sensei, my teacher, and the man who taught me to commit to my Dojo Decision, encouraging me to always maintain hope for a better future. That, ladies and gentlemen, is the secret to my success, and one which I'm honored to share with you tonight."

The crowd's energy swelled, and he could feel their eagerness to hear the secret that made him the nation's best lacrosse player. They would not be disappointed.

"In my experience," Jordan continued, "success starts with knowing exactly what you want.[117] From the first time I picked up a stick, I knew what it was I truly wanted in life. I wanted to win this trophy. And once I recognized this, I stopped listening to my well-meaning friends who constantly advised me to lower my expectations. To be fair, they had good intentions. They really did. I suppose they thought I would fail and wanted to protect me from disappointment. And again, these were my friends, the ones who were watching me when I first tried to imitate fancy new skills after watching a superstar make it look easy on TV. Like anyone, I was terrible when I tried to learn a new skill. Heck, if you were there when I first tried to throw a behind the back pass, I imagine you'd have been right there alongside my friends suggesting I explore a new hobby." He laughed, and the crowd joined him, grateful for the relief of humor.

"But I didn't care. Of course I was terrible! Here's the thing: everybody's horrible at the start of something new, long before they're good. So I never compared myself with the pros who had most likely put in the work, practicing their skills for the 10,000 hours necessary to become a master. Internalizing this helped me stay eager to learn and ignore the critics who laughed at me."

---

117 +1: Begin With the End in Mind | The Seven Habits of Highly Effective People by Stephen Covey

Jordan chuckled, shaking his head. “Funny story. Last week at a barbecue I *finally* learned to throw a football spiral. Everyone watching laughed at the wobbling passes I was throwing. And let me tell you, they were *terrible*. Just terrible. But I didn’t care. Why not? Because I knew I was just starting out. Why would I ever expect to be good already? That’d be ridiculous! I’d never even practiced. But I’ll tell you this, at the end of the day, I was throwing virtual *darts*—probably better than most of the kids watching from the deck who had been laughing, but were too freaking afraid to step into the yard.” He shook his head as he grinned, recalling their shocked and somewhat jealous faces.

“My point is that anyone can improve—*you* can improve—if you’re willing to practice and put in the hours. You can’t fail ... unless you quit.[118] My friends at the time didn’t realize I would never quit.[119] Ever. They also didn’t understand the power of goal setting. Their advice to lower my expectations and choose a safe goal could have hypnotized me into thinking I was smaller than I saw myself. It could have. Truthfully, it’s impossible to outperform the self-image you set for yourself in your mind.[120]Just like how an undersized flowerpot will stunt a tree’s growth, or a small fish bowl will keep a goldfish tiny, your limiting beliefs will curb your potential success.

“Dreaming big is like planting a tree in an open field or putting a goldfish into a big lake. When you do that, the tree or fish grows to be hundreds of times their size. Lucky for us, we don’t have to rely on someone else to move us to a lake or an open field. We have the freedom to dream big and grow to our full potential.[121] When I first understood this concept, I chose to dream big, and I always have. Little did I know my mentor was going to ask me to dream even bigger. Frankly, I was terrified.

“He told me that winning the Tewaaraton would be a nice outcome goal, a worthy goal, but it was ultimately one which remained beyond me. Not beyond my potential, mind you, but outside of my

118 +1: It’s Always Hard Before It’s Easy | How to be a Straight-A Student by Cal Newport

119 +1: To Play Any Game | The 5 Second Rule by Mel Robbins

120 +1: Self-Image 101 | With Winning in Mind by Lanny Basham

121 +1: Bonzai Trees, Goldfish, and You | Why Your Life Sucks by Alan Cohen

control. If I wanted to accomplish this, I would need to pick a goal that was 100 percent *within* my control. It also had to be so bold, so breathtaking, that even if I fell short, I would still accomplish great things as a byproduct."

Some in the crowd turned to each other and whispered, *"What goal could possibly be bigger than being named the best player in the country?"*

Jordan heard the murmurs and raised a hand, nodding. "I know, I know," he laughed. "I know what you're thinking. What goal could be bigger than winning the Tewaaraton Trophy, right? Well, what about holding the National Championship Trophy in a few days? Anyone with me?"

His teammates in the audience cheered. However, the room respectfully quieted down when Jordan continued. "Hear that? I love that sound, when people cheer me on and believe in me. But I gotta admit, as great as it is, I can't let it steer my course. I have to stay true to myself, first and foremost, regardless of who stands with me. And let's be honest, winning the NCAA Championship is also out of my control. After all, I can't control how well my opponents will perform, can I?"

Jordan shrugged, watching as the crowd nodded their heads in understanding. He was getting through to them, and he smiled wider. "Instead of choosing a goal with an uncertain outcome, my sensei-mentor taught me the difference between setting a goal and having control over its outcome. This truth is the key for any human to thrive. He'd say, 'If you want to be happy, you need to have hope that tomorrow will be better than today.' Then he'd define hope as 'having confidence that you can achieve your bold goal along with having many pathways to overcome the challenges in your path.'"

Hope = Confidence + Pathways + A Goal.[122]

To make the concept super practical, he introduced a journaling tool called W.O.O.P. that I used to fire myself up with hope each

122 +1: The Science of Making Hope Happen | Making Hope Happen by Shane Lopez

morning. That's spelled W-O-O-P, for those of you taking notes, and it stands for Wish, Outcome, Obstacles and Plan. Throughout my lacrosse career, I've been W.O.O.P.'ing my goals, big and small. The process helps me mentally prepare to face all the obstacles I expect to encounter each day.

Here's how it works. I mentally rehearse this process before any challenge. First I Wish, I picture the ideal vision of exactly what it is I want to achieve. Next is the Outcome, when I get super excited about the future outcomes I'll experience when I achieve my goal, visualizing in detail how good it will feel. This step always reignites my passion! Third is Obstacles, where I rub my wish up against reality, brainstorming all the things that could get in the way of my success. When you expect obstacles, they won't sideline you as quickly. Finally, I Plan. I create a concrete, pre-defined plan to prepare for those obstacles."

Jordan grinned. "That's it. W-O-O-P. Wish, Outcome, Obstacles, Plan. It's that simple. W.O.O.P.ing my goals helped me clarify what I truly wanted..." He paused again, unclear whether the practical benefits of this tool would register with his audience.

"You know what? This has had such an impact on my success, I'd like to take you through the process." He lifted a hand to shield his eyes from the lights and looked toward the back at the room. "Do we have time for that? Are you interested in this, or do you have somewhere else to be?"

The consensus from the crowd was unanimous, everybody seemed equally excited to learn the secret to success from someone who had accomplished exactly what they wanted to achieve.

"Good?" Jordan asked, getting the okay from the organizer off stage. "Fantastic. Okay, so let's start small. This tool isn't just for your big goals, it's also helped me stay excited about the smaller ones throughout my day. How about we W.O.O.P. what you want to get out of this speech?"

Jordan looked around the room and saw his teammates and peers in the audience, their eyes closed, big smiles spread across their faces. The audience encouraged Jordan to continue.

"Good. Now let's address the other half of the equation, rubbing the goal up against reality. What are your obstacles to learning something new during this speech? What if you think my delivery is kind of boring? Or can't stand the sound of my voice? If you're anything like me, I know you've had teachers who put you to sleep. You might be here physically, but you're not really present."

Jordan stepped around the podium and leaned against it casually. "Maybe you're thinking about what you plan to do after this. Or you might be distracted by your friends whispering next to you. Perhaps your phone vibrated in your pocket and now it's burning a hole in your pants, virtually demanding you reach down, divert your attention, and check it out." He paused and cocked his head to the side, listening closely. "Hear that? Maybe you're distracted by the chatter in the hallway outside, or someone dropping a plate back in the kitchen. Some of you probably drank too many of these free Dr. Peppers so now you can't concentrate 'cause you have to pee so bad it hurts." The crowd burst into laughter. "Trust me, I've been there!" Jordan said. "And there's no shame in going now, so if that's you, please feel free. But ... maybe wait a few seconds so everyone doesn't stare at you if you bolt right this instant."

The crowd laughed again and relaxed, slowly becoming aware of how they were currently fighting many of the distractions he described. "Just like on the lacrosse field, we all constantly face obstacles and distractions in our lives. For each distraction, we need a *plan.* Take my examples. How can you stay alert if my delivery is boring? Maybe you can mentally repeat what I say? Take notes and write questions to ask me later? Are you able to listen with the intent of one day teaching what you learn to someone else? If your friend is talking, do you have a polite response prepared, asking them to be quiet?"

He lifted a hand and gestured to his temple. "What about your attention? What if you're not present, and instead are thinking ahead or ruminating on something from the past? Can you even recognize that you're lost in your head? Recognition comes before action, of course. Or what about that nagging notification? Are you able to ignore it for a few more minutes? And hopefully commit to turning it off next time? Background noise? Dropped plate? Perhaps you check to ensure everyone is okay and make it a game to see how fast you can refocus your attention." He stood back from the microphone and shrugged. "And finally, you still have to pee, don't you? Then go pee. But maybe set your phone to record what you're missing in the meantime. Don't hold it in, fellas. It doesn't make you a bigger man, just a man with a bulging bladder. And that's not a good look, lemme tell ya."

The crowd laughed louder. Two people in the back jumped up from their tables and ran for the doors, making Jordan both smile and grimace at their plight. However, it was becoming increasingly clear that Jordan's points had hit the mark. They recognized the sheer amount of distractions fighting for their attention, and now understood the need for a pre-planned strategy to combat these hurdles.

Jordan took another deep breath, surveyed the room, and again allowed the silence to pervade the audience. "I hope you get my point. This is a useful tool that can change your life if you let it. The purpose of W.O.O.P.'ing—or really *any* goal-setting exercise—is to identify and clarify what it is you truly want. Then it's just a matter of identifying the potential obstacles and executing a plan to stay confident, fired up, and focused on your mission.

"To bring my speech full circle, I want to close by re-emphasizing the importance of selecting a system-goal that you have complete control over. It will be impossible to sustain your hope if you pick a goal out of your control. While it's true winning games and trophies are both goals that fire me up, my teammates, opponents, referees, and dozens of other factors also cast a vote about whether I'm going to be successful.

"Therefore, my systems-goal is simply to be the best lacrosse player I can be. That's a goal within my control, one I can constantly win at every single time I successfully execute my system of competing with maximum effort.[123] But sometimes that goal is still too vague to fire me up. It is. Therefore, I specified my target-goal by choosing a model of the exact player I wanted to be. I identified that player as 'Tasmanian Devil-Connor Shellenberger.' This identity excited me—*still* excites me—because I can see myself transforming into him every time I step onto the field."

The crowd laughed, questioning if Jordan was quietly and publicly losing his mind.

"Unique, I know, but I have to admit, that is the secret tactic I applied to win this Tewaaraton Trophy today. It's probably the one thing that separates me from 99 percent of my competitors, who I should emphasize are *equally* driven and talented. We all work hard and practice, but every time I practice, every single time I put on my pads, I remind myself to step into *that* version of myself. I suit up every day and set the intention to improve, fully knowing I'm still a work in progress. I love that fact, actually! Every morning I wake up with the hunger to improve. I don't have a timetable for how long that will take. By adhering to this process, I know I'm going to enter my peak flow state and feel most engaged with the world.[124] *That* is what drives me!"

The room was captivated and fell silent.

"I truly believe anyone can do this. *Anyone.* All you have to do is set a goal to show up as the best version of yourself, then measure your progress against those standards. It's that simple. And that hard. Stop worrying about goals that are out of your control, such as the praise or criticism of others. Their opinions don't matter. Only your opinion of yourself matters. You will find this is far more rewarding than winning any trophy. What's surprising is when you only focus on what you can control, the trophies and accolades will follow."

He held up his hands in protest. "Don't get me wrong, I love lacrosse and being recognized for my effort. I really, really do. But the lacrosse field is merely an arena to practice the principles of

123 +1: Systems VS. Goals | How to Fail at Everything and Still Win Big by Scott Adams

124 +1: Flow Junkies | The Rise of Superman by Steven Kotler

my original Dojo Decision. I want to be the best lacrosse player I can be. When I play, my only focus is becoming a great player and teammate, a little bit grittier, a little more confident, and a lot more focused on what it is I want to accomplish."

Jordan thanked the audience and was taken aback as he received a standing ovation. He thanked his audience once more for their time and attention and wished them luck as they committed to their own Dojo Decisions.

Back in the Dojo with Coach Brian

September 1st – Jordan's Junior Year of High School

The First Day When College Coaches Can Contact High School Prospects

No calls...

No texts...

No contact of any kind from a single college coach.

To say Jordan was feeling disappointed was a colossal understatement. For years he had dreamt of this day, the moment he'd be recruited, but right now that dream seemed to be dying a slow, painful death. It was September 1st of his junior year, the first day college coaches were allowed to contact prospects in his class, and it seemed as if his teammates' phones were all blowing up with interested coaches nationwide.

Jordan stared at the wall in his room, frustrated, confused, and borderline angry. Less than a year ago he had been the star of the team. Unfortunately, he had suffered a sudden knee injury to cap off the season, ending it in an instant. Although he was recuperating and slowly healing, the injury had nonetheless kept him from competing throughout the pivotal summer tournament circuit—the same timeframe college coaches rely on when evaluating potential recruits.

It would have been easy for Jordan to get down and feel sorry for himself. Only a year ago he was projected to be the top recruit in the country. But now coaches were questioning whether Jordan would ever regain the quickness that had always separated him from the competition.

After a few more moments of sadness, Jordan noticed his melancholy mood. He immediately stepped between stimulus and response and initiated his best-self protocol: *"If I feel sad, then I will call someone in my support group."* Jordan sighed, then immediately picked up the phone and dialed his mentor, the one person who had faithfully encouraged him through the tough times.

After the third ring, an enthusiastic voice answered. "Good morning Jordan, I was just thinking about you!"

"You were?" Jordan asked. He could picture Coach Brian's infectious smile on the other side of the phone.[125]

"Of course! It's September 1st, the day college coaches reach out to new recruits. I couldn't help wondering how it was going."

After Jordan shared his disappointment and discouragement, there was a moment of brief silence before Coach Brian responded.

"How can this be good?"[126] he asked, referencing one of his favorite mantras. He paused for effect before answering his own question. "We knew this might happen. In fact, we planned for it. Do you remember our conversations on hope?"

---

125 TOOL: Light up when you answer the phone! Let the person calling feel that they're important to you!

126 +1: Extreme Ownership | Extreme Ownership by Jocko Willink

"I do," Jordan said. "We spoke about the science of hope,[127] and how, as humans, we need to wake up excited to pursue our incredibly bold goals."[128]

"Correct! It's in enjoying the *process* of working towards our goal that we enter our peak flow state and feel most engaged with the world.[129] So I have to ask you, was getting recruited your incredibly bold goal?"

Jordan smiled. He immediately knew where Coach Brian was going with this. "No, it wasn't."

"What was your goal?"

"My lacrosse goal was to emulate Tasmanian Devil-Connor Shellenberger."

"Go on."

"I mean, did I believe I was gonna be recruited today? Did I hope for it? Sure I did. It was clearly something I wished for. But you're right, it wasn't my goal, really. It was just a benchmark, and one that is out of my control. I can't control what others think of me—friends, teammates or recruiting coaches."

"That's right," Coach Brian said. "Now, does not being recruited today impact your ongoing decision to become 'Tasmanian Devil-Connor Shellenberger'?"

"No. Not a bit. That goal still fires me up!"

"Good! Not receiving a call today is only data to let you know you still have a lot of work to do.[130] So I ask again, 'How can this setback be *good*?' I understand it seems like a misstep, but in reality, it's just a reminder you aren't there *yet*. You need to continue to

---

127 +1: The Science of Making Hope Happen | Making Hope Happen by Shane Lopez

128 +1: Ikigai, Your Reason for Getting Up in the Morning | The Happiness Equation by Neil Pasricha

129 PN: +1: Boredom, Anxiety and Flow | Flow by Mihaly Chiksentmihaly

130 +1: Edison on Failures | No Sweat by Michele Segar

work on your skills until you become so good these coaches simply *can't* ignore you."[131]

Coach paused on the other end of the line and let out a long sigh to communicate he understood Jordan's pain. "So, how can you make this happen? Do you remember the other aspects of hope?"

"Yeah. Of course," Jordan responded. "I need a big goal that fires me up. I need to keep in mind the many pathways I've put in place to overcome the inevitable obstacles. For instance, If plan 'A' fails, then on to plan 'B' and so on. And finally, I need to maintain my confidence throughout the journey."

Jordan stood up and walked across his room to sit in the chair facing the window. He watched the wind blowing the trees, leaves falling everywhere. For a moment he envisioned himself as one of those trees. The discouragements blowing into him shook him, but he stayed rooted to who he was inside.

"To be honest, Coach, I still have a strong belief I can become the 'Tasmanian Devil-Connor Shellenberger' version of myself."

"As do I," Coach agreed.

"I know by following my micro habits I have a clear path towards reaching my ultimate goal. Although I originally felt my injury was a setback, I now see it was also an opportunity to improve. It slowed me down and pushed me onto a new path, sure, but it didn't stop me from climbing the mountain toward my goal. In fact, rehabbing my knee kind of helped me realize I can train harder, grow stronger, and become even more determined than I thought I could. At the end of the day, I believe the injury will make me a better player!"

"And not getting a call from coaches today," Coach said quietly, "does that kind of disappointment make you want to quit?"

"No way!" Jordan exclaimed. "I still have two years left to show those coaches how good I can be. I need to stop thinking about what oth-

131 +1: Be So Good They Can't Ignore You | So Good They Can't Ignore You by Cal Newport

ers are saying and focus solely on becoming better! If I really am the best player in the class—and I believe I am—I'll end up exactly where I deserve to be. Nothing will get in the way of achieving my goal!"

TAKE ACTION: HOPE

(Use your Journal page or your *Heroic App*)

- Goals Check In! For each of your *Big 3* Identity Goals:
  - W.O.O.P. it! (Wish, Outcome, Obstacle, Plan)[132]
    - Does that goal or identity still fire you up?
    - Do you believe you can achieve it?
    - What are the potential obstacles or distractions standing in your way?
    - What's your plan to address each obstacle?
- Download the W.O.O.P. App (scan the QR code or visit https://woopmylife.org/en/home) to practice on your phone!

132 +1: WOOP! There it is | Rethinking Positive Thinking by Gabrielle Oettingen

5.

W.O.O.P CHECK IN

Blackbelt Mentality Athletes have Hope.

We always believe our future will be better than our present circumstances. This is the core definition of hope. If we don't believe this, we are, quite literally, hopeless. Being hopeless is a fast, one-way ticket to depression.

We have the confidence that we can—on cue, like flipping on a light switch— achieve our goal to transform into our incredibly bold, best-self identity. We also use our small, can't miss, micro habits to maintain our momentum and plan for any obstacles in our way. We are willing to do whatever it takes, for however long it takes, to reach that goal. No matter the setbacks!

Your effectiveness as a leader is always driven by your ability to accomplish one crucial task: Inspire hope. You can't inspire hope in others if you don't first have hope yourself!

Hope = Confidence + Planning for obstacles + Striving toward a goal.

You can W.O.O.P. (Wish, Outcome, Obstacle, Plan) any goal, to establish your confidence, plan for obstacles, and make sure you have HOPE.

Step 1. Get really excited about what you want to accomplish!

W **Wish:** Picture the ideal vision of exactly what it is you want to achieve.

____

◇ Turn it into an Identity goal. Who do you need to become to achieve that goal?

____

O **Outcome:** Take a moment to get excited about the future outcomes you'll experience when you achieve your goal, visualizing in detail how good it will feel. This step will ignite your passion!

1. _______________
2. _______________
3. _______________

Go to dojodecision.com for inspiration!

Step 2. Rub your goal up against reality. Plan for setbacks!

O Obstacle: Now, brainstorm everything you can think of that could get in the way of your success.

1. ______
2. ______
3. ______
4. ______
5. ______
6. ______
7. ______
8. ______

P Plan: Finally, create a concrete, pre-defined plan to prepare for every obstacle.

1. ______
2. ______
3. ______
4. ______
5. ______
6. ______
7. ______
8. ______

Go to dojodecision.com for inspiration!

Hope (+1's)

Visit DojoDecision.com, scan the QR code below, or search the keywords in the *Heroic App* to learn the origins of the lessons introduced in this chapter!

115. +1: OMMS–the Hero's Mantra | Spartan Fit by Joe De Sena and John Duran

116. +1: The Oak Sleeps In The Acorn | As a Man Thinketh by James Allen

117. +1: Begin With the End In Mind | The Seven Habits of Highly Effective People by Stephen Covey

118. +1: It's Always Hard Before It's Easy | How to be a Straight-A Student by Cal Newport

119. +1: To Play Any Game | The 5 Second Rule by Mel Robbins

120. +1: Self-Image 101 | With Winning in Mind by Lanny Basham

121. +1: Bonzai Trees, Goldfish, and You | Why Your Life Sucks by Alan Cohen

122. +1: The Science of Making Hope Happen | Making Hope Happen by Shane Lopez

123. +1: Systems VS. Goals | How to Fail at Everything and Still Win Big by Scott Adams

124. +1: Flow Junkies | The Rise of Superman by Steven Kotler

125. TOOL: Light up when you answer the phone! Let the person calling feel that they're important to you!

126. +1: Extreme Ownership | Extreme Ownership by Jocko Willink

127. +1: The Science of Making Hope Happen | Making Hope Happen by Shane Lopez

128. +1: Ikigai, Your Reason for Getting Up in the Morning | The Happiness Equation by Neil Pasricha

129. PN: +1: Boredom, Anxiety and Flow | Flow by Mihaly Chiksentmihaly

130. +1: Edison on Failures | No Sweat by Michele Segar

131. +1: Be So Good They Can't Ignore You | So Good They Can't Ignore You by Cal Newport

132. +1: WOOP! There it is | Rethinking Positive Thinking by Gabrielle Oettingen

6

Gratitude

Black Belt Athletes know if they want to be happy, they must remind themselves of their blessings. This practice gives them instantaneous access to transform into their best self. They choose to practice this in victory or defeat.

This chapter is dedicated to Sam Harris and his Waking Up App. Download the app to assist your gratitude reflection process.

Jordan's Championship Season - Present Day

Jordan's Team Had Just Won the NCAA National Championship Game

Jordan crawled out from beneath his team's celebratory pile-up, gasping for breath just in time to see the shower of confetti fluttering down from above the stadium. Reality began to sink in as he heard Freddie Mercury belt out the lyrics to, *"We Are the Champions,"* blasting from the stadium's loudspeakers and perfectly capturing the moment and emotion. Jordan and his teammates had just won the National Championship!

As he looked up into the stands, Jordan beamed with pride, recalling all the decisions that had led to this special moment. He would never call these decisions *sacrifices,*[133] but he acknowledged the rigor of the early morning workouts, the early bedtimes, and the numerous times he'd resisted the temptations that could have easily derailed him from reaching his goal.[134]

Tears of joy streamed down Jordan's face. He scanned the many faces of his teammates, those who had supported him on his journey. One by one, Jordan began to lock eyes with them, followed by his family and friends, all of whom had motivated him to commit and continue to recommit[135] to the Dojo Decision he had made all those years ago.

At the end of the day, those were the people he played for. They were the ones who motivated him to transform into *The World's Best Teammate* on the field, *The World's Best Student* in the classroom, and *The World's Best Friend, Brother,* and *Son,* in each of his relationships.

Deciding to transform into these inspirational identities guided him to this moment. Before rejoining his teammates in celebration, he studied the crowd one last time until he saw the man who had

133 +1: Sacrifices vs. Decisions | The Way of the Fight by Georges St-Pierre

134 +1: The Choice of Hercules | How to Think Like a Roman Emperor by Donald Robertson

135 +1: Recommitment | Willpower by Roy Baumeister

taught him the importance of developing these alter-egos. Coach Brian stood alone at the top of the stadium stairs with a victorious fist raised in the air. The pride in his eyes said it all, and Jordan mouthed, “Thank you,” as a fresh wave of gratitude surged through him. True to his training, Jordan had a habit installed for when he felt this emotion: “If I feel gratitude, then I soak it in and share it with others.”

Back in the Dojo with Coach Brian

Jordan’s High School State Championship Game

Five Years Before the NCAA Championship Game

“Three ... Two ... One ... Game Over!” The referee’s whistle was harsh and shrill, perfectly punctuating the emotionally-draining experience. The game was finished. Jordan’s team had lost.

He dropped to his knees and watched his opponents storm the field to celebrate their high school state championship victory. Jordan was utterly drained, his emotions threatening to swell up and overwhelm him as he scanned the field. Just like him, many of his teammates were in tears. As he watched the scene unfold, almost as if time itself were slowing down, it began to sink in that this defeat would be his final high school game.

Jordan sighed, sharing his teammates’ despair. He couldn’t help but feel sad, and who could blame him? The loss felt so finite on so many levels. They had laced up their cleats to play with one another for the last time. There would be no more practices, no more games, no more moments to work toward their dream of winning a state championship.

This was it, and it had been a rollercoaster ride every step of the way. His team had experienced endless ups and downs, absorbed life lessons that could have only been gained by competing with a tight group of friends, bonding as a team over many years. Battling through their shared adversity had built strong bonds.

All of a sudden, Jordan frowned. He noticed the defeated mindset settling on his mind like a dark fog and began to practice the response he had prepared for this occasion. *If I feel sad, then I practice gratitude,* he thought. This triggered his always-accessible ability to drop out of his head and into his heart,[136] and he began to steer his thoughts in the opposite direction, attempting to appreciate the current moment rather than resent it. Practicing gratitude was Jordan's response to overcome many negative emotions because it was so easy to invoke, and so amazingly effective in helping him *flip the switch* to quickly experience a more positive mood.

With this newfound positivity, Jordan picked himself off the turf and began to make his way to his team's bench, hugging and consoling each of his teammates along the way. His team huddled together as his coaches said a few words of encouragement before they lined up to shake hands and watch their opponent's accept their championship trophy. Jordan embraced these final moments on the field and thanked his coaches and teammates before making his way to the bleachers to personally thank his family, friends, and fans who had traveled all this way just to support him. He then sought out Coach Brian, waiting patiently in the back of the procession. Jordan reached out and hugged his mentor, inviting him to walk with him back to the locker room.

"I know this isn't the outcome you hoped for," Coach began, "but you should be proud of your season and how you competed on the field tonight. How do you feel?" He understood how Jordan might be slow to accept the deserved praise after the heartbreaking ending to an otherwise great season.

Jordan took a deep breath. After taking a moment to investigate his current state, he said, "Strangely enough ... I think I feel okay. I know we left it all out on the field tonight. We controlled what was in our control, you know? Our opponents played well. *We* played well! But in the end, they were the better team tonight. That's really all there is to it."

---

136 +1: Grateful Flow | The Tools by Phil Stutz and Barry Michels

Coach Brian paused, knowing Jordan needed a moment to lean into his emotions. “Can you still say you have a lot to be grateful for, Jordan?”

“Oh, absolutely! No question! We had a great season, Coach, and I’m grateful for all the moments I was able to share with my teammates. This game is just a passing mist in time, but those relationships? Those connections? Those will last a lifetime.”

“They absolutely will! I’m glad to see you’re practicing gratitude. In victory or defeat, it’s always a smart decision. Gratitude is not only a positive emotion, it’s a great tool that allows you to *flip the switch* and become happy in *any* moment.”

“In *any* moment?” Jordan asked. He knew gratitude was a positive emotion to experience, but never thought of it as an activity to practice. “That sounds kinda hard to believe.”

“It is, but it’s true. Gratitude is one of the best tools you can deploy to instantly lift your mood,” Coach Brian answered. “Take a moment to look back at your teammates. I’m sure some of them are grateful for this moment, for others the emotion will hit them in a few hours when they reflect on your season together, but at this moment, how many would you say appear to be practicing gratitude?”

Jordan stopped walking toward the locker room and glanced back toward the field. He saw many of his teammates with their heads in their hands, still in tears, overwhelmed and drowning in their misfortune. As Jordan witnessed their pain, he couldn’t help but feel an echo of sadness overwhelm him once again as his mind turned inwards. He began to think, *My teammates and I have a good reason to feel sad. We worked hard for this day, preparing for an outcome, but we fell short. This is the end. We will never play together again. We failed.* Just like that, Jordan began to feel sorry for himself once again.

However, just as quickly as the waterfall of negative emotions began to leak through his dam of positivity, he was able to catch himself lost in thought and realize how his emotions could turn on a dime.

He turned his attention outward to Coach Brian.[137] "So, I'm guessing now's a good time to practice gratitude?"

"It is." Coach Brian smiled, celebrating Jordan's ability to catch himself lost in thought and recommit to their conversation. "There's never a bad time to practice gratitude. But more to your point, whenever you feel sad, let down, afraid, angry, frustrated, jealous, or really *any* negative emotion, *that* is a perfect time to practice gratitude." He motioned behind them. "Look back at your teammates once more. However, this time, don't let your emotions run the show. Instead, proactively command yourself to practice gratitude. When you do, you will find it's virtually impossible to feel sad when you feel grateful. In the worst of times, no matter how sad or painful, it is still easy to find *something* to be grateful for. And once you do, you will start to turn the tide inside your mind."

"I like that," Jordan said. "Almost sounds poetic."

"The alternative is feeling depressed," Coach continued. "If you enjoy that feeling, then, by all means, compare yourself with the opponent who just beat you. Think of their post-game celebration and all their good fortune you won't experience because of today. But be forewarned, that's a one-way ticket to 'Sadtown.'"

Jordan thought about Coach's words. He didn't want to complain about the calls that hadn't gone his way, the shots he almost scored, and the many events that could have gone differently throughout the game, but didn't. It was in the past, and Jordan wanted to feel good in the present. He *chose* to feel good in the present. He slowly turned back to look at his teammates and actively rifled through an assortment of happy thoughts which began flooding his mind. "I am grateful for the moments I spent training with my teammates," he said aloud. "And I'm grateful for all the friends and family who supported me in the stands today. And I'm grateful for a Coach who was willing to put so much effort into preparing us for the game."

---

137 +1: The Space Between Stimulus and Response | Man's Search for Meaning by Viktor Frankl

"Excellent observations," Coach Brian said, interrupting Jordan's brainstorming. "How do you feel?"

"Much better!" Jordan replied and continued, "It's amazing how changing my frame of mind instantly changed the way I feel. And I could go on! The more I accentuate the positive, the more things came to mind I could be grateful for."

"Gratitude is a powerful force."

"It's kinda obvious now. It's not what happens to me that affects my emotions or mood, but how I *think* about them. For instance, I thought I was going to be fine the first time you had me look back at my teammates. But when I saw them agonizing over the loss, trying to practice gratitude was suddenly the furthest thing from my mind. However, when I had a plan and stepped between stimulus and response, I was able to fill that void with a thought of gratitude. I was totally in control of my feelings!"

Coach Brian was pleased to see Jordan's excitement. "I'm glad it worked! But I've held you up long enough. I've got a feeling you'll have to practice this process a few more times tonight. If you would like to talk more tomorrow, I'd be happy to introduce you to a few additional gratitude practices that have greatly impacted my happiness and general state of well-being over the years."

"Sure thing! Can we meet at the coffee shop around the corner tomorrow morning when we get back in town?" Jordan asked.

"I'll see you there at nine," Coach said, nodding his head. "Have a good night, Jordan. And again, congratulations on getting this far!"

"Thanks, Coach. See you tomorrow!"

After showering and changing, Jordan boarded the bus for a quiet, reflective ride home. When he arrived back at school, he said a heartfelt goodbye to his teammates and drove home to join his family, who were gathered around the kitchen table, eagerly waiting to discuss the game. At first, his parents and siblings were quiet and let Jordan lead the conversation. They didn't want to ask too many questions or comment about the game for fear of triggering a cascade of emotions. However, once Jordan took the time to thank them for attending and for waiting up late to talk with him, they saw how he was handling himself and began to relax, sharing their insights and observations.

Jordan was amazed at how much better the interaction went with them when he took on an air of gratitude. Compared to past conversations when he thought he was entitled to emotional outbursts, it was a marked improvement. He cringed when he thought about how he would regularly erupt when his parents or siblings asked the wrong question, catapulting him to relive a passionate moment. With his newfound control and perspective, even tough topics weren't enough to throw him off course.

After the kitchen talk, the night soon wound down and Jordan headed to bed. He nodded off quickly, thinking how lucky he was for all his blessings. He was excited to meet Coach Brian in the morning to continue learning additional strategies he had credited for his almost constant state of stoic optimism.

When morning came, Jordan woke once again, thinking about the game. It took a moment of sadness before he caught himself lost in thought, and began to shower his consciousness with all things he was grateful for this morning. He was alive. He was healthy. And he was about to have eggs and bacon with someone who cared for him!

Jordan arrived at the restaurant to see Coach Brian already chatting away with many locals. It seemed as if Coach knew everyone in the room, and each person he spoke with left the conversation happier. Jordan was eager to continue to learn the tactics the Coach used to brighten everyone's day, and he had a hunch it might have something to do with the topic of the day: gratitude. When Coach Brian saw him, he greeted Jordan kindly and gestured for him to take a seat at the corner table.

They exchanged pleasantries and once their order was in, Coach jumped right into the heart of their conversation. "So you still want to know the strategy that enables me to be happy no matter what is going on around me?"

"Of course!" Jordan pleaded. "Whatever it is, it's gotta be priceless!"

"The stoics call the strategy 'negative visualization.' I use this strategy whenever something doesn't go my way. For example, let's say I just lost the state championship..."

Jordan winced at Coach Brian's very specific example. "That doesn't sound very positive, but please go on," Jordan muttered. He leaned back, put his hands behind his head and prepared for Coach Brian to explain.

"I should point out that I also use this strategy when dealing with minor everyday occurrences. Perhaps our food is already cold when it arrives, or it's not exactly what we ordered. Or maybe we're just stuck in traffic and will be late for practice."

Jordan nodded, understanding Coach's point. It wasn't a strategy to be saved for the big things. This advice was supposed to be used throughout mundane occurrences, minor events or setbacks that happened a dozen or so times every day.

Coach Brian continued his discussion. "When these things happen, I try to think of more, really bad things that *haven't* happened to me. I might think I haven't suffered a career-ending injury, and I haven't been diagnosed with a life-threatening illness. And then I begin to think of all the people who *have* suffered those sorts of despair in their lives."[138]

"Huh," Jordan said, frowning. He was genuinely surprised, and didn't expect that dark of a turn in the conversation. However, he naturally began to think of how lucky he was that neither he nor his loved ones had experienced either of those calamities.

Coach Brian continued. "I then reflect how, if I were in their shoes, I would be desperate and grateful to get back to the exact situation I'm facing now—just having lost an important game I really wanted to win. Or stuck in traffic, eating cold food or whatever, but without any other real care in the world."

---

138 +1: Stoic Negative Visualization | A Guide to the Good Life by William B. Irvine

Jordan agreed. He felt a wave of appreciation wash over him as Coach reframed his conversation. "You're right, Coach," he said. "Last night, when you had me look back at the field, I started to catch a gloomy mood when I saw my teammates and our fans reacting to our loss. Everyone seemed so sad, upset, and defeated. Some fans were even angry about it! But in the grand scheme of things, that one game is nothing to get upset about, and no reason not to find joy in each other's company. As you said, we have a *lot* to be grateful for!"

"Yes, we do," agreed Coach Brian. "But stick with my analogy for a moment longer to let me drive the point home. Let me ask you this: What if you had lost the semi-final game and never even had the opportunity to *compete* in this state championship game? What if you didn't even make the state playoffs?

"The truth is, because you have the freedom to listen to me right now, you are in an unusual situation. Think of the billions of people on earth at this very moment who would consider their prayers answered if they could change places with you. Hundreds, no, thousands of people would be grateful to have played in and lost the most important lacrosse game of their lives. To be healthy enough to run around a lacrosse field, pain free. To have teammates, friends, and a loving family to share the experience of a championship loss with. Even more, to possess the luxury of free time in which they could pursue their lacrosse goals!"[139]

Jordan's eyes grew wide. "Oh, wow," he said, envisioning everything Coach Brian was saying.

"Having these things is an incredible gift, and a reason to practice gratitude! Jordan, just think of what it would be like to *lose* all these things you hold dear, to see them crumble in your hands like dust, and then have them magically restored to the very moment you find yourself in now. What would you give for the opportunity to be reunited with your teammates at this very moment, having lost the championship, but nonetheless celebrating a pretty remarkable season?"

139 Waking Up App: A Lesson On Gratitude | by Sam Harris

Jordan had never thought of this and began to think about how much he would savor being back in that exact moment, right now. His mood was totally transformed. It gave him instantaneous access to his best self and to a feeling of pure gratitude for his teammates and how his lacrosse season had ended. “That’s really, really amazing. Powerful!”

Coach Brian could see the sense of gratitude spread across Jordan’s face. “It’s easy to get caught up in the sadness and focus on what you lost. And the loss is real, and painful, for sure. But when you contrast your current situation with that of a billion people who would consider their prayers answered to change places with you, you can’t help *but* feel grateful. The best part is it only takes a brief moment to reboot your mind through this thought exercise. This, Jordan, has been a crucial tool in helping me create and maintain a happy life.”

Jordan took a deep breath, smiled, and was in the midst of reflecting on the lesson when he glanced down and noticed his food had arrived. Without effort, his thoughts naturally flowed toward how lucky he was to have the opportunity to enjoy this delicious breakfast with someone who truly cared about him.

Jordan wasn’t even on the second bite of his breakfast before Coach Brian asked, “Ready for my next strategy?”

“Ummm…” Jordan said through a mouthful of food. “I just started…”

“This one will only take a second, and will instantly make you feel more present and more focused.”

Jordan nodded, swallowed, and gulped down a big swig of water.

“Don’t worry, you can practice this even as you take your next bite of food. Go ahead, pick something from your plate.”

Jordan eyed Coach Brian suspiciously, wondering what he had planned as he stabbed his fork into a juicy piece of bacon. He popped it into his mouth before Coach could protest. As soon as the flavor hit Jordan’s taste buds, Coach Brian grinned. “Okay, now, as you chew that piece of bacon, I want you to ask yourself, 'What if this is the last piece of bacon I will ever eat for the rest of my life?'"

Jordan followed Coach's instructions and immediately began to enjoy the sweet, smoky, and salty flavor infusing his taste buds. He chewed longer and slower than usual to savor the experience a little bit more.

"And? How was it?" Coach Brian asked eagerly. "Would you say it was the best piece of bacon of your life?"

Jordan wasn't willing to go that far. Still, he had to admit, taking the time to mindfully enjoy each second of the bite made him savor it that much more. "I guess. I mean, I've eaten thousands of pieces of bacon in my life, so mathematically, it's doubtful this was my absolute best piece of bacon, but paying more attention certainly made me feel that it was."

"Good," Coach Brian said. "That was exactly the point I was trying to make. Contrary to what the world will try to tell you, your true source of wealth is not money, but attention. *Your* attention."

"Woah, woah, woah..." Jordan said, holding his hands up in protest. "Hold on. If you're talking about money, I'm gonna need you to go nice and slow. I don't want to miss a thing." He took out a notepad and pen and started to scribble, repeating the message slowly. "My true wealth ... is my ... attention ..." He looked up. "Got it. Continue, please."

Coach smiled, looking down at the notepad. "I'm glad to see you remembered your notepad today. As I was saying, when you remind yourself that there will come a day when you do an activity for a final time, you immediately enjoy it a bit more. Knowing this will change your experience of it in the current moment. Every moment, no matter how mundane, will become somewhat more precious to savor."

Jordan nodded as he wrote, knowing Coach Brian was talking about more than just bacon. As he thought of going through his day and doing everything for a finite number of times, he considered all the moments he took for granted—the beautiful moments as well as the seemingly unenjoyable moments, like losing a game. Moments he previously just tried to 'get through.'

Coach Brian continued. "My point is that life is precious, and you must constantly remind yourself of this fact so you don't take a single moment for granted. Each time you do something, that is one last time you will ever do it."[140]

The weight of that insight hit Jordan and he whispered, "Wow! That is so true."

"When you do something a final time, you rarely recognize it in the moment. For instance, the last time I played lacrosse, I wasn't remotely aware it would be my last time. If I had known ahead of time, I'm sure I would have enjoyed each shot a little bit more. Even the moments I didn't enjoy at the time, for instance, when I got the ball checked out of my stick and was out of breath, frantically trying to chase down my opponent—that was still a precious moment to celebrate."

Jordan thought of Coach Brian playing his last lacrosse game before reflecting on many of his teammates who likely played their last organized lacrosse game last night. "I think I get it. So, as I go about my day, I just need to rehearse, 'What if this is the last time?' in the midst of any activity and I will get more enjoyment out of it."

"Precisely! If there is a single lesson to remember that will bring more joy into your life, this is it. Jordan, don't wait. Don't wait until you play your next lacrosse game to decide you will enjoy it as if it's the last time you will play! Make that decision now. Then shine your attention in the same manner on *whatever* you're doing! The only alternative is to be lost in thought. Don't waste any time!"

Coach leaned in closer. "Having a mantra, ready-at-hand, is the easiest way to remind yourself to mindfully enjoy each and every experience. You can apply this technique to the simplest activities,

140 Waking Up App: What if This Is The Last Time? | By Sam Harris

even down to each breath you take. In the moments of your game, ask yourself how you'll approach and appreciate them:

What if it's the last time you put your lacrosse gear on?

The last time you get to sprint down the field?

What if this is the last time you take a shot?

The last time you celebrate scoring a goal?

The last time you encourage a teammate?

What if this is the last time you play a lacrosse game?

What if this is the last deep breath you take to calm your mind and re-engage your focus?

Jordan understood Coach's message. He knew this approach to living was the tactic Coach Brian used to guard himself against the stress that tormented most people. It was effective, powerful. Therefore, Jordan made a note to build this new tool, one which promised to bring more joy and excitement into any moment—even the negative experiences—into his routine.

The two continued their small talk, sharing their plans for the summer before saying their goodbyes and parting ways. As Jordan walked home, he used this tool to frame the rest of his day. He mindfully enjoyed each step as he thought, *What if this is the last time I walk home from breakfast?* When he walked through his front door, he used the technique again to greet his parents. *What if this is the last time I see my Mom?* He greeted her with a hug and asked engaging questions about her day. Because he was more present, their interaction was more pleasant than ever before. He realized every moment was precious, and represented a finite opportunity to practice gratitude in his life. He would be sure to make every moment count!

TAKE ACTION: GRATITUDE

(Use your Journal page or your *Heroic App*)

- Choose (1) Gratitude Exercise:
  - Write five things you're grateful for.[141]
  - Write a gratitude letter.[142]
  - Negative visualization exercise.[143]
  - Grateful Flow—Observe what you're grateful for in your current surroundings.[144]
  - "Thank You" Mantra plugged into your emotional response routine.[145]

---

141 +1: Gratitude, Science Says: It Works! | Thanks! by Robert A. Emmons

142 +1: Gratitude Letters (+ Visits) | Gratitude Works! by Robert A. Emmons

143 +1: Stoic Negative Visualization | A Guide to the Good Life by William B. Irvine

144 +1: Grateful Flow | The Tools by Phil Stutz and Barry Michels

145 +1: Thank You. Thank You. Thank You | Words to Live by Eknath Easwaran

6.

How to Enjoy the Journey!

Practicing gratitude is a great response to battle the daily onslaught of negative emotions, because it is so easy to invoke and amazingly effective in helping you to quickly experience a more powerful, positive mood. Gratitude is one of the best tools you can deploy to instantly lift your mood whenever you feel sad, let down, afraid, angry, frustrated, jealous, or really any negative emotion. Anytime you're pulled down, that is the perfect time to practice gratitude.

IDEA 1: Write down simple things you're grateful for :

Brainstorm non-obvious things you're grateful for and why you're thankful for them. Don't just write down your family members! Flex your imagination muscle to get the full effect.

1. **For example,** If you're journaling with a pen in hand, start there. You're grateful for the invention of an instrument with which you can easily record your thoughts. Imagine a world where pens don't exist!

2. **For example,** Then think how grateful you are for the person who invented the pen. How about the people who work at the factory who manufactured the pen?

3. **For example,** The ink?

4. **For example,** How about the pen cap itself, preventing the pen from exploding or leaking in your pocket?

1.	5.
2.	6.
3.	7.
4.	8.

When you look for what's good in the world you will unconsciously tend to see more of it! (And it sure beats looking for and focusing on the negative!)

IDEA 2: Select one important person from your past who has made a major positive impact in your life.

Think of someone who's still alive whom you have never fully expressed your appreciation.

Step 1: Write a simple, one-page letter to them. Take your time composing it.

Step 2: It is important you read this letter to the person face-to-face if at all possible, not just reading over the phone or sending it in a text or e-mail. (Note: Do not tell the person the purpose of the visit in advance.)

Write your initial thoughts here: _______________

IDEA 3: Negative Visualization

Write down a list of bad things that have never happened to you and then think of all the people who are suffering those sorts of despair in their lives right now. There are at least a billion people on earth at this very moment who would consider their prayers answered if they could only change places with you, even just for one day!

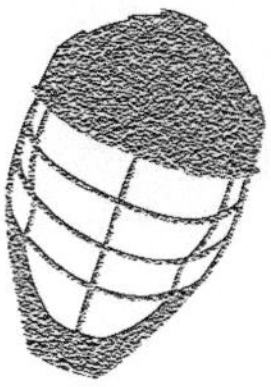

i.e. Perhaps you haven't suffered a season-ending injury, you have time to train and don't have to spend all your time working, you have friends and family who care about your success, you can afford lacrosse equipment, etc.

1. ________	4. ________
2. ________	5. ________
3. ________	6. ________

Go to dojodecion.com for inspiration!

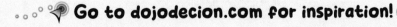

IDEA 4: Think of things you will do today which you might be doing for the last time.

you never know when will be the last time you do an activity!

Cherish the good in your life! Pay more attention to it! Appreciate it for what it is! As you go about your day today, consider everything you're doing with this lens. Everything represents a finite opportunity to enjoy your life.

i.e. Last time you play a game? Celebrate scoring a goal? Take a shot? Put your lacrosse gear on? Encourage a teammate? Sprint down the field? Take a deep breath to calm your mind and re-engage your focus?

1.	8.
2.	9.
3.	10.
4.	11.
5.	12.
6.	13.
7.	14.

Go to dojodecion.com for inspiration!

Check out, WakingUp.com

for more ideas on gratitude referenced here!

Gratitude (+1's)

Visit DojoDecision.com, scan the QR code below, or search the keywords in the *Heroic App* to learn the origins of the lessons introduced in this chapter!

133. +1: Sacrifices vs. Decisions | The Way of the Fight by Georges St-Pierre

134. +1: The Choice of Hercules | How to Think Like a Roman Emperor by Donald Robertson

135. +1: Recommitment | Willpower by Roy Baumeister

136. +1: Grateful Flow |The Tools by Phil Stutz and Barry Michels

137. +1: The Space Between Stimulus and Response | Man's Search for Meaning by Viktor Frankl

138. +1: Stoic Negative Visualization | A Guide to the Good Life by William B. Irvine

139. Waking Up App: A Lesson On Gratitude | by Sam Harris

140. Waking Up App: What if This Is The Last Time? | By Sam Harris

141. +1: Gratitude, Science Says: It Works! | Thanks! by Robert A. Emmons

142. +1: Gratitude Letters (+ Visits) | Gratitude Works! by Robert A. Emmons

143. +1: Stoic Negative Visualization | A Guide to the Good Life by William B. Irvine

144. +1: Grateful Flow | The Tools by Phil Stutz and Barry Michels

145. +1: Thank You. Thank You. Thank You | Words to Live by Eknath Easwaran

PART II
LEADING OTHERS

In Part I, Jordan learns how to lead himself.

Now, Jordan will learn how to lead his team.

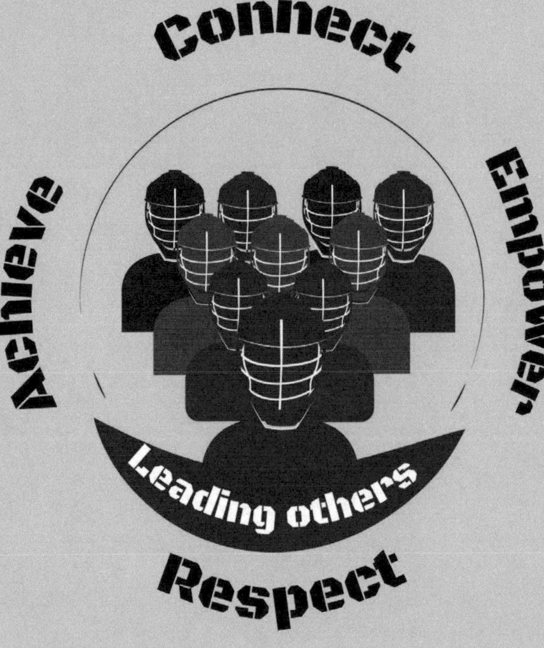

7

Teamwork

Black Belt Athletes know why they train for mastery: to share more moments of joy with their teammates, friends, and family. They do this by practicing the principles of the C.A.R.E. loop.

Connect. Achieve. Respect. Empower.

***This chapter is dedicated to Alden Mills for the wisdom shared in his books* Unstoppable Teams, Be Unstoppable, *and* Unstoppable Mindset**

Jordan's Championship Season – Present Day

Three Minutes Left in the NCAA Championship Game

Only moments ago there had been six minutes left in the game and Jordan's team was up by three goals. Now only two minutes remained—and the game was tied.

Their opponent had come roaring back. Jordan's team was often told that lacrosse was a game of runs, and like magic, as they focused their attention on that belief, their self-fulfilling prophecy was brought to life.[146]

"Timeout!" Jordan's coach yelled.

His team ran off the field. Huddled on the sidelines, all eyes were now fixed on their coach as they listened to his inspiring words, attempting to regain their composure. Jordan's coach said his piece and then passed the spotlight over to his lone captain, the only one he trusted to lead the team in moments like this.

"Fellas, we've been here before," Jordan began, meeting the tired eyes of his teammates. "I know you're exhausted, overwhelmed, and have been told that runs like these are bound to happen. They are. But in moments like this, when our backs are against the wall, well, that's when we gotta double down on the protocol that got us here in the first place.[147] Remind yourself of who you can be at your best and recommit to your Dojo Decision. Listen to the inspiring voice in your head that's urging you to push past your discomfort. You gotta dig deep and leave everything you have left out on the field! Everything! Ignore any negative voices. It's just your inner whiner telling you to give in. Gentlemen, that voice is *not* your friend. That voice is the enemy, and you have my full permission to ignore it. We have prepared for decisive moments like this!"

He shook his head. "Look, each of you has shared with me the superhero you plan to transform into on the field. You've all practiced

146 PN: +1: The Pygmalion–See the Best | The Art Of Connection by Michael Gelb

147 +1: Operationalizing Antifragile Confidence | The Stoic Art of Living by Tom Morris

the habits you need to make that transformation happen. Now is the time to unleash your superpowers! So do it! Get into that mental phone booth in your head and leave Clark Kent behind. It's your time!"

The huddle erupted into cheers, and Jordan grinned, impressed he was able to come up with such an example off the top of his head like that. He had his team right where he wanted them; focused and confident, yet loose, ready to dominate. "I love you guys. And you can bet the superhero version of me is going to show up for you. Don't show up for me out of obligation. Instead, show up because you love your teammates. I know you want to make each other proud. Let's go!"

Jordan's tone connected with each teammate. They all knew he would show up to lead them toward the goal they had decided to achieve together. On this team, they all felt respected and empowered. They truly cared for one another. As the huddle broke, his team took their positions on the field with a newfound confidence that they would finish what they started.[148] They would see their mission through to the end!

Back in the Dojo with Coach Brian

Jordan's Junior Year in High School

Six Years Before the NCAA Championship Game

It was a Monday in April, and Jordan's high school lacrosse team was halfway through their Spring season. To date, his team had accumulated six wins and one loss. They were ranked second in their division, and although poised to make a postseason run, he could sense they were headed toward a defining point in their season. He would soon find out if his team would commit to being exceptional,

148 +1: Heroes Have Quests: What's Yours? | A Joseph Campbell Companion

or if they would be content to drift toward a mediocre end to their season.[149]

It was spring break, and many of his teammates had plans to skip practice and travel on vacation. Others planned to use their time off from school to ski, hang with friends, and play video games. The problem was they still had a lacrosse game scheduled for the end of the week.

It didn't help that they were playing a team they had previously beaten in a landslide victory. This led many of Jordan's teammates to mistakenly assume it would be easy to replicate their earlier win. They were taking their opponent lightly, and as a result, their preparation had suffered. Jordan could feel a potential upset brewing.

He pleaded with his teammates to prepare the same way they had for all previous games. He had been taught how winning or losing was a byproduct of enjoying the preparation process itself, and desperately tried to share this insight with his teammates. Unfortunately, It didn't matter how hard he tried; his words seemed to fall on deaf ears.

Jordan didn't understand. He knew his teammates enjoyed winning, yet they seemed happy to put in the minimum effort to achieve this outcome. Jordan was wired differently; he wanted to be his very best. He was frustrated with how they were willing to settle for *good enough* and weren't pushing themselves to see just how good they could become.

They all saw him doing extra work and had witnessed his rapid improvement firsthand. However, the majority of them still had no interest in joining him in his early morning workouts or staying after practice to hone their skills. Jordan was disappointed as he recognized how they were currently happy to live as White Belts. They played lacrosse for fun. They loved game day and hanging out with the team, but had little ambition to play lacrosse in college or compete to become their absolute best.

149 +1: Mediocrity Vs. Excellence–How to Avoid Getting Stuck in the Middle of a Rugged Mountain | Die Empty by Todd Henry

Jordan wanted his teammates to commit to the level of training necessary to win, but didn't know how to motivate them. Luckily, he had a training session scheduled the following day with someone who might have the answer.

What Is a Team?

Spring break had arrived and Friday's game was now only four days away. Jordan woke up early and headed to the field to train with Coach Brian. It wasn't long into the workout when Coach sensed Jordan had a question burning on the tip of his tongue. "What's going on today?" he asked. "You seem a little ... off."

Jordan let his guard down and explained his frustration. "Sorry, Coach," he said, shaking his head. "My team's taking our opponent lightly, and I just feel we're gonna lose our game this Friday if they don't pull it together."

"Oh," Coach Brian said, nodding his head in recognition. "I hear you. That can be very frustrating."

"I just don't get it!" Jordan fumed. "We have a great bunch of guys on our team! We've been playing together since we were little, and we're practically best friends. But I still can't seem to motivate them to care about winning this week. It's our spring break, and they all seem to feel our time off from school means time off from training."

Coach Brian listened to Jordan's frustration, giving him more space to vent without interruption or advice.

"Coach, I don't understand why they won't listen to me! I'm the best player on the field! I work harder than anyone else, and our coach has appointed me captain! That should *mean* something, shouldn't it?!"

Coach Brian took a moment to let Jordan calm down before replying. "Jordan, I know you think they *should* listen to you, but I'm afraid that isn't how leadership works."[150]

---

150 +1: Shoulding On Yourself: Stop! | Awaken The Giant Within by Tony Robbins

"What? Why not?"

"Do you really believe being named captain will influence your friends to follow you? Would *you* follow someone just because they had talent? I hope not."

Jordan sighed. "I really don't get where you're going with this—"

"Nothing will sink a team faster than if a team's best player is appointed captain, yet he is unworthy of the position," Coach Brian said bluntly.

Jordan grew silent, unable to respond as he stared at Coach with his eyes tearing up.

"Jordan, the authority you wield over them, along with your God-given skills, aren't enough to win you the respect you're after."

Jordan sighed, knowing once again, Coach Brian was right. "That hits hard."

Coach Brian nodded. "It does. I get it. But let's take a step back. Do your teammates believe you work hard for the good of the team? Or do you think they believe your effort is selfishly-driven, only to promote your individual recognition?" He paused for a second. "These types of questions require a large amount of maturity and self-awareness to ask, so take your time responding."

Jordan hadn't thought about this. He always wanted to be a leader, but he now questioned his motivation. "Sadly, I think it might be more of the second one. Door number two."

Coach Brian placed a hand on Jordan's shoulder. "It seems you're on the verge of making a leadership breakthrough," he said, smiling down at him.

Jordan was surprised. "You really think so? I was starting to think you were gearing up to tell me I was leading all wrong!"

"Well, not *all* wrong..." Coach admitted sheepishly.

"Oh, here it comes..."

"Listen, you're doing a lot of things right. To start, it sounds like your teammates know you genuinely like and respect them. I don't know if you've noticed, but this alone is more than most teams can say about their leaders. However, if you're interested in transforming your band of merry men into a championship caliber team of warriors, they must also *feel* you care about them."

"But I do care about them! They're some of my best friends!"

"Feeling cared for is very different than feeling liked. There is a big difference. When your teammates only feel liked, they will work just hard enough to not let you down. They will nod their heads and say the right things and appear to follow your advice. However, when times get tough, it will be easy for them to find an excuse to not follow through—or worse, quit."

He continued, "It seems you have a group of talented friends who enjoy playing lacrosse together. That is different from a team. If you want to lead them, then you must show them you care."

Jordan was confused. "We *are* a team. That's what our school calls us—a lacrosse *team*."

Coach Brian was happy to clear up this common misconception. "Yes, our culture uses the words 'groups' and 'teams' interchangeably. However, if you can distinguish the difference, you can start building a genuine team."

"So what's the difference?" Jordan asked, still a bit confused.

"A team comes together to achieve a bold, lofty goal. The path to reaching that goal will be riddled with obstacles. On the journey, the team will face challenges that test each member's capacity to love one another."

"Love?" Jordan asked, frowning. He didn't typically use that word except with his family or girlfriend. "That sounds pretty serious."

"Indeed it is!" Coach Brian answered. "Love is a powerful word that should never be used lightly. However, members of a team genuinely and truly *love* and *care* for one another. Championship teams use those two words interchangeably."[151]

He continued. "Groups, on the other hand, merely work together. In your case, they may even really *like* each other. Groups are common. You see them every day in the workplace, in athletics, and while working on projects at school. However, *teams* are more than *groups*. Teams share a bond, and that bond is love."

Jordan was starting to understand where Coach Brian was coming from. He was reminded of post-game interviews given by professional teams who had just won their championship game. The players and coaches were always talking with reporters about the love they shared with their teammates, how they struggled to overcome setbacks, and how they eventually came together to achieve their outstanding victory.

He was starting to understand. There was a clear difference between good and great teams. But he still didn't know how they became a team. They must have started as groups, right? "So how do I transform my gang of lacrosse-playing friends into a team?" Jordan asked, careful not to use the word 'team' casually.

"Playing a sport is great because it gives you the opportunity to build a team," Coach Brian answered. "The ingredients are all there. You will spend a ton of time together pursuing a common goal. Through your season, there is bound to be conflict, right? Obstacles to overcome? Highs and lows?"

"Uh, yes. That's kind of an understatement."

"I'm guessing you will also have to control your emotions in victory and defeat?"

151 101 Class: +1: #11 Bonus: Love (43:57) | Unstoppable Teams by Alden Mills

"Hello? Moody teenager with raging hormones here," Jordan said, then reined back his sarcasm a few notches. "I mean, the answer is yes. Emotional control is a struggle, and it is real."

Coach smiled. "In essence, you will experience a short season of life with your teammates. If you commit to caring about them, you will become a team and reap the rewards of shedding your individual selfishness. You will learn to work with others to achieve something you couldn't have dreamed of accomplishing on your own. This is why sports seasons are so special. Most people never get to experience such a transformational opportunity. That is why many employers want to hire athletes—they know athletes have dealt with many life-changing trials which many non-athletes never dare to experience."[152]

Shifting thoughts, Jordan asked, "What about my family? Are we a team?"

Coach Brian liked where this conversation was going. "Yes. At a certain point, the words 'team' and 'family' can also be used interchangeably. Families may get annoyed with each other, but at the end of the day they love and care for one another. There is no quitting or kicking someone out of a family. Sure, there are dysfunctional families just like there are dysfunctional teams. However, a family won't disband when they face this adversity. Instead, they will lean on their leaders to guide them through the tough times."

Jordan snapped back to thinking about his lacrosse predicament. "And that's what I'm trying to do with my team! I see how my teammates aren't dedicated to preparing properly for Friday's game. Is there anything I can do about it now? It feels like it's too late to change the course of this flight, and gravity's about to kick in any second..."

Coach Brian understood his frustration. "To lead, you must first develop the skills necessary to show your teammates you care about them. It starts with leading yourself![153] Don't consider leading an-

152 +1: How To Win Forever: After Losing For Over 16 Years | Win Forever by Pete Carroll

153 +1: Lead Yourself First (The Forward) | Lead Yourself First by Raymond Kethledge & Michael Erwin

other person, let alone an entire team, unless you first have control of your own mind. As flight attendants say, 'You have to put your own oxygen mask on before you can begin helping the person sitting next to you.'"

Jordan grinned. "You continue to impress me, Coach."

"Thank you," Coach Brian said. "I've learned to adapt in the moment. And lucky for you, you have already begun to lead yourself. You started when you first began training to master your mind."

Jordan reflected on his prior lessons and realized he had become very good at leading himself. After all, he had set a goal for himself, devised a plan to achieve it, and energized himself every morning to wake up and pursue it. But leading others couldn't be that simple, could it? "You're right," he said. "You taught me how to lead myself, but there has to be a lot more that goes into leading others. I mean, how do you set goals and then motivate your teammates to achieve them? They all have different personalities and different interests that drive them. It's like herding cats!"[154]

Coach Brian laughed. "Herding cats," he chuckled. "That's a new one."

"Saw it in a Super Bowl commercial when I was a kid. Pretty funny."[155]

"I'll have to watch it. And you're right, it's more difficult to lead a group of people who all have their own, unique personalities. However, once you help each individual feel cared for, you can then lead the team using the same process you used to lead yourself."

"Hold up," Jordan said, flipping through his notebook. "I think I have this one..." He grinned when he reached the page he was looking for. "Ah, here you go. So you're saying I need to: one, set a collective team goal?"

"Check."

---

154 PN: +1: Shapers = Heroes + Actualizers | Principles: Life by Ray Dalio

155 YouTube: EDS/Hewlett Packard: Cat Herders Commercial

"And two, establish the habits and routines critical to my team's success?"

"Two for two," Coach said, nodding.

"And three," Jordan continued, "I need to get busy encouraging my teammates to execute those routines! Am I right?"

"You are correct, sir!"

"Yes!" Jordan cheered. "Nailed it! Honestly, I'm excited to apply this stuff and encourage my teammates to work together. It's a lot easier with a clear plan. I felt like I was flying blind!"

"Later, we will dive into specific techniques that will show your teammates you care about them. If you think about it, however, you'll find you already know how to make people feel loved and cared for."

"I do?" Jordan asked.

"Of course!" Coach Brian answered. "Just follow the golden rule—treat others the ways in which you feel cared for.[156] More often than not, you don't have to look much further for advice. You see, as a leader, it's your job to be an example of the characteristics you want your teammates to express."

Coach Brian continued, "You must set an example. Your teammates are going to watch you, and they will eventually model your behavior. They will do the good things you do half as well, and the negative, twice as bad."[157]

"Ohhh ... are you serious? I had no idea they were watching *everything* I did. That sounds bad. Are you saying I always have to be on? Like, perfect? Being a leader sounds exhausting." Jordan felt his energy wane just thinking about the constant commitment ahead of him.

---

156 +1: The Golden/ Platinum Rule | The Pursuit of Perfect by Tal Ben-Shahar

157 +1: Parenting Tips: Model the Behavior You Want To See | Mindset by Carol Dweck

"Leading is only exhausting when you're acting out of integrity with your core values," Coach Brian said. "However, I agree with you; nobody can be on all the time. Even the best leaders have moments when they are off.[158] They just have more moments when they are on. I think you will discover when you truly love your teammates, more and more of your actions will be aligned with your feelings. Your words will naturally inspire hope, which is a key ingredient to leading others!"[159]

Jordan nodded in understanding, so Coach Brian continued explaining the role of a leader. "You will help each individual teammate develop a vision of who they can be at their best, and then encourage them to practice those habits throughout the season. As a leader, you will take the time to learn each of your teammate's individual goals and make sure they know that when they contribute to the group's success, they will *also* be contributing to their own individual success."

Jordan smiled as he heard Coach's message. "Alright. Please tell me if what I'm going to say is too big of a leap. Is it fair to say my job as a leader can be condensed into a single mandate: to develop other leaders?[160] As in, all my teammates should see themselves as leaders of the team, right?"[161]

"I love it—simple, direct, and actionable! However, be prepared for some growing pains. Some players don't want extra responsibilities. They want things to be easy. It's important to remind these teammates of *The Story of Hercules*. Do you remember it?"

"I do. He was given a choice. The Greek gods offered him an easy life disguised as pleasure, or a hard life filled with joy. His happiness was directly related to the amount of responsibility he took on. Stories were written about him because he chose a hard life full of adventure."

---

158 +1: There Are No Perfect People | Motivation and Personality by Abraham Maslow

159 +1: Hope, How to Increase Engagement from 1% to 69% | Making Hope Happen by Shane Lopez PhD

160 101 Class: +1: Leaders Develop Other Leaders | Unstoppable Teams by Alden Mills

161 +1: Lead From Any Seat | The Art of Possibility | by Ben & Rosamund Zander

"Good memory! And just like Hercules, your teammates are faced with the same choice. The value they will get out of your season will be directly proportional to the degree they commit to serving each other. They will resist at first. After all, they were enjoying the easy life. They will give you excuses, saying things like they don't have leadership qualities. However it's your job to see the best in them and guide them toward a vision beyond what is, to help them see what is *possible*. It is important that when you encourage them to take on more, you balance the high standards you set for them with a large amount of love, grace, and encouragement!"[162]

"That makes sense," Jordan said. "Balancing the negative with the positive, so to speak."

"When your teammates take on more responsibility, they will inevitably be compelled to take ownership of your team's mission. When this happens, your teammates will begin to happily concede their selfish pursuit in exchange for a selfless commitment to helping everyone become the best they can be. *That* is when you'll know you have developed a championship culture!"

Jordan took a moment to absorb the message. He knew he had some work to do if he wanted to be a great leader. "Coach, this is amazing. It's kinda painful, but I now realize I could be doing a better job as my team's captain. A lot better, honestly. So being called a captain alone doesn't really make me a leader, does it?"

"Yes and no," Coach Brian answered. "Your title gives you power. However, if you rely solely on your position of authority, then your teammates will follow you for only as long as they have to, and they will do so begrudgingly. Your teammates with the most integrity are the real leaders of your team. When times get tough, your teammates will turn to those who have the most character, not the biggest title. In fact, your team will implode if a high character leader quiets his voice out of blind obedience, allowing an unworthy captain to speak. This often happens on teams where a player is appointed merely because of his talent. Leaders must also have the courage to speak up."

---

162 +1: To Bring Forth | Grit by Angela Duckworth

Coach Brian was excited for the next part of the conversation. It was time to teach Jordan the actionable skills necessary to lead. "Are you ready to learn the skills that will show your teammates you truly care about them?"

"Oh, yeah! Bring it!" Jordan flipped to a new page in his notebook. He was lapping up every word. His coach had appointed him captain; therefore, he felt he had a responsibility to lead. However, after this conversation, Jordan saw where his current approach was failing. His title influenced his teammates to follow his instruction, but they did so without enthusiasm. To become a great team, his teammates would need to be empowered to give more. However, to become worthy of following, he would need to develop his leadership skills.

"Like all the processes I have taught you, these skills are simple. They are easy to do, but just as easy not to do.[163] You can remember to practice these skills using an acronym you've been hearing me use interchangeably with love—care. You have to C.A.R.E. about your teammates, spelled C—A—R—E. With each individual teammate, you must practice these four steps: You must Connect. Before your teammates will listen to your words, they will need to trust you. Then you must Achieve, showing your teammates a vision of success. Thirdly, you have to show Respect. Your teammates must feel comfortable contributing without the fear of judgment. And finally, you have to Empower them, giving your teammates opportunities to lead."

TAKE ACTION:

Measure Your Relationships With Your Teammates

163 +1: Two Easies | Leading An Inspired Life by Jim Rohn

7. Teamwork

Here's the truth: nobody cares how much you know until they know how much you care. Do your teammates know that you care about them? What have you done to show them this?

In this exercise you will assess your team. For each team member, you will assess if you think each teammate honestly feels that you C.A.R.E. about them.

1. After reading this chapter, fill in the names of 10 teammates that you want to improve your relationship with.

2. For now, only fill In the first column. Answer quickly and generally, detailing your feelings about your relationship with each one (1-10).

	Teammate:	First Glance?	Connect	Achieve	Respect	Empower
1.						
2.						
3.						
4.						
5.						
6.						
7.						
8.						
9.						
10.						

After you finish each chapter (Connect, Achieve, Respect, Empower) circle back to this page and in the corresponding column, rate where you think your relationship is at for each teammate, coach, friend, or family member that you CARE about. (1-10, with (1) being not at all and (10) being very much so)

Teammates can be any relationship in your life! Your parents, siblings, coaches, friends, significant others, etc.

Have more teammates?
Go to dojodecision.com for additional worksheets

Teamwork - What is a Team (+1's)

Visit DojoDecision.com, scan the QR code below, or search the keywords in the *Heroic App* to learn the origins of the lessons introduced in this chapter!

146. **PN: +1: The Pygmalion–See The Best | The Art Of Connection by Michael Gelb**
147. **+1: Operationalizing Antifragile Confidence | The Stoic Art of Living by Tom Morris**
148. **+1: Heroes Have Quests: What's Yours? | A Joseph Campbell Companion**
149. **+1: Mediocrity Vs. Excellence–How to Avoid Getting Stuck in the Middle of a Rugged Mountain | Die Empty by Todd Henry**
150. **+1: Shoulding On yourself: Stop! | Awaken The Giant Within by Tony Robbins**
151. **101 Class: +1: #11 Bonus: Love (43:57) | Unstoppable Teams by Alden Mills**
152. **+1: How To Win Forever: After Losing For Over 16 Years | Win Forever by Pete Carroll**
153. **+1: Lead Yourself First (The Forward) | Lead Yourself First by Raymond Kethledge and Michael Erwin**
154. **PN: +1: Shapers = Heroes + Actualizers | Principles: Life by Ray Dalio**
155. **YouTube: EDS/Hewlett Packard: Cat Herders Commercial**
156. **+1: The Golden/ Platinum Rule | The Pursuit of Perfect by Tal Ben-Shahar**
157. **+1: Parenting Tips: Model The Behavior You Want To See | Mindset by Carol Dweck**
158. **+1: There Are No Perfect People | Motivation And Personality by Abraham Maslow**
159. **+1: Hope, How To Increase Engagement from 1% to 69% | Making Hope Happen by Shane Lopez PhD**
160. **101 Class: +1: Leaders Develop Other Leaders | Unstoppable Teams by Alden Mills**
161. **+1: Lead From Any Seat | The Art of Possibility | by Ben and Rosamund Zander**
162. **+1: To Bring Forth | Grit by Angela Duckworth**
163. **+1: Two Easies | Leading An Inspired Life by Jim Rohn**

— Connect —

The next morning they met to continue their chat on how Jordan could better lead his team. Friday's game was only four days away, and Jordan desperately needed expert intervention to help him encourage his teammates to give their opponent the proper respect as they prepared for the game. However, Jordan soon discovered there was no quick fix when it came to connecting with his team.

"How'd it go with your teammates?" Coach Brian asked. "I don't imagine you made much progress overnight."

Jordan laughed. "How'd you guess?" he said, shaking his head. "At practice last night, I was like a fire hydrant of knowledge! I blasted them with all the lessons you taught me." He laughed again, now realizing it was possible he came on too strong. "Perhaps it was a little too much, too soon."

Coach Brian laughed as he thought about all the times he had also rushed to share a new idea before he had first mastered the concept. "Do any of your teammates think you're a bit full of yourself?"

"Of course!" Jordan surprised himself as he barely hesitated to respond with an answer that would embarrass most people. He sensed he had to explain himself. "But that's just because they don't share my passion to improve. They have a White Belt Mentality, Coach! Which is exactly what I'm trying to change in them."

"It sounds more like a connection problem to me," Coach Brian said, bringing Jordan back to earth. "It seems like your teammates don't relate to you."

"You may be right, but that's not my fault," Jordan said indifferently.

"Well, it may or may not be your fault, but it certainly is your *problem* if you want to lead them," Coach answered, slightly inflecting his tone to show his disagreement. "To have any shot at influencing a teammate's behavior, you must first meet them where they're at.

The tone of your voice, your body language and your words must all resonate with them so they can't help but think, 'Jordan is a guy I respect. I like myself more when I am around him, and I trust he has my best interest at heart.'"

Jordan took a moment to let Coach's message sink in. "I hear what you're saying, Coach. I do. But I've always been a guy who soars with the eagles, you know? I don't want to spend my time on the ground clucking with the chickens;[164] the White Belt chickens, clucking around without a clear goal. That's just not who I am, not who I want to be. I try to stay away from the petty locker room talk and always let my work ethic speak for me. How is that *not* the way to lead?"

"That's one way to lead," Coach answered. "And you're right, your actions will always speak louder than your words. Every time. On the lacrosse field, I'm sure your teammates know you walk the walk. However, does your inspiring work ethic show your teammates you care about them?"

Jordan thought long and hard before he answered. "I ... no. I guess not. If I'm being honest, I'd have to say my work ethic only shows that I care about my own success." He then thought about his dismissive interactions off the field. "Dang. And it probably doesn't help when I choose to distance myself from their small talk in the locker room, does it?" A pained expression crossed his face and Jordan winced. "Coach, the truth is I *do* care about my teammates! I really do! I just ... I need to learn how to show them that."

"Correct," Coach agreed. "This is the key. You need to learn how to bring your teammates along to soar up in the sky *with* you, instead of behind you! Rather than building walls, you need to build bridges. You must show your teammates the reason you work so hard is because you're committed to helping *them* win. Again, your words, your tone, and your body language must align to reinforce your actions. That's how you will communicate your credibility and show them *they* are your priority."[165]

---

164 Book: The Chameleon by Merrick Rosenberg

165 +1: The Gift of Greatness | Peak by Anders Ericsson

"Tell me, how did you become good at lacrosse?" Coach asked.

Jordan frowned. "Uh ... I practiced. Like, a *lot*."

"Yes, you *practiced*! And just like you practice lacrosse, you can also practice being a leader," Coach Brian remarked.

"Okay, but how? *How* can I practice being a leader?" Jordan protested.

"Well, whenever I learn a new skill, I like to break it down into its smallest pieces. For instance, if I want to be a really good lacrosse player, then I know I will need to develop four things: my stick skills, my lacrosse IQ, my fitness, and most importantly, my mental game."

Jordan held up a finger to ask Coach to pause for a minute while he scribbled what Coach had said on a notebook page. "'Kay..." he said. "Go on."

"To that end, if you want to be a great leader, you must master the three essential roles of a leader. You must be able to set a vision, communicate that vision and then encourage your team to work toward that vision. It's that easy ... and that difficult."[166]

Reviewing the list, Jordan started to recognize the obvious. "Okay. So, it seems that if I want to be a great leader, I have to first become a great communicator. Am I close?"

"That's right. If you can't communicate your vision, your teammates will tune you out.

When you speak, is your chest up, your chin down, and do you exude an air of confidence?"

"I ... sometimes? Maybe?"

"How about your tone? Do you speak clearly and with enthusiasm, or do you disguise your sincerity with sarcasm, a laugh, or a ques-

166 +1: Two Easies | Leading An Inspired Life by Jim Rohn

tioning up-pitch at the end of your statement because you're afraid of being judged?"

Jordan thought about this for the first time. He had never put much consideration into the delivery of his message. Instead, he usually just spoke freely based on whatever mood he was in at the time. "I guess you could say I speak with confidence when I'm sure of my message, or when I know I'm speaking with an audience who wants to listen."

"That's great. And it's important to speak from the heart," Coach Brian replied. "However, you will rarely have all the answers, or an audience where everyone is eager to hear what you have to say. In those instances, you can't allow your emotions to run the show. Too often, those who have yet to master their minds do just that. They feel an unwanted emotion; for instance, they may *feel* anxious at the end of the game. This causes them to start *behaving* anxiously. Finally, they start *identifying* themselves as an anxious player who chokes when the game is on the line. This identification will only trigger the cycle to repeat. Leaders do something different."

Using their previous lessons as a guide, Jordan finished Coach's thought. "Let me guess. Leaders have strong identities they turn to when their negative emotions attempt to hijack their confidence."

"Well said! Leaders have strong identities that must always be driving their actions. Instead of being at the mercy of their emotions, their confident self-image drives their confident behaviors, and those behaviors determine the confident way they feel."[167]

"That makes sense. That's why you taught me to keep my Tasmanian Devil-Connor Shellenberger identity front-of-mind, ready to be called upon in the moment I need it."

"Exactly."

"As long as I can remember *who* I want to be, I can decide *how* I want to behave, and that will leave me feeling great!"

---

167 +1: Identity-Behaviors-Feelings | Resilience by Eric Greitens

"Right."

"But I don't want to transform into the Tasmanian Devil when I'm trying to connect and encourage my teammates, do I? I need to be confident, but I think I also need to be calm, empathetic, and make sure I listen before I speak."

"Good point," Coach Brian answered. "The identity you rehearse in your relationships will most likely be different than the identity you rehearse when you're trying to transform into a dominant lacrosse player on the playing field. Let's brainstorm an identity you can model in your relationships. Can you think of a teammate you admire who has exhibited the habits you want to model?"

He held up his hand. "Before you answer, maybe there's a fictional character from a movie or a book? Take your time to think about someone who really resonates with you. For now, as a placeholder, let's just use the identity, 'World's Best Teammate.' A specific identity of an actual person that you can visualize would have a greater impact, but this is a bold goal that will still serve your purpose."[168]

Jordan nodded, writing down some more notes before looking up, still trying to envision someone in his mind.

"Imagine if all your teammates competed for that title," Coach Brian said, smiling.

"I'd expect we'd have a pretty strong culture," Jordan answered.

"Exactly. You could even make it a game.[169] You can measure who has the most moments of encouragement and appreciation throughout a practice."

"Love that!" Jordan said, already beginning to plan how he could win that game. He could win with his teammates using the same method he used to win on the field. He would take inventory of all the habits he currently practiced, double-down on the ones that served him best, eliminate the ones that hurt him, and later add

---

168 +1: Thrown a Perfect Game Lately? | Wooden by John Wooden

169 +1: Make it A Game: Turning Chores Into Gifts | No Sweat by Michelle Segar Ph. D

tiny habits to help remind him of the game he was playing. He envisioned himself in a variety of scenarios. Opening the locker room door and rehearsing a mantra and smile. Then when he left, he could compliment a teammate as they walked to the field together. If he found himself standing behind a teammate in a drill, he could encourage them to play with confidence.

Thinking about it, Jordan realized the opportunities to transform into the *World's Best Teammate* were endless. He re-entered the present moment when he saw Coach Brian smiling at him with an '*I know what you're thinking*' glance.

"I think I'm beginning to get it, Coach," Jordan said. "So, just like on the field, I can rehearse my relationship identity before I interact with a teammate. This will help me align my body language, my tone, and help me find the words to encourage and appreciate my teammates."

Coach Brian answered, "Yes. At the very least it will give you a moment to pause, collect your thoughts, and choose the best way to connect with your teammates."

"Ha! Yeah, sometimes a moment of clarity is all I need to cool down before I say something unproductive. Or worse, damaging."

"That's a life-changing insight in itself, right there!" Coach responded. "Here's something to think about; all your teammates are different, right? So do you think you will have to change your body language, tone, and words to best connect with each individual?"

"I guess. I never really thought about it much. But won't I kinda be sacrificing my integrity if I don't express myself the way I normally would? Authentically?" Jordan asked, understandably confused once again.

"You're somewhat right. You do need to be true to yourself, but you also need to make the effort to connect with each individual. Let's state the obvious, you make friends with people who sometimes remind you of yourself, right?"

“Of course,” Jordan answered. “Everyone does. I naturally want to be friends with people who have things in common with me. I mean, I give people who have different interests the proper respect, of course, but I’ll always choose to spend time with those who inspire me.”

“Agreed. However, you will always have teammates who were raised in different environments. Therefore, they will look different, talk different, and have different beliefs than you. Before you can connect with them, you will have to show them you’re open to listening to their ideas. This is how you motivate—you first create a bond of trust! You can’t do this by dismissing their way of doing things. Their walls will go up. Instead, you must meet them where they are at. Once you do so, you can begin to influence them to align their behavior to serve your team’s goals. As you demonstrate the next pillar of the C.A.R.E. loop, they will want to be the best version of themselves.”

Intrigued, Jordan asked, “What’s the next dial in the C.A.R.E. loop?”

Coach paused to playfully let the suspense build before answering. “You will need to show your teammates you’re going to do whatever it takes to achieve your goals. With your work ethic, this part of the equation will come easy. Your behavior will inspire them to do the same!”

TAKE ACTION:

CONNECT

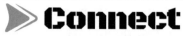

Connect

Teams are strong when they have clear communication, credibility, and a commitment to each other.

Use the definition above to assess how much your teammates think you C.A.R.E about them. (1-10, with (1) being not at all and (10) being very much so)

CONNECT – Relationships start with connection to build trust.	
Choose a relationship you want to improve.	
1. Do you make this teammate feel connected? (1-10)	
2. Does the tone of your communication encourage this teammate to listen to you or do they tune you out? (1-10)	
3. Does this teammate feel that you're committed to the team? (1-10)	
4. Does this teammate feel that you're credible? Do you do what you say you will do? (1-10)	
Average (1+2+3+4)/4 =	

Now, circle back to your initial Teamwork Exercise. In the CONNECT column, fill in this score and repeat this exercise for each of the 10 teammates you've selected.

	Teammate:	First Glance?	Connect	Achieve	Respect	Empower
1.						

Go to dojodecion.com
for ideas on how to show your teammates you're committed to connecting with them.

Teamwork - Connect (+1's)

Visit DojoDecision.com, scan the QR code below, or search the keywords in the *Heroic App* to learn the origins of the lessons introduced in this chapter!

164. Book: The Chameleon by Merrick Rosenberg

165. +1: The Gift of Greatness | Peak by Anders Ericsson

166. +1: Two Easies | Leading An Inspired Life by Jim Rohn

167. +1: Identity-Behaviors-Feelings | Resilience by Eric Greitens

168. +1: Thrown a Perfect Game Lately? | Wooden by John Wooden

169. +1: Make it A Game: Turning Chores Into Gifts | No Sweat by Michelle Segar Ph.D.

— Achieve —

"Jordan, now that you know how to turn up the 'C' in the C.A.R.E., it's time to teach you about the 'A'."

"Yes! *Achieve!* Can't wait!" Jordan said, eager for more. "After our last talk, I immediately began to practice what I just learned. And I've gotta say, it worked wonders with my teammates! When I made it a game to see just how engaged I could be within each conversation, my teammates began to share their feelings more, and I think our relationships improved. We were able to find common ground, accept our differences, and connect on a deeper level."

"That's great!"

"Yeah, and it worked so well that after I left practice and arrived home, I decided to use your same techniques to better communicate with my family."

"How'd that go?"

"Great, actually! I was exhausted from practice and just wanted a minute alone to decompress after a long day. However, as I walked in the door, my Mom bombarded me with a million questions. Granted, I know she was only showing interest, but I was pretty tired and not really in the mood for chit chat."

"Perfectly understandable."

"On most days, I would have tuned her out, maybe half-heartedly answered her questions to appease her while I watched TV or engaged in some other selfish behavior. That would've inevitably led to a series of conversations where we'd become more and more annoyed and withdrawn from one another."

"A common pattern," Coach Brian said.

“However,” Jordan said, holding up a finger. “Because I paused, smiled, and intentionally decided to follow the golden rule and actually listen to her the way I’d want to be listened to, our conversation was one of our best ones yet. And because she was in such a great mood, it seemed like my entire family was happier.”

“Amazing, right? Positivity is contagious!”

“No doubt,” Jordan agreed. “It really helped me connect with the people I care about.”

“As I mentioned before,” Coach said, “teams come together to achieve something greater than themselves. Your coach may set the vision, but as a leader, it’s your job to inspire your teammates to share that vision. So let me ask you, would you say all of your teammates are committed to your team’s goal? Do they know what they are going after, or why it’s important to them?”

Jordan raised an eyebrow as he considered the question. “I … think so? I mean, our coach posted our goal at the beginning of the year. We see it as a reminder every time we enter or exit our locker room. The sign reads, ‘W.I.N. the Day, WIN the Championship.’ He told us we’ll inevitably get distracted along the way, and this acronym reminds us that when this happens, we need to ask ourselves, ‘What’s important now?’[170] It’s an easy reminder that helps us reset and think about the next immediate action we can take to push closer toward our goal.”

“That’s great. Written reminders are powerful tools. They make sure everyone is on the same page. I have my goals written in erasable markers all over my bathroom mirror so it’s the first thing I see when I wake up each morning. However, simply posting a sign doesn’t guarantee your teammates will connect emotionally with your goal.”

Jordan knew this all too well. He’d been in many locker rooms where he was overwhelmed by an abundance of inspirational posters on the walls. He had also seen many of his friends post inspiring messages on social media that seemed to do little more than signal

170 +1: First Things First | The 7 Habits of Highly Effective People by Stephen Covey

virtue, rather than remind Jordan of how his friends actually lived their lives.

Coach Brian then asked a series of questions for Jordan to contemplate. "Do you believe all your teammates really care about winning the State Championship?"

"They seem to," Jordan said with a shrug. "But I'd be lying if I didn't say their commitment levels vary."

"That makes sense," Coach Brian replied. "I'll bet those who are committed can visualize what winning that Championship would feel like. When they close their eyes, I'm sure they can imagine themselves hoisting that trophy over their heads. However, do you think they will associate this achievement with learning the process to achieve anything they set their mind to?"

On cue, Jordan closed his eyes and imagined celebrating a State Championship victory with his teammates. He smiled as he envisioned all his hard work paying off. He could vividly see how leading his team to a Championship would directly impact his personal goals. It would put him on the radar of every college program in the country!

Jordan then thought of his teammates. He could imagine them storming the field to celebrate winning the Championship. But as hard as he tried, he couldn't seem to visualize how winning would directly impact each of their personal goals. After all, they didn't all aspire to play college lacrosse. As he thought about his teammates, he suddenly realized he didn't even know many of their goals. Well, that wasn't exactly true, he knew his goalie, Cam, wanted to be a doctor someday. And Riley, his team's star defenseman, only played lacrosse to stay in shape for his football season, his real passion.

Jordan finally answered. "I think all my teammates would be stoked to win, but I now see I haven't exactly taken the time to learn their goals. I mean, I know the goals of my closest teammates, but their goals don't seem to have anything to do with lacrosse, let alone winning the State Championship. If their passion isn't lacrosse, how is it possible for them to connect with our team's goal?"

“Great question! Good leaders must take time to learn each teammate’s personal goal. Then, they show each individual how their personal goal aligns with the greater goal of the team.”

“What if their goal isn’t connected?” Jordan thought of his teammates who chose to not fully commit to practice. “Cam’s real passion is studying to become a doctor, and Riley wants to play football in college.”

“Good point,” Coach Brian acknowledged. “However, although their individual goals may differ, each of your teammates, like all humans, share the same big, all-encompassing purpose. Do you remember what that is?“

Jordan did. In fact, he rehearsed it every morning after his first push-up as a part of the sequence of mantras he repeated to prepare his body and mind for the day ahead. He recited it from memory. “To create more moments of joy and to share those moments with the people I care about.”

“Good memory!” Coach Brian said, visibly impressed. “That is correct. Not all your teammates will prioritize their lacrosse training to the same extent as you. However, they will care about showing up and winning the game we call life. It’s your job as a leader, and as a friend, to help them see that they are always playing this game, and every moment they spend playing is precious.”

Jordan knew Coach Brian was right, but didn’t think his message would resonate with his teenage teammates. “Coach,” he said, “I understand where you’re coming from, and I agree with you, they *should* care. However, I don’t believe just knowing this fact alone will be enough to motivate my teammates to train harder. For instance, Cam could be a great lacrosse player, but he only plays for fun. His true passion is training to become a doctor. How do I convince him that committing to his lacrosse training will also help him become a better doctor?”

“I think you know the answer.”

Jordan frowned. “I … do?”

"Have you really practiced for all of those hours just to win a State Championship? Or to get recruited to play lacrosse in college?" He didn't give Jordan a chance to respond before answering his own question. "I sure hope not! Just like your friend Cam, you need goals that transcend your lacrosse success."

Jordan realized where Coach Brian was going. "You're right; my goals extend far beyond lacrosse. I mean, I love to play, and I definitely want to win, but I also love the feeling I get when I'm in the process of training to see just how good I can become."

"Exactly. That is your goal—to see just how good you can become. Therefore, just like your friend Cam, winning a State Championship is only your benchmark goal. It's a short-term measuring stick you both share. Chasing it together will keep you motivated. It will allow you to track your progress and keep you on target to hit your big, pie-in-the-sky goals!"

Jordan knew Coach Brian was right. "Okay, but how do I get Cam to understand how important this lacrosse season is to his career goal?"

"That's simple," Coach Brian answered confidently. "You need to teach him how training to improve his character on the lacrosse field will also strengthen the same mental skills that will help him focus, learn, and stay disciplined to achieve the grades necessary to get into medical school."

"Oooh ... nice."

"By going all in on this lacrosse season, he will develop the life skills he needs to dominate in all areas of his life. He will develop his confidence, grit, focus, and leadership skills. Those are the skills all the best doctors possess. In fact, this is the reason employers want to hire athletes. As a high school student, there is no better opportunity for you to learn these skills than dedicating yourself to a cause greater than yourself!"

"That makes sense," Jordan reasoned. "And I think it would resonate with Cam. Now that I think about it, that strategy would work with most of my teammates! I just need to help each of them understand that by dedicating themselves to the team, they're simultaneously dedicating themselves to their individual goals!"

"Exactly! I don't imagine all your teammates want to be doctors, but I would bet they all have individual goals they want to achieve—even your teammates who aren't inspired to build successful careers. Some may want to have better relationships with their parents, or their siblings. Others may want to be great fathers someday. Whatever their individual goal, once you help them understand that working hard to achieve your team goal is their ticket to learning the skills necessary to achieve their own personal goals, you will have them on their way to making their Dojo Decision and beginning to train like a Black Belt!"

Jordan grinned as he scribbled more notes into his notepad. He couldn't find fault in Coach Brian's logic. Now that he knew how to actively develop trust and connect with each of his teammates, he could see how having individual conversation would further strengthen his relationships.

He was excited to discover each of his teammate's personal goals and then support and encourage them to achieve them. "I'm excited! It makes perfect sense. If I can help each of them connect their personal vision of success with our team's success, then they will want to give full effort in every drill of every practice!"

"Good," Coach Brian said. "It may take time, but once you connect with each of your teammates and you help them align their personal goals with your team's goal, you will be ready to address the other half of 'Achieve' in the C.A.R.E. Loop.

"Wait. A *second* half?"

"Now that you've shown your teammates you're committed to helping them achieve their personal goals, you must model the behaviors you want to see in them. This is how you will reinforce your team's values. As a leader, it is how you will demonstrate your integrity and what will give you the credibility to lead.[171] If you can do that, Jordan, your team will trust you have what it takes to lead them on the darkest days, through every obstacle, until you reach your goal."

"Well, I certainly do that!" Jordan responded reflexively. "I lead our team in points, and everyone sees me putting in the effort to help us succeed."

"You're right. You speak with your effort, and your talent gives you instant credibility. Your teammates will want to follow you because they are inspired by your skill and commitment. You will give your teammates a vision of what's possible. When you show them your greatness, you give them the courage to pursue their own greatness.[172] It doesn't matter what we want to achieve; anyone seeking mastery in life will need a role model to show them what's possible. That's what leaders do; they inspire hope!"[173]

"Thanks, Coach. Everything you've said so far makes a lot of sense. But you'll forgive me if I say it still doesn't sound like enough to motivate my team to prepare for our upcoming game."

"You're right. But that's because you are still missing half of the equation," Coach Brian continued. "It sounds like your teammates believe you're committed to achieving your *personal* goals. But ask yourself: do they think you're willing to put the team's goal of winning a championship *above your individual success*?"

Jordan thought for a moment. "I see where you're going with this; showing my work ethic is great, but my teammates also need to know I'm working for *them*, and not just myself. I need to spend more time sharing how my individual goals are a hundred percent in line with our team goal."

171 +1: Do You Do What You Say You Will Do? | The Leadership Challenge by James Kouzes & Barry Posner

172 PN: +1: Show Me Your Achievement | The Fountainhead by Ayn Rand

173 +1: Hope: How To Increase Engagement from 1% to 69% | Making Hope Happen by Shane Lopez

Yes!" Coach Brian agreed. "Once your teammates see that you're grinding for them, they will grind for you. Humans are wired to reciprocate. For example, has anyone ever held a door open for you? Did you hold it for the next person?"

"Of course, I don't want to be a jerk."

"Exactly. The majority of people will respond the same way. When someone knows you care for them, they will start to care for you." He paused, grinning. "Or put another way, if they see you don't act like a jerk, they won't want to be a jerk to you, either."

"Well said," Jordan laughed.

Coach Brian continued, "Okay, let's review. You've set the strategic vision, your team has bought into your common goal. Your teammates are aware of each other's personal goals and believe that each is aligned with your team's common goal. And your actions have established you're committed to helping them achieve that goal. What's next?"

Recalling Coach Brian's lessons, Jordan said, "So far, your advice on leading others has mirrored the principles you taught me to lead myself, which you said was essential before I ever attempted to lead another person. Once I made my Dojo Decision, there were three rules you told me I'd need to follow. First, I'd need to know what I want to accomplish. Next, I had to brainstorm the habits I'd need to practice in order to accomplish that goal. Lastly, I'd have to bring the juice every day!"

"Excellent."

"So far, the extra step in leading others is to make sure everyone is committed to our common goal. With that in mind, I gotta make sure my teammates are not only committed to our goal, but they're excited to learn our playbook, policies, and then practice all the habits necessary to reinforce our team's identity."

"Very good," Coach Brian said. "And what will you have to do each day?"

"Bring the energy! Model the behaviors I want to see from my teammates. When I showcase my integrity, my teammates are gonna hold themselves accountable to be their best every day."

"Correct. But don't assume just because your team has a playbook, policies, and pillars to guide them, your teammates have individual habits in place to actually live your team's culture. Your job as a leader is to help them establish their own personal habits. These habits must be aligned with your team's identity and easy to execute.[174]

"That makes sense. Our team guidelines provide a general direction of the behaviors that will help us succeed, but each individual's habits will have to be specific to them. I can share what has worked for me, but they will need to develop their own process. Once they do that, I can hold them accountable and encourage them to hit the habits they choose for themselves."

"That's right," said Coach Brian.

"That completes the three steps to self-mastery you laid out for me. What's next?" Jordan asked, believing this lesson must be complete.

"Now, you must do something that may sound counterintuitive. You must let go and assume your teammates know what they're doing. For instance, I imagine you have played for a coach that needed to control every nuance of your play? How'd that feel?"

"Smothering. It felt like there was no room to grow," Jordan immediately thought.

"I'll bet it did. When you micromanage someone, you kill their creativity and their sense of ownership of your team's mission."

"It did! My coach constantly tells me there is no time or place to shoot underhand. However, I see pro players shooting underhand all the time. I have practiced that release and I am frustrated my coach won't budge in his approach."

---

174 +1: Making Yourself Proud | Rethinking Depression by Eric Maisel

Even though Coach Brian was never one to advocate for underhand shooting in youth players, he could relate to Jordan's frustration. "Although I understand why your coach preaches the importance of fundamental, overhand shooting, your example works well to exemplify my point. A coach should take the time to explain the reason *behind* his policy. As long as you're respectful, he would be wise to listen to your feedback. However, if he's tyrannical in his approach, you will resent it. All his players will. Inevitably you will stop taking chances, stop speaking up, and your team won't get the most out of you."

"I agree 100 percent. Maybe I'll share this with my coach after our next practice. I'd like to believe he'd want to hear how he can bring out the best in us."

"Most likely he will, as long as you're respectful and don't challenge him in front of your team, of course. A good method to help him see your side is to ask questions *before* offering a recommendation. Put him in your shoes. Ask him, if he were you, how would *he* like to be coached? Listen between the lines and you will identify the reason behind his current policies. Once you discover the key, you can lead him to a compromise by summarizing his words back to him. Remember, everyone likes hearing themselves talk!"

Jordan agreed, and tried out this approach with Coach Brian. "So you're saying I need to think win-win."[175] Before Coach could respond, Jordan's eyes lit up. "Oh! Hold on! I can totally act this out!" He stretched his neck from side to side, focusing on his character and scene.

"Coach," he said, "It makes perfect sense that you want us to shoot overhand. It allows us to still back up our shot and keep possession if we shoot the ball over the goal. And if we miss low, our shot will still bounce into the goal. Unlike a side-arm shot where if we don't release the ball at the perfect point, we will miss the goal completely, or even worse, shoot it right into the goalkeeper's stick."

---

175 +1: Think Win-Win+ | The Seven Habits of Highly Effective People by Stephen Covey

Jordan turned his head to the left and sat up straighter. “That’s right,” he said in a deeper voice, taking on the role of the coach. “I’m glad you see where I’m coming from, Jordan.”

“I do see where you’re coming from!” Jordan said in his normal voice, looking in the other direction. “Yet, would you agree some of the best shooters in the world utilize an underhand release?”

“Sure, but they are pros. They’ve been perfecting their shot for years.”

“You’re right. And I’m sure they had a coach who made them learn to shoot overhand first. However, those pros must have also had a coach along the way who gave them the freedom to prove they could help the team by expanding their skill set.”

Jordan looked the other way and frowned. “Well ... yeah, but we just don’t have time for that.”

“I agree, we don’t have time. But how do you feel about this: if I meet your standards by shooting overhand throughout practice, would you be willing to watch me practice shooting with my underhand release afterwards? If you like what you see, maybe I could have your blessing to try it out in a game?”

“That seems reasonable,” Jordan said in his deep coach voice.

“And, scene!” Jordan said, ending the roleplay and grinning at Coach Brian. “How’d I do?”

“That was impressive,” Coach said, nodding. “You made your coach feel as if the two of you came up with your idea together. It’s important he feels involved in any tweaks to your team’s strategy. After all, he is also human and needs to feel like he’s doing his job as a coach. And as a captain, your job is similar to that of your coach. You also need to give your teammates freedom to create. It will be more fun to explore their ideas. Hopefully, they work, but if not, what’s the downside? At worst, you have fun learning tactics to avoid. That’s still a win. Maybe you learn your shot isn’t ready for game time, but you will be encouraged to practice more.”

Jordan nodded. "I wouldn't get down on them. I'd put my arm around them and help them figure out a way to improve the next time we practice together. Plus, I'll make it a goal to never crush a teammate's creativity! I will appreciate their effort and what they're going through."

Coach Brian grinned. "Jordan," he said, "You are going to be a fantastic leader."

TAKE ACTION:

ACHIEVE

7.

Achieve

Teams come together to achieve something greater than themselves.

- ◆ Your coach might set the vision, but as a leader, it's your job to inspire your teammates to share that vision.
- ◇ Use the definition above to assess how much your teammates think you C.A.R.E about them. (1-10, with (1) being not at all and (10) being very much so)

ACHIEVE – Now ask yourself:	
Choose a relationship you want to improve. ______________________	
1. Do you believe this teammate feels your effort and attitude is actively contributing to the goals of the team? (1-10) What are you doing to show them you're committed? Maybe it's your work ethic on the field, but maybe there's also something off the field you're doing to promote your team's identity? ______________________	_____
2. How well do you know this teammate's personal goals? (1-10) If so, what do they personally want to accomplish? ______________	_____
3. Does your teammate understand how achieving your team's big picture goal will help him/her achieve his/her personal goal? How closely linked? (1-10)	_____
4. Does this teammate feel that you're committed to the team? (1-10)	_____
5. Do your words and actions give this teammate confidence you will help the team achieve it? (1-10)	_____
ACHIEVE SCORE: Average (1+2+3+4+5)/5 =	_____

Now, circle back to your initial Teamwork Exercise. In the ACHIEVE column, fill in this score and repeat this exercise for each of the 10 teammates you've selected.

	Teammate:	First Glance?	Connect	Achieve	Respect	Empower
1.						

Go to dojodecion.com

for ideas on how to show your teammates you're committed to helping them achieve their goals!

Teamwork - Achieve (+1's)

Visit DojoDecision.com, scan the QR code below, or search the keywords in the *Heroic App* to learn the origins of the lessons introduced in this chapter!

170. +1: First Things First | The 7 Habits of Highly Effective People by Stephen Covey

171. +1: Do You Do What You Say You Will Do? | The Leadership Challenge by James Kouzes & Barry Posner

172. PN: +1: Show Me Your Achievement | The Fountainhead by Ayn Rand

173. +1: Hope: How To Increase Engagement from 1% to 69% | Making Hope Happen by Shane Lopez

174. +1: Making Yourself Proud | Rethinking Depression by Eric Maisel

175. +1: Think Win-Win+ | The Seven Habits of Highly Effective People by Stephen Covey

— Respect —

Coach Brian continued where they left off. “Alright, we’ve reviewed the steps you can take to better **Connect** with your teammates. You’ve also learned the importance of showing your team a vision of success, along with a plan to support them in **Achieving** that vision. The next dial you can actively crank up in the C.A.R.E. loop is **Respect**. To achieve the level of success you’re after, you’ll need to create a culture where all of your teammates are both eager and willing to contribute to your team’s success.”

“Haven’t you already taught me how to create that, some kind of positive environment?” Jordan asked, frowning. “I mean, I feel if I’m able to connect with my teammates and they believe I’ll help them achieve their goals, then they should feel comfortable speaking their mind and sharing their thoughts with me, right? Isn’t that enough?”

“It may be,” Coach Brian said, shrugging. “However, your teammates’ willingness to contribute will largely be determined by the degree they feel respected. The word respect is overused in this sensitive world. So much so that its meaning is often lost.

“For instance, it’s not okay to weaponize the word if someone accidentally smudges your sneaker or voices a different opinion than yours. That’s not disrespect.”

“It’s not?”

Coach shook his head. “Intent matters. Teammates are going to disagree and accidents will happen. That’s life. You can’t spend it walking on eggshells, afraid that if you breathe the wrong way it will offend someone someday.”

Jordan nodded. “I guess that makes sense…”

“Jordan, let me ask you this: what does respect mean to you?”

"I guess I'd define it as treating someone as an equal. Or maybe reassuring your teammates their feelings and opinions are important to you."

"Good. I actually agree with both definitions."

"Ummm ... thank you?" Jordan said, smiling.

"However, there will be situations where you can easily treat someone with respect, but it will be more difficult to treat them as an equal. An obvious example is parenting. Even though parents respect their children, they can't always treat them as equals. For instance, do you think it would be wise for a parent to give in and compromise when their kid is throwing a tantrum?

"Absolutely not," Jordan said. "Although I do know some people who parent that way..."

"Is it effective?"

Jordan balked. "It most definitely is not."

"Exactly my point," Coach said. "And just like a parent, as a leader you will need to know how to respond when an emotional teammate throws a tantrum.

"You will also have disagreements. A friend's opinion may not be important to you; in fact, you may actually hate their opinions. I've decided the most accurate definition of respecting someone is to listen to someone's opinions, feelings, and wishes without judgment."

"I like that," said Jordan.

"It's simple, right? You don't have to agree with someone, or even like their opinion, but it's still important you make sure they feel heard. When you listen without judgment, you create a safe space where ideas will flow freely. Truthfully, the most likely alternatives in a disagreement are for one party to stay silent, or for the conversation to escalate into a shouting match or a physical altercation."

Jordan hadn't thought about that. He tried to think of additional outcomes, but he had to agree. "You're right. Nothing good comes out of an interaction when one side doesn't feel acknowledged."

"Exactly. It's a universal law of creating positive relationships. Even if a teammate thinks the world of you, they need to feel respected. Therefore, leaders need to take precautions to make sure they don't unintentionally isolate themselves from their teammates. Their teammates must see the leader as approachable, otherwise they may clam up around him, or even worse, become a 'Yes Man.'"

"A 'Yes Man?'" Jordan asked. "Isn't that a movie? With Jim Carrey?"

"I don't watch a lot of movies," Coach admitted, "but a 'Yes Man' is typically someone who's too scared to voice their opinion. They sit in silence when they disagree; they don't share their ideas, and they don't tell their leader the hard truths he needs to hear. They may think their absolute loyalty and silent submission is helpful, but nothing is more harmful for a team than creating a culture of 'Yes Men.'"

"I hear you," Jordan said. "I've always believed leaders need to surround themselves with teammates who will speak their minds. However, I can see how this could be challenging." He looked off into the distance for a moment, processing everything he'd just heard. Opening his mouth to speak, he shook his head and closed it.

"What?" Coach asked.

"It's nothing," Jordan said.

"Jordan. Don't be a Yes Man. Speak up."

Jordan laughed. "Fine," he said. "I was just thinking it must be pretty lonely as a leader. Difficult to not come across as high and mighty when you're constantly challenging your teammates to be their best."

"It can be accomplished, as long as you stay humble. When you step into a leadership role, it's important to maintain the balance between delivering high standards and high warmth.[176] Your teammates need to know you're going to be there, that you won't let them slip from their path. They need to know when they do make mistakes, you'll be right there, standing beside them, saying, "That's okay. We'll figure out how to do better tomorrow.'"

"I love that. Those are the leaders I respect."

"Of course you do. We all do. And that's the equation you must follow to bring out the best in people. Because you have been named team captain, your teammates will listen to you. Unfortunately, many leaders choose to scream and boss people around, and while that may achieve results in the short term, if you choose to lead with an iron fist there will come a day when your teammates will tune you out. Fun fact: nobody enjoys getting yelled at."

"Oh, you don't have to tell me," Jordan said, smiling. "Been there. Done that."

"I have a buddy who is a famous show-dog trainer," Coach said. "One day he confided in me that the dogs who win championships are always trained with positive reinforcement.[177] They're rewarded with kindness or a treat when they demonstrate positive behavior. However, many of his competitors still choose to train their dogs by scaring them into submission—a strategy which rarely helps them reach their potential. When you think about it, animals can teach you a lot about human behavior. After all, humans are still just animals. For instance, do you know any pet owners who believe their pet can do no wrong?"

Jordan laughed as he thought of Deeogee, his buddy's dog who walked all over him. "Oh, yeah, and it's not a pretty sight. Those dogs have absolutely zero discipline. They're always pushing their boundaries to see what they can get away with!"

"Precisely. Which is why you need to treat both animals and humans with respect. In your relationships you must maintain the

176 +1: Bring Forth | Grit by Angela Duckworth

177 Book: Don't Shoot the Dog by Karen Pryor

balance of providing high standards they can aspire to, with an equal abundance of love. You will have problems if that balance tilts in either direction. You already know what happens if you're a tyrant, but conversely, if you only provide love without holding your teammates to a high standard, then they will lack the structure they need to reach their full potential."

Jordan wrote in his notebook, internally determined to maintain that balance with his teammates. He also wanted to make sure he found the balance between coming across as sincere yet welcoming, so his teammates wouldn't hesitate to approach him. He thought back to something Coach Brian had mentioned earlier. "Can we talk more about charisma? As in, I've noticed certain people just seem to exude the confidence I naturally respect and want to follow. They're never dictators, but they aren't pushovers, either."

"Of course we can, Jordan. You know, there is a science to charisma as well."

"That makes sense."

"I imagine the charismatic people you are referencing are not the loudest in a crowd, nor do they always come from a position of power?"

"For sure. I don't usually like spending time with loud people. You know, the ones who always need to be the center of attention?"

Coach Brian chuckled. "I get it. We all gravitate toward those who follow the equation to balance their power, presence, and warmth."

Jordan was intrigued. "What do you mean? I've always been kinda quiet, and thought the best way I could lead was through my actions."

"Anyone can learn to be more charismatic. It's easy to learn, but it's a constant, never-ending balancing act. To be charismatic you need to dial up and down those three scales.[178] We already talked about power. We don't want to be a dictator, as they are unapproachable.

178 +1: How To Be Charismatic | The Charisma Myth by Olivia Fox Cabane

And we don't want to be a pushover or appear weak. The ideal state is right dab in the middle—high standards and high warmth."[179]

"Got it," Jordan said as he continued to write.

"Next, we have presence. The ideal state here is calm confidence.[180] You want to be engaged. You want to make the person you're talking to feel like the most important person in the room. However, you can go overboard on this continuum as well. Have you ever felt smothered?"

"Oh, for sure. It's so annoying when someone's asking questions just to hear themselves talk. They're nice, but man, can they be overwhelming!" Jordan thought of a certain person he routinely avoided because he knew sparking a conversation would lead to a half hour of lost time.

"Exactly, do you see the balance you need? Engaged but not annoying. Just being aware of these spectrums can go a long way toward improving your interpersonal skills. You want to make the other person light up when you speak to them. This is easy to do if you *flip the switch* and enter a state where you really and truly want what's best for them. Do you remember any habits you can practice to instantly enter that state?"

"I suppose I could remind myself of my identity, World's Best Teammate, before entering a conversation."

"Good! Now, on the other end of the spectrum you have indifference, which is signaling that your partner in conversation doesn't matter. This is not only hurtful, but if you can't stay present, you will appear as if you're always searching for the next best thing. Can you guess what behavior you would engage in to instantly become the *least* charismatic person in a room?"

Jordan snickered. "Coming across as negative, insecure, or uncomfortable?"

---

179 +1: Bring Forth - How To Be a Wise Parent | Grit by Angela Duckworth

180 +1: Calm Confidence | Eat Move Sleep by Tom Rath

"Yes. But what behavior do you practice when you feel uncomfortable or insecure in a conversation?" He cocked his head to the side. "When people are typically uncomfortable these days, they will tend to pull out this device instinctively..."

Jordan didn't have to think long. "Phones," he said, nodding. "We start to play on our phones."

"Bingo! When you pull out your cell phone you instantly become the least interesting, least charismatic person in a room. When you are looking at your phone you signal to whomever you are with that they are far less important than virtually any other input in the world. In fact, did you know that simply having your phone in view at the dinner table has been proven to drastically diminish the quality of your interaction?"[181]

"Really? Wow, I had no idea." Jordan was shocked that the mere presence of a phone could have such a strong effect.

Coach Brian explained, "You see, everything registers. Everything is important. Even habits as simple as where you store your phone will make a difference toward the quality of your life.[182]

"And then there is warmth, the third input necessary to create a charismatic presence. On one end, there are those who are cold or mean. It's easy to see why you don't want to be around these types of people. But on the other end, you have people who will smother you with their kindness. I'm sure you've seen these people as well. They have good intentions and want to solve all your problems, but in doing so they take away your autonomy. We need the opportunity to struggle if we want to develop into the person who can deal with any obstacle in our path. As a leader, it's essential to find the balance to allow others to feel independent. You do this by empowering your teammates to meet you halfway. That is the final lever of the C.A.R.E. loop; you need to empower your teammates to take ownership of your mission."

---

181 +1 The iPhone Effect | Are You Fully Charged by Tom Rath

182 +1: Crimes Against Your Nature | Towards A Psychology of Being by Abraham Maslow

"Coach," Jordan said as he finished writing on one page and moved to the next. "This is really, really good stuff."

TAKE ACTION:

RESPECT

7.

Respect

"Leaders create a culture where all of their teammates are both eager and willing to contribute to their team's success."

Use the definition above to assess how much your teammates think you C.A.R.E about them. (1-10, with (1) being not at all and (10) being very much so)

RESPECT – Begins by listening to someone's opinions, feelings, and wishes without judgment.	
Choose a relationship you want to improve. ____________	
1. Does this teammate enjoy being around you? (1-10)	_____
2. Does this teammate feel they can speak freely and comfortably in front of you without fear of embarrassment, judgment or criticism? (1-10)	_____
3. Does this teammate feel comfortable contributing to conversations and offering thoughts when around you? (1-10)	_____
Average (1+2+3)/3 =	_____

Now, circle back to your initial Teamwork Exercise. In the RESPECT column, fill in this score and repeat this exercise for each of the 10 teammates you've selected.

	Teammate:	First Glance?	Connect	Achieve	Respect	Empower
1.						

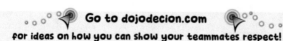

Go to dojodecion.com
for ideas on how you can show your teammates respect!

Teamwork - Respect (+1's)

Visit DojoDecision.com, scan the QR code below, or search the keywords in the *Heroic App* to learn the origins of the lessons introduced in this chapter!

176. +1: Bring Forth - How To Be a Wise Parent | Grit by Angela Duckworth

177. Book: Don't Shoot the Dog by Karen Pryor

178. +1: How To Be Charismatic | The Charisma Myth by Olivia Fox Cabane

179. +1: Bring Forth - How To Be a Wise Parent | Grit by Angela Duckworth

180. +1: Calm Confidence | Eat Move Sleep by Tom Rath

181. +1 The iPhone Effect | Are You Fully Charged by Tom Rath

182. +1: Crimes Against Your Nature | Towards A Psychology of Being by Abraham Maslow

— Empower —

Jordan was hungry for more. As he waited for Coach Brian to dive into the next lesson, he took the intermission to mentally recite what he had just learned. He was ready to be a great leader, and that meant extending his Dojo Decision to serve others. He had the blueprint. He would first **connect** with his teammates, then show them a vision of success, along with a plan to support them to **achieve** that vision, and finally show them **respect** so they would *want* to willfully contribute to their team's mission.[183]

"And now, the 'E,'" Coach Brian continued. "The final dial of the C.A.R.E. loop that you can actively turn to improve your relationships. You need to **empower** your teammates."

"Empower my teammates," Jordan echoed, scribbling the truth down on the page. His mind churned, deciphering what that would involve. "I guess that means I need to give them more responsibility? But before you tell me how to best accomplish that, you mind if I suggest a few empowering behaviors I can delegate to my teammates?"

"Be my guest!" Coach Brian exclaimed, further igniting Jordan's desire to contribute.

"To empower my teammates, I need to provide them with opportunities to lead, *including* opportunities to lead me."

"That's right," Coach Brian said. "Great leaders create other leaders. If you can remember that one rule, you will be a better captain than most.[184] The fact is, your teammates can't lead if they are always following you."

---

183 PN: Unstoppable Teams by Alden Mills

184 +1: Level 5 (Heroic!) Leadership | Leadership by Doris Kearns Goodwin & Good to Great by Jim Collins

Jordan chewed on this, realizing that although everyone had the ability to lead, few saw themselves in this light before taking the jump into leadership. "Well, I hope the example I've set will encourage them to start building their own C.A.R.E. loops with each other."

"This will have a cascading effect," Coach Brian said. "Once they start to reap the rewards, they will begin to create C.A.R.E. loops that extend outside your primary team. Your example will spark them to improve all their relationships—with their friends and family, their teachers and advisors, as well as their fans, alumni, and donors. This is how your team can level up their performance 10x or more. Imagine the impact you will make when you treat everyone who touches your program as a teammate!"

Jordan heard Coach Brian loud and clear. The lesson had clicked, and he loved it. "So what you're saying is it's my responsibility to create a team of great leaders. When my coach appointed me captain, his intention wasn't to give me a platform to show off all the cool things I know."

"Shocking, isn't it?" Coach joked.

Jordan laughed. "On the contrary, he tasked me to serve my teammates. A good captain isn't that authoritarian figure you see in the movies, screaming and barking orders. He exudes a calm confidence. His respect comes from his actions, not his title. A good leader is ... a teacher?"

"You got it! Keep going!" Coach Brian encouraged.

"Just like you've taught me to master my thoughts and my emotions, now it's my job to pass on your teaching to my teammates so *they* can start leading themselves. I need to teach them the tools they need to succeed. I need to help each of my teammates develop a vision of who they can be at their best, then brainstorm the habits and routines they'll use to transform into their best-self identity. And finally, I need to hold them accountable to practice the habits they've chosen. This will help them become the person they want to be."

"Bingo!" Coach Brian exclaimed.

Jordan continued. "And if I can do that, then there'll be no need to yell at my teammates to do the right thing. Instead, I'll just have to gently remind them to transform into *who* they had previously decided to be at their best. That's all it will take for my teammates to want to go all-in, committing 100 percent to the team. Remind them of who *they* want to be! And then together we'll become a team of Black Belts pursuing our common goal!"

Coach Brian beamed at Jordan's revelation. "Please," he said, spreading his arms wide. "Do continue."

"The more my teammates feel responsible for our common mission," Jordan said, "the higher the probability our team will achieve our goal. To create a championship culture, we need a team of leaders who feel personal ownership of our goal."

Coach Brian agreed. "Exactly! Now let's bring your understanding of this idea down to earth. How can you operationalize this? What can you actually do to empower your teammates to lead? None of my teachings are valuable unless you apply them through your daily habits. You will need to give your teammates a realistic plan of action."[185]

Jordan took a few seconds to think before answering. "As captain, I don't think I need to be leading the majority of our team's speeches."

Coach Brian nodded, silently acknowledging how far Jordan had come and encouraging him to continue his thought process. He nodded, raising his eyebrows in expectation.

"For instance," Jordan continued, "I could take one of my teammates aside before a team huddle, ask him what he was seeing on the field, what we're doing well and get his input on how he thinks we could improve." He frowned. "Would that actually work?"

185 +1: Warriors vs. Librarians | The Philosophy of Cognitive Behavioral Therapy by Donald Robertson

Coach Brian was impressed again. “It would be most effective. Plus, I imagine within that conversation you’d have ample opportunity to share your opinion and create a complimentary opinion of your current situation.”

“Right! And then I could share how much I appreciate his insight and give him the honors of expressing it to our team.”

“Great idea! I bet such a course of action would make him feel like he is *also* a leader of the team!” Coach Brian said.

“Exactly. I know that’s how I would feel.” However, after a moment of reflection, Jordan began to question himself. ”I mean, it sounded like a great idea in my head, but I’m starting to wonder if I’d kinda be doing my team a disservice.”

“Why is that?” Coach Brian asked.

“Well, I suppose my teammate won’t be as well versed in speaking in front of the team as me. He may not come off as confident and well-spoken. It may be good for that teammate, but would it be at the team’s expense?”

Coach Brian saw where Jordan was coming from and didn’t hesitate to respond. “It will always be scary when you let go of control and give your teammates more leadership opportunities. Giving up control is intimidating because of the unknown. However, it’s okay for your teammates to not talk, act, and lead exactly like you would. In fact, it would be a boring world if they did!”

“Uhhh...” Jordan said, not hiding his dismay. “Was that a back-handed compliment you just paid me there?”

Coach grinned, shrugging. “We all have different life experiences and different personality traits that predispose us to attack problems from different perspectives. And you’re right, they won’t have as much practice and will likely not be as well-spoken as you.”

“See? *That’s* a compliment! Thank you!”

Coach grinned and ignored the interruption. "However, none of this is a problem. I guarantee that the autonomy you give your teammates will encourage them to rise to the occasion. In fact, all your teammates will see this and will take it as an indication that they have the same opportunity to contribute and lead your team. Plus, in the worst-case scenario, you will still have the opportunity to jump in at the end and reshape the message. Right?"

Jordan agreed. "Of course. And giving my teammates the opportunity to speak will give me an additional opportunity to provide feedback and encourage them to continue expanding their leadership roles. This is awesome!"

The conversation continued as Jordan and Coach Brian brainstormed additional ways he could empower his teammates with leadership opportunities. They were only scratching the surface, and Jordan was astonished by the list of responsibilities he could pass off to his teammates. He planned to assign leadership groups to take ownership of a variety of areas:

- field set-up responsibilities
- team-building activities
- travel responsibilities
- community service outreach
- improving the experience when potential recruits visited campus
- ensuring their alumni felt connected to the program
- making sure everyone was studying film and understanding their playbook material

When Jordan thought about it, he saw that the leadership opportunities were endless. He understood how, as a leader, he could create a system to transform his team from a group of individuals who put their own interests first into a team of selfless leaders, excited to serve.

From this day on, Jordan's leadership goal would be to teach his teammates to lead. He would mentor his teammates, filling their minds with words of encouragement. Contrary to what he had originally believed, the less he had to talk, the more he felt the team would succeed. He would help his teammates become better leaders than him!

Being appointed a leader gave him the opportunity to dissolve his ego. *He was here to serve.*

TAKE ACTION:

EMPOWER

Empower

Leaders provide their teammate with opportunities to lead, including opportunities to lead them. Great leaders create other leaders!

Use the definition above to assess how much your teammates think you C.A.R.E about them. (1-10, with (1) being not at all and (10) being very much so)

EMPOWER - Leaders create other leaders.	
Choose a relationship you want to improve. _ _ _ _ _ _ _ _ _ _ _ _ _ _ _	
1. Have you personally and intentionally helped this teammate become a leader? (1-10)	_ _ _ _ _
2. Does this teammate know that you see potential in them? Do they feel you're actively encouraging them to reach it? (1-10)	_ _ _ _ _
3. Have you given this teammate an opportunity to lead in your place? How about an opportunity to teach or lead you? (1-10)	_ _ _ _ _
Average (1+2+3)/3 =	_ _ _ _ _

Now, circle back to your initial Teamwork Exercise. In the EMPOWER column, fill in this score and repeat this exercise for each of the 10 teammates you've selected.

	Teammate:	First Glance?	Connect	Achieve	Respect	Empower
1.						

Go to dojodecion.com
for ideas on how you can empower your teammates!

Teamwork - Empower(+1's)

Visit DojoDecision.com, scan the QR code below, or search the key-words in the *Heroic App* to learn the origins of the lessons intro-duced in this chapter!

183. PN: Unstoppable Teams by Alden Mills

184. +1: Level 5 (Heroic!) Leadership | Leadership by Doris Kearns Goodwin & Good to Great by Jim Collins

185. +1: Warriors vs. Librarians | The Philosophy of Cognitive Behavioral Therapy by Donald Robertson

— Dealing With Difficult People —

As the conversation continued, Jordan hit a snag in his plan. He began brainstorming the many leadership opportunities he planned to assign to his teammates, thinking of Casey, one of his more stubborn teammates who always seemed to be disagreeable. Jordan knew Casey would be hard-pressed to take any assigned leadership responsibility seriously. Throughout the season, it didn't seem to matter how much time Jordan spent nurturing his C.A.R.E. loop with Casey. No matter how hard he tried, they never seemed to connect or see eye to eye.

Casey simply didn't seem committed to their team. Worse, he seemed to feed off distracting his teammates from *their* goals. He was always joking and recruiting his teammates to goof off with him. Although he would never do anything so blatant as to attract negative attention from their coach, his sarcasm and indifference was clearly becoming toxic for team morale.

Jordan took this opportunity to pitch the problem to Coach Brian. "How do I deal with difficult people? Like, the ones who don't seem to care about our team's success? For example, I've tried to establish a C.A.R.E. loop with Casey, but he's always criticizing, complaining, and undermining my coach's message. He never gives full effort and makes fun of those who do. He actually seems to enjoy taking on the role of team clown."

"I'm glad you asked," Coach Brian replied. "Dealing with difficult people is unfortunately an inescapable part of life, whether you're on an athletic field or in a boardroom. Like any contagious sickness, it must be operated on quickly before negativity spreads throughout your team. Just like you must remove your negative habits before you can begin to install more positive routines, if you allow a teammate to linger and spread his negativity, he will sabotage your best intended team building efforts. Therefore, my rule for dealing with difficult people is swift and simple: always forgive once, but then be prepared to take decisive action and extinguish their troublesome behavior."

"Always forgive once?" asked Jordan, his tone suggesting he wasn't convinced. "That sounds great in theory, but it also sounds like it's easier said than done. Listen to some of the stunts he's pulled—"

"Jordan," Coach Brian cut him off, not concerned about the specifics. "Let me stop you there. You're right, forgiving is never easy. But I guarantee you will live a happier life if you always try to see the best in people. Therefore, before you jump to conclusions, it's always a good idea to listen and learn where a person is coming from.[186] After all, he may just be having a bad day, or he may not even realize how he's coming across."

Jordan sat back and crossed his arms, trying his best to listen with an open mind. "Go on," he said, frowning.

"A good question to ask when you don't agree with someone or you don't understand their behavior is, 'How did you come to believe this?' or 'Are you okay'? Those questions will show respect, while disarming the difficult person of their emotion. This will give them an opportunity to save face and change their behavior. When you confront someone, you don't want to back them into a corner where their only option of escape is to fight through *you*. Most people tend to yell, blame, and make a scene when they're thrust into such a position. Those actions rarely motivate anyone to change their opinion *or* their behavior."

"That makes sense," Jordan agreed, still visibly frustrated with his predicament. "However, to be honest, we *have* talked with him, *and* forgiven him, *and* compromised with him, and all with respect. The problem is he always acknowledges his bad behavior and agrees to make an effort to change, but after a few days he's right back to disrupting practice again. It's almost like he takes pleasure in being difficult! Coach, I feel like I spend all my time and energy addressing this one teammate! Time I feel would be better spent encouraging

---

186 +1: Think Win/Win | The 7 Habits of Highly Effective People by Stephen R. Covey

those who are actually *committed* to our team!" He shook his head and glanced out the window, catching his frustrated reflection staring back at him. "If we follow your rule, it sounds like it's probably a good time to kick him off the team, right? Time for some swift action to remove the cancer!"

"Let's slow down and take a breath," Coach said. "You're right."

"I am?"

"If you've confronted him with respect and he continues to whine, complain, and disrupt practice with his sarcastic jokes, then his counterproductive behavior must be removed from the team.[187] Just like I've asked you to banish your internal, lower-self voice that constantly tries to whine, complain, and make excuses, if you want to achieve your goals you must banish this person from the group. The saying, 'one bad apple can spoil the bunch,' is absolutely true. Your job as a leader is to remove the voices of discouragement while doubling down your focus on the voices that are encouraging your team's mission!"

"Okay. Thank you," Jordan said, honestly surprised at what he was hearing. His mind raced with thoughts on how best to get rid of Casey.

"But permanently removing Casey from your team might not be your answer," Coach Brian said.

"Go on," Jordan said half-heartedly. He was almost convinced kicking Casey off the team as quickly as possible was the only course of action.

"If you can determine *why* Casey continues to act out, then you might be able to convert him into your most powerful ally."

"My most powerful ally? Are you serious?"

"I am."

---

187 Book: Barking Up the Wrong Tree by Eric Barker

"How?!" Jordan asked in disbelief. "He's offensive and a disruption on the team! He's destroying us from within and he has *always* been this way! I mean, I could maybe see how we could pull him along until the end of the season, but it seems pretty dang impossible for him to completely transform into a positive influence on the team." Jordan sat back in the booth again, shaking his head. "I can't wait to hear where you are going with this!"

"Well, number one, you should never get offended," Coach Brian said. "Don't give others that kind of power over you! Most people are so focused on their own thoughts and actions they're almost never deliberately trying to hurt you. You're just getting caught in the crossfire. Not getting offended might be the toughest skill to develop—it may take a lifetime to develop that superpower! But yes, throughout history those who were once enemies have often wound up becoming great allies. Have you ever heard the saying, 'keep your friends close, but your enemies closer'?"[188]

"I have, but doesn't that just mean keep an eye on them so they don't stab you in the back?" Jordan said. "Unfortunately, I've been forced to watch a few reality TV shows with my girlfriend, so I know all about that. The people in those shows behave horribly, but those shows are addicting ... what a waste of time!"

"Jordan, please stop watching those shows! They depict the worst of human interactions and normalize awful behaviors. You will become who you surround yourself with and your brain can't differentiate the difference between real people and fictional characters."[189]

Coach Brian shook his head, baffled that Jordan would subject himself to such negativity. "On the contrary, 'keep your friends close, but your enemies closer' means to befriend them," Coach Brian said. "Your friends might follow you out of loyalty, but a so-called enemy—someone who has no reason to be trusted and who has failed you in the past—will work hard to prove his loyalty. Therefore, Casey, this teammate of yours you continue to butt heads

---

188 Book: Law #II Keep Your Friends Close but Enemies Closer | 48 Laws of Power by Robert Greene

189 +1: Building Agency: Step #2 | The Power of Agency by Dr. Paul Napper and Anthony Rao Ph. D.

with, might need some befriending. Instead of kicking him off the team, might it be wise to simply suspend him for a few weeks?"

"I guess," Jordan said reluctantly. "That *might* work..."

"That way, you can swiftly separate him from the team as a trial, but you can simultaneously reach out to him privately. Tell him you believe in him, re-establish your C.A.R.E. loop, and see if he will consider rising to the standards of your program."

"Coach! I feel like you're missing the point! I've been trying to follow the C.A.R.E. principles with him and have bent over backwards trying to connect, help him achieve, and show him respect! But he still won't..." Jordan trailed off as he realized he may have forgotten one element of C.A.R.E.

Coach Brian continued. "When you reflect on your C.A.R.E. loop, always do so from a vulnerable, questioning perspective. Before you blame your deteriorating relationship on a teammate, consider how you may have contributed to the problem. It always takes two to tango! Leaders must be humble. When you're mad at someone, you're usually mad at the traits you observe in yourself. More often than not, when you catch yourself yelling or acting out of character, it's a great idea to revisit your C.A.R.E. loop and shine more attention upon the relationship-building step you may have neglected."[190]

"I don't suppose you have some examples?"

"Of course. Ask yourself these questions: Does your relationship need more connection?

Do you need to demonstrate that you can achieve your goal? Do you believe your teammate feels respected? And finally, have you honestly given them enough freedom to shine?"

Jordan looked down at his notebook, turning to a new page as he quietly recorded Coach Brian's words. When he was done he looked up and nodded, saying nothing.

---

190 +1: Fingers and Lectures | The Dark Side of The Light Chasers by Debbie Ford

"Everyone, including troublemakers and attention seekers, has something to offer. It's important to identify their superpowers and channel their strengths to help serve your team. On prior teams I have coached, I've encouraged my players to take the Troutwine Athletic Profile.[191] This is a twenty-minute online assessment used by championship teams like the New England Patriots, San Antonio Spurs, and Kansas City Royals. It identifies the unique traits each athlete can use to help their team succeed. I have found it's easy to show your teammates respect when you take the time to let them know what they're good at and share how they can use their skills to help the team."

"Sounds cool," Jordan said quietly, reflecting on his relationship with Casey. If he were honest, he had to admit Casey *did* have superpowers. He was charismatic and able to influence a crowd. Unfortunately, he typically used this power as a super villain, wreaking as much destruction as possible. Jordan wondered if he could help him harness his superpower for the good of the team. After reflecting, he now felt that Casey deserved another chance. He still thought he needed a good kick in the butt. However, Jordan knew before dismissing him from the team, he would acknowledge where he might have let Casey down and make amends. As he took inventory of their relationship, he recognized how he'd never truly empowered Casey to lead. Instead, he had micro-managed Casey, which only made the situation worse.

"So, I think Casey, and other players I dub as troublemakers, might need more leadership opportunities," Jordan admitted.

Coach nodded and listened intently.

"At worst, giving them more responsibility will accelerate our team building process. It'll quickly become clear if they want to be a part of the team or if they need to move on," Jordan said, excited to have stumbled upon a eureka moment.

Coach Brian couldn't agree more. "Those who seem less capable of leading need opportunities to lead *more* than anyone. Do you

191 https://dojodecision.com/tap

remember our discussion about personality research? The science is there, and nothing changes someone's personality faster than giving them responsibility. For instance, what if you named Casey a captain? Do you think his personality would change?"

"A captain!" Jordan balked. But then he resisted the urge to over-dramatize his feelings and instead controlled his reaction, giving the idea some serious consideration. "Well, yes. But he'd be a tyrannical jerk that everyone would probably hate." He shuddered at the thought of Casey in a position of power.

"You're right. Most people aren't ready to lead. But do you believe his personality would change?" Coach Brian continued without waiting for a response. "Jordan, it's your job to help *guide* him and *develop* his C.A.R.E. skills so, in time, he *will* be able to step into a leadership role."

"Coach!" Jordan couldn't contain his disagreement. "No way. That's too much responsibility. It would ruin our team!"

"I'm not saying to overload Casey with responsibility. I'm saying let your actions show that you see his potential, that you believe in him, and doing so will encourage him to reach that potential. Once he sees how you care for him, he will care for you. Reciprocity is a natural human instinct.[192] Who knows? Casey may continue to grow and transform into an impactful leader within your team, or perhaps within a different team whose goals align closer with his aspirations. That's when you can bask in the highest compliment a leader can receive."

"Oh yeah? And what's that?" Jordan asked.

"There's nothing more gratifying than watching your teammates build their *own* teams, with their *own* C.A.R.E. loops," Coach Brian said. "It's the biggest compliment a coach can receive. Nothing satisfies me more than watching my players build amazing families and businesses that make the world a better place."

---

192 Book: Influence by Robert Cialdini

“Thanks Coach. I needed to hear this. I’m only human, I guess. And I get so caught up in petty arguments that I feel are so important in the heat of the moment that I forget my adversary is also human. They are acting the way they are for a reason. Maybe being a jerk was the only way they got attention in the past. Maybe they have something deeper going on that I’ll never be able to understand. But you’re right, I have a responsibility to teach my teammates how to successfully interact on *my* team. Hopefully, Casey will see the light in time to salvage his position on the team. Regardless, I’m happy to share a new way of behaving that he may choose to embrace when the time is right for him to make a change.

TAKE ACTION:

DEALING WITH DIFFICULT PEOPLE

7.

Dealing with Difficult People

1. Everyone, even difficult people, have strengths. Can you see the best in them (even if they don't see it in others or themselves?)

2. Is there a component of C.A.R.E you may have neglected with this person? How can you encourage them to be their best going forward?

	Difficult person in your life	(1) Their Strength?	(2) C.A.R.E Component neglected?	(3) How can you encourage them to be their best going forward?
1.				
2.				
3.				
4.				
5.				

Take the Troutwine Athletic Profile

use [Dojo20] for a 20$ discount!

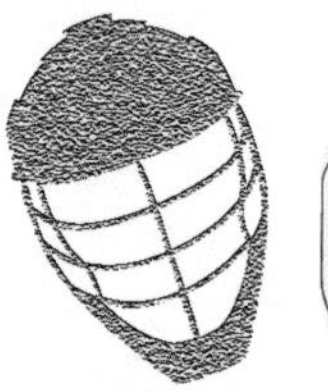

This is a twenty-minute online assessment used by championship teams. It identifies the unique traits each athlete can use to help their team succeed. I have found it's easy to show your teammates you care about them when you take the time to let them know what they're good at and share how they can use their skills to help the team.

Openers you can use to repair your relationships!		
IF: You disagree with someone:	THEN: "How did you come to believe this?"	Showing interest leads to trust and understanding. Nobody is usually 100% wrong!
IF: Someone is emotional:	THEN: "Are you okay?"	It's important to know what people are going through. If they're emotional, their probably thinking about themselves, and less interested in ruining your day!
IF: Someone is sharing a problem:	THEN: Ask, "Comfort or solution? Do you want me to help solve your problem? Or do you want me to listen, appreciate, and support you?"	Instinctively, many people jump to solve problems. Sometimes, people just want to feel heard!

Go to dojodecion.com for ideas on how to improve your relationships!

Teamwork - Dealing with Difficult People (+1's)

Visit DojoDecision.com, scan the QR code below, or search the keywords in the *Heroic App* to learn the origins of the lessons introduced in this chapter!

186. +1: Think Win/Win | The 7 Habits of Highly Effective People by Stephen R. Covey

187. Book: Barking Up The Wrong Tree by Eric Barker

188. Book: Law #II Keep Your Friends Close but Enemies Closer | 48 Laws of Power by Robert Greene

189. +1: Building Agency: Step #2 | The Power of Agency by Dr. Paul Napper and Anthony Rao Ph. D.

190. +1: Fingers and Lectures | The Dark Side of The Light Chasers by Debbie Ford

191. https://dojodecision.com/tap ← Take the Troutwine Athletic Profile (TAP)!

192. Book: Influence by Robert Cialdini

CONCLUSION

8

Passion

Black Belt Athletes are present and enthusiastic while they pursue their goals. They passionately strive for constant, never-ending improvement, fully knowing they will always be a work in progress, never arriving at their final destination! They understand excellence is a lifestyle, and they teach this through their actions to their teammates, friends, and family.

Jordan's Championship Season - Present Day

One Week After Winning the NCAA National Championship

Eight Years After Jordan First Began His Training with Coach Brian

A week had passed since Jordan won the National Championship and was named the most valuable player in all of college lacrosse. He had achieved his season goals, celebrated on campus with his teammates, and was now returning to his hometown to spend a few well-deserved weeks off with his family.

It was his first morning home, and Jordan woke up early as usual to perform his AM routine. He then walked a few blocks down the street to train at his old high school lacrosse field, the place where his training with Coach Brian first began, hoping to catch up with his old mentor at the field after his workout. It was still dark when he arrived, and despite the years, it felt as if nothing had changed. The field didn't care whether he was an All-American or an eighth grader first making his Dojo Decision. Reveling in the reverie, Jordan laced up his cleats with a grin, dumped out his bag of balls, and began paying homage to the field that had given him so much.

By the time Coach Brian arrived, the sun was out, birds were chirping, and Jordan's music was blaring from his nearby speaker. Coach found Jordan drenched in sweat, just finishing what looked to be an intense practice session.[193] He took a seat in the bleachers and watched as Jordan finished the final few drills of his training routine. As he observed him, Coach Brian couldn't help but feel a swelling sense of pride. Not many people in Jordan's shoes would be practicing this intensely, especially mere days after being named the best player in the country.

But Coach knew Jordan's internal motivation. He was training because he loved the game, pure and simple. He loved improving, and he loved the process of building his confidence, grit, focus, joy,

193 +1: Channeling Mia Hamm | The Champion's Mind by Jim Afremow

and leadership skills. The media called him a National Champion, but Jordan had decided long ago he wouldn't play solely for titles or external validation. He was too busy walking his own path.[194] He woke up every morning excited to pursue his ultimate goal—to embody the best version of himself. That, and that alone, was a mountain he knew he'd have fun climbing every single day for the rest of his life.[195]

In fact, he was always having fun, climbing three different mountains simultaneously. Winning the National Championship was only one of his mountains. From day one, Coach Brian had him set goals for each of the big three areas of his life: lacrosse, school, and his relationships.

Lacrosse was Jordan's passion. He loved it. He could almost always show up with enthusiasm to practice, even on the days he didn't feel motivated to train. However, he quickly learned that the confidence, grit, focus, and leadership skills he had developed from pursuing his lacrosse dream were the differentiators which helped him excel in the classroom *and* in his relationships. He had those character skills to thank for landing the prestigious internship he would start next week. He also had those life skills to thank for creating more magical moments of connection with his parents, siblings, and friends.

When he finished his training, Jordan practiced the art of sweeping the sheds. This was a discipline he had picked up from the legendary New Zealand All Black rugby team. It referred to the idea of leaving the field in better condition than it was found.[196] After the field was clean, he took a moment to acknowledge Coach Brian with a wave before making his way to the sidelines to take off his gear and end his training session. Before rushing over to greet him, Jordan methodically placed his equipment in his bag, and pulled out a notebook to reflect on his performance.

194 +1: The 5 Greek Keys to Optimizing | Ego is The Enemy by Ryan Holiday

195 +1: Ikigai, Your Reason for Waking Up In The Morning | The Happiness Equation by Neil Pasricha

196 PN: +1: Sweeping Sheds | Legacy by James Kerr

Coach Brian knew what Jordan was writing. After each performance, he had taught Jordan to pause and focus on the past and the future. Identify three things he felt had done well, note one as 'needs work,' and then specifically detail how to improve that area.[197]

Coach Brian was impressed. He had taught Jordan the easiest way to improve his performance was to measure it.[198] And there Jordan was, not only putting the lesson into practice, but taking his reflection process to the next level. Coach had instructed Jordan to mentally rehearse his post-practice performance review, a great start to begin reflecting on all the important tiny habits most people tend to overlook. However, Coach Brian knew there was magic to putting pen to paper.

When Jordan journaled, not only did he pay more attention, but he committed deeper to the lessons he was trying to install into his life. He knew how simply reflecting on his goals would increase his probability of success by 42 percent.[199] Jordan, like almost everyone, knew *who* he wanted to be at his best. The difference which separated him from his peers was his commitment to take action multiple times each day to remind himself to act like that person. He also knew there was a destructive force in the universe distracting him from being that person, and it was his responsibility to recommit daily to fighting those distractions.

When Jordan finished journaling, he put his notebook in his bag and eagerly walked across the field to meet Coach Brian. He greeted him with a smile and a hug, genuinely excited to share the many stories from his championship season. After exchanging pleasantries, Coach Brian said, "I'm impressed with your training routine, Jordan. It has come a long way. Do you remember when we first met on this field and you began to introduce your first simple micro habits into this routine?"[200]

"Of course!" Jordan answered. "You taught me how to become a habit building *machine*, Coach! Since then, I've been improving my

---

197 +1: Win or Learn | With Winning in Mind by Lanny Bassham

198 +1: Want to Improve? Measure! | Eat, Move, Sleep by Tom Rath

199 +1: Spiritual Windshield Wipers | Stillness is the Key by Ryan Holiday

200 +1: 100% on ONE Keystone Daily Micro Habit | Mini Habits by Steven Guise

training routine by constantly taking inventory of what habits are working, deleting the ones getting in the way, and adding tiny habits that improve my success. All of this helps me improve each time I follow through with the process."[201]

"Yes, you've certainly been busy leveling up since our early training days! I'll bet you rarely have bad training sessions when you practice your micro habits."[202]

"Well, yeah, my bad days definitely aren't as bad as they once were. And my good days tend to be even better. I took your lessons to heart! You told me champions don't rise to the occasion, but rather fall to their level of preparation."[203]

"If I had only watched this one training session," Coach said, "I would have seen enough to predict your success."

"It's been fun," Jordan answered humbly. "You taught me how success isn't an accident—it's a series of choices anyone can make. And ever since I committed to my Dojo Decision, I've been choosing excellence in every choice I face."

"Have those decisions been difficult for you?" Coach asked.

"Sure, at first. I mean, not with the big decisions, but there are still times when I hesitate in the minor 'who cares' decisions. For instance, it would've been easy to end my training early this morning, not journal on my performance, and rush over to say hello to you. Heck, that's what I *wanted* to do, and I still have that annoying voice inside my head that tells me, *Who cares? It's no big deal, it won't compromise your success*. It tempts me, sure, but I silence that voice when I remember to ask myself 'What do I truly want?'[204] When I prompt myself with *that* question, it only takes a moment to

---

201 +1: Marginal Gains—Here's How To Win | Black Box Thinking by Matthew Syed

202 +1: Scaffolding - Constructing Your Destiny | The Monk Who Sold His Ferrari by Robin Sharma

203 +1: Raise The Basement | The Art of Learning by Josh Waitzken

204 +1: What's Important Now | No Limits by Michael Phelps and Alan Abrahamson

reignite my desire, and then it's easy for me to recommit to my Dojo Decision."[205]

"Do you still have the same goals?"

"Yeah, pretty much. I'm committed to excellence. You helped me become extremely clear on exactly what I wanted to achieve, so I still want to be the Tasmanian Devil version of Connor Shellenberger every time I step on the lacrosse field. It also helped me when you told me how there would be a price to pay if I wanted to *be* that person; a price most other people wouldn't be willing to pay. It's a price I'm paying every day, whenever I make those tiny, positive decisions."

"Good. Very good," Coach Brian said. "There will always be pain in life. It's inevitable, but you are making the smart choice when you choose the pain of discipline rather than the pain of regret. Tell me, did you find most of your friends were unwilling to pay that price?" [206]

"Oh, yeah. Absolutely. And to be honest, it actually fired me up! I saw my advantage. So, I became a disciplined, habit-forming machine. I looked back through my life and took inventory of the bad habits that were holding me back. It was hard to remove them at first, but once I became more aware of them, I was able to stop sabotaging my success. I could replace the negative habits with positive ones. Once I started, I gained momentum and kept going to see just how good I could become. And, well, as you saw today, I start again each day paying that price. Still feels fantastic!"

The two continued to chat as Jordan shared the peaks and valleys of his NCAA Championship season. There were ups and downs, obstacles he had to overcome, and deep relationships built and a few lost along the way. It was truly a season filled with life lessons. As the two talked they lost track of time until Jordan's phone alarm brought them back to the present moment. They realized they were about to be late for the family party his parents had planned in his honor.

---

205 +1: Easy To Do. Easy Not To Do | Leading An Inspired Life by Jim Rohn

206 +1: The Little Things Aren't That Little | Go Long by Jerry Rice

As he and Coach Brian drove to the party, Jordan's phone rang. He looked down to identify the caller, and saw his girlfriend's name light up on his screen, 'Jen-Beam Love.' It was a lengthy contact name, but it served as a simple relationship reminder, prompting him to reset, drop from his head down into his heart, and answer the call with patience and warmth. [207] "Hey, babe. We're on our way! I'm with Coach Brian ... can't wait to see you!"

Coach Brian was impressed with Jordan's simple technique to remind himself to transform into his best self when transitioning from his lacrosse pursuits to his relationship goals. He was witnessing Jordan *flip the switch* firsthand, and was proud to see him practicing this important strategy from years ago.

"What a great strategy," he said to Jordan. "I'll have to add that 'best self' reminder into my repertoire of tools. Today the pupil has become the teacher!"

"Sharing what we've learned is the secret to living the Black-Belt Lifestyle, right, Coach?" Jordan laughed, remembering his lessons.

"You got it! Once you master a system, you need to constantly look for improvements and then share what you've learned with others.[208] Teaching others is the easiest way to guarantee you will continue to sharpen your skills.[209] So, who are you teaching this Black Belt Mentality to, Jordan?"

"I'm glad you asked," Jordan said. "I have a freshman on my team, Blake, that I've taken under my wing. The kid has a ton of potential and is eager to improve. I started mentoring him when he noticed some of my more unique habits and started asking me questions. That was two years ago! Now we both have many players on our team who we're teaching to become Black Belts."

---

207 +1: Active Love | The Tools by Phil Stutz and Barry Michels

208 +1: Constant and Never-Ending Improvement | Legacy by James Kerr

209 +1: Want To Make It Stick: Explain Like I am 5 | A Mind for Numbers by Barbara Oakley Ph.D.

"That's great! Speaking with your actions is the best way to build a culture of excellence."[210]

"Ain't that the truth! I learned *that* the hard way! When you first taught me, I wanted to share the lessons that helped me with everyone. Looking back, I now see it wasn't until I fully embodied these ideas that my teammates started to seek me out."

"True, you don't want to preach. As you've seen, your teammates will come to you when they're ready. When you have enough teammates practicing the process, excellence will become the norm. Then, when you have a player who isn't living the mindset, he will stick out like a sore thumb and quickly realize that a White Belt Mentality won't cut it on your team."

"Yeah, that's something we've systematized. We always have someone to mentor and someone who will hold us accountable. If you have a White Belt Mentality, you can't hide on our team!"

With that, they pulled up to the party. Jordan hated being the center of attention. He always had to fight his tendency to become irritated when people wanted to celebrate his success.

As they unbuckled their seatbelts and opened the car door, the two looked at each other and rehearsed their 'best self' relationship identities.

"World's Best Son," Jordan said, smiling.

"World's Best Friend!" Coach Brian responded with a nod.

They laughed and bumped fists as they simultaneously *flipped the switch* and re-committed to bringing their best selves to this moment.

That was the game they were both playing—to close the gap between their current behavior and how they were capable of behaving at their best.[211]

---

210 +1: Today's 'To-Be' List | Primary Greatness by Stephen Covey

211 +1: How to Close the Gap | Ego is the Enemy by Ryan Holiday

It was time to *flip that switch* and Jordan was calm and content, knowing he would never be exonerated from this process. After all, every moment was another opportunity to show up as his best. That was how he would continue to win the game of life.[212]

TAKE ACTION: PASSION

(Use your Journal page or your *Heroic App*)

A. Who will you teach the Black Belt Mentality to? (Teaching someone else is the best way to hold yourself accountable and practice what you've learned!)[213]

B. Commit to constant, never-ending improvement! Review your identities and habits:

  - Do they still fire you up?
  - Which micro habits have you mastered?
  - Which micro habits need to be tweaked to improve?
  - Which micro habits have fizzled along the way?
  - What *new* micro habits do you want to add to transform yourself into your ideal identity?

---

212 +1: Constant and Never-Ending Improvement | Legacy by James Kerr

213 +1: How to learn FASTER | Limitless by Jim Quik

8. passion

Leaders strive for constant, never-ending improvement, fully-knowing they will always be a work in progress, never arriving at their final destination! They understand that excellence is a lifestyle, and they teach this through every interaction with their teammates, friends, and family.

You will always be a work in progress, never arriving at your final destination! And that's a good thing! Even after you've finished this course and reached your goal, every future moment presents another golden opportunity to show up at your best. Committing to your Dojo Decision and living with your Black Belt Mentality is how you will continue to win the game of life.

Therefore, Live one Day at a Time. Make Every Day a Masterpiece!

IMAGINE SOMEONE IS DOCUMENTING EVERYTHING YOU DO TODAY...
AND AT THE END OF THE DAY, HE/SHE WRITES A SUMMARY
A DAY IN THE LIFE OF...
1
THIS DESCRIPTION IS THE EMBODIMENT OF WHO YOU ARE!

Reflect on how you will continue to live the lessons you've learned:

Review your current habits. What habits have you practiced, mastered, and implemented into your daily routine?

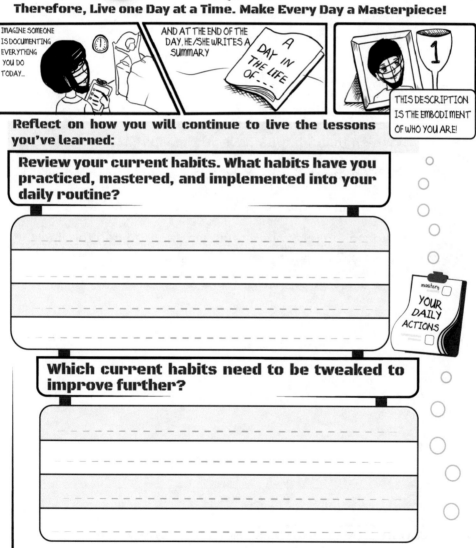

Which current habits need to be tweaked to improve further?

Are there any habits or goals you were once interested in that no longer fire you up? (Delete them from your protocol!)

What new habits do you want to add to transform yourself into your ideal identity? (Keep on the lookout for micro-habits that will improve your performance!)

◇ **How do you plan to continue to live what you've learned in this book? What were your favorite lessons?**

1.
2.
3.
4.
5.

Go to dojodecision.com for inspiration!

This is a process you can continue to hone forever.

Take inventory of your habits

Delete what's not working

Experiment to add improvements

Repeat!

Continue to install and delete micro habits indefinitely to keep your optimal protocol up to date!

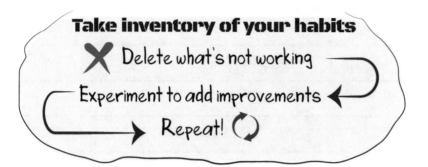

What apps / tools will you use to hold you accountable?

[Heroic App]

[W.O.O.P App]

[Habit Share App]

Go to dojodecision.com for inspiration!

Masterpiece Day - Conclusion

Got the hang of building your routines? Go through an ideal day.

Start when you wake up and end when you go to sleep.

Feel free to sprinkle in non-sequential micro habits that leave you feeling more energized, productive, relaxed, hopeful, courageous, grateful, caring, and passionate!

1.	IF: You wake up:	Then:
2.	IF:	Then:
3.	IF:	Then:
4.	IF:	Then:
5.	IF:	Then:
6.	IF:	Then:
7.	IF:	Then:
8.	IF:	Then:
9.	IF:	Then:
10.	IF:	Then:
11.	IF:	Then:
12.	IF:	Then:
13.	IF:	Then:
14.	IF:	Then:
15.	IF:	Then:
16.	IF:	Then:

17.	IF:	Then:
18.	IF:	Then:
19.	IF:	Then:
20.	IF:	Then:
21.	IF:	Then:
22.	IF:	Then:
23.	IF:	Then:
24.	IF:	Then:
25.	IF:	Then:
26.	IF:	Then:
27.	IF:	Then:
28.	IF:	Then:
29.	IF:	Then:
30.	IF:	Then:
31.	IF:	Then:
32.	IF:	Then:
33.	IF:	Then:
34.	IF:	Then:
35.	IF:	Then:
36.	IF:	Then:
37.	IF:	Then:
38.	IF:	Then: You fall asleep.

Go to dojodecision.com for inspiration!

Masterpiece Daily Journal :

Date:

Things to do today :

Map out your day here!

Remember, We have 100% control over our AM and PM routines that prime you for the day. Remember your day starts the night before! For daily journaling tips check out: https://bulletjournal.com

Open Space:

This is your space to draw a picture, recite a quote, a mantra, to remember something you read or heard throughout the day: Need an idea for a topic?

- How will you use your strengths to serve the world?
- Did your Coach send out a bit of wisdom, a YouTube video? Reflect on this in your own words here!
- No time? Draw a picture that reminds you of who you want to be!

AM

PM

Three things you will do today to step outside your comphort zone:

-
-
-

Gratitude:

What are you thankful for? Science shows writing this down will make you 10% happier!

-
-
-

	Energy/Your Sport	Work/School	Relationships
Identity	Identity: Who do you want to be: Energy/Athletics? i.e. "Elite Athlete"	Identity: What's your "school/work" Identity i.e. "Straight A Student"!	Identity: What's your "relationship Identity i.e. "World's best teammate"!
Virtues	Virtues: To be that Identity, what virtues to you need to embody today? i.e. "Confidence, Resilience"	Virtues: To be that Identity, what virtues to you need to embody today? i.e. "Smart, Confident, Proactive, Prioritized, Organized, Take Action	Virtues: To be that Identity, what virtues to you need to embody today? i.e. "Confident, Kind, Present, Patience.
Behaviors	What's your #1 behavior to focus on today? i.e. 100% effort at practice! - #1 bad habit to eliminate? i.e. I won't eat Sugar!	What's your #1 behavior to focus on today? i.e. do HW before w/o phone on before TV!	What's your #1 behavior to focus on today? i.e. "Listen before speaking" - #1 bad habit to eliminate? i.e. No phone when talking with parents!

(Work/School Behaviors continued: - #1 bad habit to eliminate? i.e. I won't procrastinate!)

Targets

0	1	10	100	1K	10K	25
A moment of stillness/meditation	1 moment of stretch upon wake-up	10 reps of upon wake-up	100 reps of movement throughout day	Endurance exercise?	10k steps?	25 min workout?

DEEP +	TEAM +	MONKEY +	PLAY =	TOTAL
phone free work?	team work?	Distracted or Busy Work?	Play?	

0.0	1.0	2.0	3.0
Love Yourself?!	Present w/ a Loved one?!	Micro Moment w/a Stranger?	Encourage or Appreciate someone?!

HRs of Sleep?
8 hrs.?

mention here:

Sleep is a necessity, not a luxury! Put yourself in a position to show up at your best today!

Did You Journal this AM?
Cross it off!

Spend a "goal" of 1 minute a day reaffirming the person you want to be today!

Pre-Input Win:
Time you were creative before reactive?

to do:
- ☐ Win in Energy?
- ☐ Win in Work?
- ☐ Win in Love?

Use the time when your mind is fresh wisely! Get a win in each area of your life to build momentum for the day!

Daily Rhythms:
I will get up and move every:

mention here:

I will only work this long before a break

mention here:

Moving several times an hour will keep you more alert than a cup of coffee!

Shutdown Complete:
What time do you transition from work to focus on your relationships?

mention here:

Do you have any routines to help you switch from work to relationship mode?

Digital Sunset:
What time will you turn off Electronics? Aim for <1hr before bed

mention here:

THE #1 obstacle to getting a good night of sleep is using your technology way too late.

Bed Time

Go to dojodecision.com for inspiration!

Passion (+1's)

Visit DojoDecision.com, scan the QR code below, or search the keywords in the *Heroic App* to learn the origins of the lessons introduced in this chapter!

193. **+1: Channeling Mia Hamm | The Champion's Mind by Jim Afremow**
194. **+1: The 5 Greek Keys to Optimizing | Ego is The Enemy by Ryan Holiday**
195. **+1: Ikigai, Your Reason For Waking Up In The Morning | The Happiness Equation by Neil Pasricha**
196. **PN: +1: Sweeping Sheds | Legacy by James Kerr**
197. **+1: Win or Learn | With Winning in Mind by Lanny Bassham**
198. **+1: Want to Improve? Measure! | Eat, Move, Sleep by Tom Rath**
199. **+1: Spiritual Windshield Wipers | Stillness is the Key by Ryan Holiday**
200. **+1: 100% on ONE Keystone Daily Micro Habit | Mini Habits by Steven Guise**
201. **+1: Marginal Gains—Here's How To Win | Black Box Thinking by Matthew Syed**
202. **+1: Scaffolding - Constructing Your Destiny | The Monk Who Sold His Ferrari by Robin Sharma**
203. **+1: Raise The Basement | The Art Of Learning by Josh Waitzken**
204. **+1: What's Important Now | No Limits by Michael Phelps and Alan Abrahamson**
205. **+1: Easy To Do. Easy Not To Do | Leading An Inspired Life by Jim Rohn**
206. **+1: The Little Things Aren't That Little | Go Long by Jerry Rice**
207. **+1: Active Love | The Tools by Phil Stutz and Barry Michels**
208. **+1: Constant And Never-Ending Improvement | Legacy by James Kerr**
209. **+1: Want To Make It Stick: Explain Like I am 5 | A Mind for Numbers by Barbara Oakley Ph.D.**
210. **+1: Today's 'To-Be' List | Primary Greatness by Stephen Covey**
211. **+1: How to Close the Gap | Ego is the Enemy by Ryan Holiday**
212. **+1: Constant and Never Ending Improvement | Legacy by James Kerr**
213. **+1: How to learn FASTER | Limitless by Jim Quik**

APPENDIX

— Tactical Recruiting Information —

THE TRAITS ALL COACHES WANT TO RECRUIT:

As a Black Belt Mentality Athlete, you have a huge advantage over your competition! You have learned how to use your lacrosse training to become:

- More confident.
- More focused on your goals and open-minded to learn.
- More able to stay present and enjoy your lacrosse training.
- A grittier competitor.
- A better leader and teammate.

These are the traits that ALL college coaches are looking for. Think of it through this lens: if you're blessed to be recruited, your coach is inviting you to join their family. Everything you do—good or bad, on or off the field, for the rest of your life—will reflect on them and their program.

Therefore, it makes sense for a coach to first and foremost recruit players of character.

WHAT YOU THINK YOU NEED TO FOCUS ON TO GET RECRUITED:

Athletes that possess high character also perform better and improve over time. Parents and players ask me all the time what they need to improve and what they need to do to get recruited. It's amazing how they always believe it's something tactical they need to improve on. I commonly hear:

- "If I improve my left hand, will I be good enough?"
- "Do I just need to get in better shape? Become faster? Stronger?"
- "Do I need to shoot harder and more accurately?"
- "Do I need to improve my lacrosse IQ?"

I almost always tell them YES! to everything above. However, I also try to share the secret no one seems to want to hear. That secret is approaching every single practice and every single game with a desire to improve the traits listed above. If you do, your stick skills, physical ability, and lacrosse IQ will take care of themselves. Don't believe me? Begin to implement the habits and routines written in this book and watch your skills improve!

Therefore, if you want tactical advice regarding what college coaches are looking for, it can be summarized in one sentence: "*Be so good that college coaches can't ignore you!*"[214] If you adopt this mindset, I guarantee coaches will seek you out!

OFF-FIELD BEHAVIOR

The adage "Be so good that coaches can't ignore you" applies off the field as well. Your performance—both in and out of the classroom—are just as important as your performance on the field. Some would even argue they're more important! It would be unfortunate to miss out on incredible opportunities due to poor grades or foolish behavior you've forever documented on social media. Coaches are always watching: on the field, on the internet, and on the sidelines.

- How do you treat your teammates? Do you encourage them? Or are you quick to ridicule them when they make mistakes?
- Do you show your coach respect? Listening to their instruction and trying to play within their system on the field?

214 +1: So Good They Can't Ignore You | So Good They Can't Ignore You by Cal Newport

- How about your parents? Do you regularly express your gratitude for their support? Conversely, are you pulling your own weight in the relationship? Are they over-involved, paving every obstacle in your path, handling your recruiting outreach and carrying your equipment from field to field for you?

Coaches are eager to recruit mature, independent leaders. Players who are actively on the lookout for opportunities to add value, not just take value from their program. It's worth repeating—if you're blessed to be recruited, your coach is inviting you to join their family. Every single thing you do from that point on—good or bad, on or off the field, for the rest of your life—will reflect on them and their program. Therefore, choose to make your team proud with every action you take. But most importantly, make yourself proud! Become the person you know you're capable of becoming!

WHAT LEVEL OF LACROSSE SHOULD YOU LOOK TO PLAY?

Now, if you're attending recruiting tournaments and you continue to be contacted by schools experiencing a similar level of on-field success, then you've most likely identified the level of lacrosse where you belong. This is almost always true (unless you know something about yourself that these coaches don't!). For instance:

1. Are you willing to use your Black Belt Mentality to work harder than players who are currently higher than you on college coaches' recruiting boards?
2. Will you grow to become bigger, faster, and stronger over the next few years?

If you said "Yes," then, by all means, continue to follow your Division 1 dreams! If you're correct about your work ethic and your ability to grow, then schools which were once a reach might become an option. Just make sure you look at the recruiting timeline shared at the end of this chapter. This will help you understand where these programs are most likely at in their recruiting process.

Now, if you have yet to attend a recruiting tournament and therefore don't have the *coaches evaluation market* to help you determine which level you should explore, then I urge you to have a conversation with your high school coach, your club coach, or your mentors to set up a plan to decide exactly what it is you want to gain from your lacrosse experience. Some questions you should get clarity on include:

- **Why are you participating?**
    - To have fun and hang out with your friends?
    - To develop skills to help you later in life?
    - To make your parents happy?

- **Decide if you really want to play a sport in college?**
  There is a place for everyone who has the passion and desire to do so, but it's important to have knowledge about the following:
    - The commitment level and time requirement asked for each Division (D1, D2, D3, JUCO, MCLA).

- **What is the recruiting calendar for each school?**
    - When should you reach out to your desired school?
    - What is the best method to reach out to each school (*email, phone, text, in person*)?
    - What tournaments or prospect days do you need to attend to be seen by each school?

Options & Recruiting Calendar:

Differences Between College Divisions

	D1	D2	D3	MCLA
EXPERIENCE				
	Your lacrosse experience will be a full-time job. Academics and lacrosse will be your priority. Your social life will be sacrificed. You will have mandatory study times. Time management is very important, social life comes last.	Each program is different. The time commitment during the season may be similar to DI. However, the off-season (Fall) is usually more relaxed. Coaches are limited in the time they can spend with their team. However, your captain's practice may be just as intense!		
SCHOLARSHIPS				
	The NCAA currently allows 48 athletes to receive a full scholarship. However, this does not mean 48 athletes will receive a full scholarship. Each school will determine the percentage of scholarship to allocate to each player.	10.8 athletic scholarships are allowed but not necessarily allocated. Some athletic scholarships are offered. Financial and academic aid available. (This could be more lucrative than an athletic scholarship. Make sure you bring this up to the coach!)	Financial need and academic aid will be available (Could be more lucrative than athletic scholarships. Make sure you talk to the coach!)	The MCLA Program is not part of the school's athletic department. You may have to pay to participate on the team once you get into the school.

RECRUITING TIMELINE

	D1	D2	D3	MCLA
Before the Fall of your Sophomore year:	Your focus should be on Improving your skill, IQ, physical ability, and mentality! Most college coaches aren't watching! Complete Black Belt Mentality Course and improve your confidence, grit, focus, and leadership skills! That's how you improve your lacrosse IQ, physical ability, and stick skills to become "So Good Coaches Can't Ignore You!"			

RECRUITING TIMELINE

	D1	D2	D3	MCLA
Fall of your Sophomore year.	A handful of coaches may watch you if their previous classes are full and they want to plan for next summer.	A handful of coaches may watch you if their previous classes are full and they want to plan for next summer.		
Winter & Spring of your Sophomore year:	You can begin to reach out to schools you're interested in. Communicate where you will be playing over the summer. Coaches can't reply, except to invite you to prospect days. Recruiting may not be their priority because they are in-season, focused on coaching their teams!			
Summer after your Sophomore year:	Attend prospect days and recruiting tournaments where these coaches will be evaluating.			

July 1st, heading into your junior year: first day US service academies can reach out to potential recruits

September 1st of your junior year: all schools can reach out to potential recruits

RECRUITING TIMELINE

	D1	D2	D3	MCLA
September and October of your Junior year:	Visit schools! Coaches are on campus and inviting players to visit. They will make verbal scholarship offers after your visit if they are sold on your character and ability. A verbal commitment is not binding but 99% of colleges honor it. However, you're not locked in!	A handful of coaches may watch you if their previous classes are full and they want to plan for next summer.		
November of your Junior year:	Coaches will still be evaluating the junior class. Many will be watching the players that have already verbally committed to their school. However, most coaches are still identifying new players to recruit -If you're playing a fall sport, and you haven't been contacted by a DI school yet, then you should try to attend these November events to get noticed.			
December of your Junior year:	Sparse opportunities to be seen by college coaches due to the NCAA recruiting calendar. However, if you can attend the IMLCA convention tournament, that is the best recruiting event of the Fall because all staff members of most programs will be in attendance.			
Winter & Spring of your Junior Year:	Lacrosse season for NCAA schools. NCAA Coaches aren't attending many recruiting events. If you haven't committed to a DI school, continue to reach out; however, it's time to start reaching out to DII and DIII schools as their recruiting intensifies.	If you have been focused on DI, it's time to start reaching out to DII, DIII, and MCLA schools to show interest. Most DI players are signed, and they will begin to double down their recruiting efforts on the players they have evaluated over the past summer and fall.		

<table>
<tr><th></th><th>D1</th><th>D2</th><th>D3</th><th>MCLA</th></tr>
<tr><th colspan="5">RECRUITING TIMELINE</th></tr>
<tr><td>Summer of your Junior Year:</td><td>Continue to compete with your club team. If committed, your coach will want to continue to watch you play.

If uncommitted, DI Coaches may come to watch you play. Try to correspond with them beforehand. Most likely, they will come to events to watch and see how you perform against top competition.</td><td colspan="3" rowspan="2">Attend prospect days and recruiting tournaments where these coaches will be evaluating. You should email them prior to a tournament to watch you play. If they don't respond, then you're not on their radar.</td></tr>
<tr><td>Fall of your Senior year:</td><td>DI Coaches will spend 90% of their time watching juniors. Coaches will watch their committed kids, especially if they think you're still considering alternative options.</td></tr>
<tr><td>November of your Senior year:</td><td colspan="3">You will sign your letter of intent to play at your chosen school. You are committed at this point and may face ramifications if you uncommit and attend another school. (if you're recieving an athelete scholarship.)</td><td>No need to sign a letter of intent.</td></tr>
<tr><td>After November of your Senior year:</td><td>Most rosters will be full. However, if you're good enough, you will find an opportunity!</td><td colspan="3">Review your list of schools and reassess your options. Colleges will continue to evaluate and reach out.</td></tr>
</table>

TAKE ACTION:

Tactical Recruiting Information (use your Journal page)

1. **Continue to improve!**
   a. **IMPROVE YOUR MENTAL GAME:** College coaches are actively looking for good players. If you're good enough and you work hard in the classroom, you will get noticed! To improve your mindset, consider reaching out to Coach McDermott about his *Black Belt Mentality* Training Program (https://dojodecision.com/).
   b. **IMPROVE YOUR SKILLS:** If you want to play lacrosse in college, lacrosse should be a labor of love. If you're not playing wall ball every night, you are not putting yourself in a position to succeed in college. If not, that's okay! Find something you're passionate about and practice it. If lacrosse is your passion, then time yourself completing a wall-ball routine and measure your improvement.[215] Share it with your accountability partner! Show your mentors you're committed to improving![216]

2. **Email your coach a list of the schools you may want to attend.**
   a. A helpful prompt is to list: 1) a reach school, 2) a good fit, and 3) a safety school.
   b. Research: Campus size, location, potential majors, the projected roster size of the team's roster (40 players vs 70 players) is a very different experience!

215 +1: Want to Improve? Measure! | Eat Move Sleep by Tom Rath

216 +1: The Audience Effect | How Bad Do You Want It? by Matt Fitzgerald

3. **Prepare to write your introductory email to College Coaches.**
   a. You can use the template below.
   b. Put together a highlight film reel! Coaches need to see you play!
      - IMLCA Recruits is a great resource: https://www.imlcarecruits.org/
   c. Share your intention and draft email with the help of your Club/High School Coach or lacrosse mentor.
      - He/She will be able to offer good feedback!

4. **Take Athlete Types Assessment!**
   a. Coaches want to know more about you. There are no right or wrong answers, but this will let them know if you may be a good fit for their program.
      - Take the Troutwine Athletic Profile (TAP) *[Scan the QR code and use the discount code **Dojo20** for $20 off]*

5. **Email specific College Program - *(cc) your Club/High School Coach!***
   a. If you cc your club coach, ask him to follow up with the college coach on your behalf to gauge the college's interest. Keep in mind, if it's before September 1st of your junior year, the college coach isn't allowed to respond to you directly.
   b. *Don't worry about the cost of tuition before reaching out. Programs at all levels can put together substantial academic financial aid packages for you if you have the grades!

Recruiting Plan:

You can begin working on your recruiting plan any time, Continue to revise as you get closer to reaching out to college coaches (follow the recruiting timeline included in the appendix!)

What are you doing to improve? Whenever you learn a new skill, It's important to break it down into its smallest pieces.

Stick Skills	i.e. Wall ball routine
Lacrosse IQ	i.e. Watching film. Subscribing to learning websites.
Fitness, Athleticism, Speed	i.e. Goin a gym. Measure your emprovement.
Mental Game	i.e. Practice your habits. Commit to your Dojo Decision!
Leadership Skills	i.e. Listen to leadership 101 on the Heroic app/Volunteer/Take on responsibilities!

Brainstorm a list of schools you are interested in. Take into account: academics. Do you have the ability to play at this school? Big school? City school? Have you considered the region of the country you want to live in? Consider the weather—can you deal with snow? Is your distance from home important?

Reach Schools:	Reasonable Schools:	Safe Schools:
1.	1.	1.
2.	2.	2.
3.	3.	3.

Create an IMLCA recruiting profile. (Keep in mind coaches may not view it until your sophomore or junior year). IMLCA Recruits is a great resource: https://www.imlcarecruits.org/

What events can you attend where the colleges coaches you're interested in are actively recruiting? Brainstorm here!

1.	2.	3.
4.	5.	6.

Introduction Letter to a College Coach

Keep it brief, informative and memorable! Coaches receive thousands of emails!

For best results, follow the recruiting timeline shared in the Dojo Decision appendic chapter, "Tactical Recruiting Information".

Subject line: NAME: POSITION: YEAR

Coach Name (personalize), I'm very interested in your school (personalize)! I believe I can help you accomplish your goal of winning a National Championship (personalize).

I'd be grateful for you to watch me play via my film or at the events I will be attending in the upcoming months (listed below).

After watching me play, please reach out to my coaches or I if you think I have what it takes to play for your program! If interested, I'd be excited to showcase my skills and demonstrate my interest by attending your prospect camp.

- FILM/PROFILE LINK: Use QR Code to create an IMLCA recruiting profile or post your film on YouTube for FREE _ _ _ _
- STATS & ACCOLADES: i.e. 60 goals/50 assists | MVP | Captain | 6'4, 215lbs
- COACHES CONTACT/TESTIMONY:
  - Name/Contact Info: Coach/Club Team Coach
  - Testimony: "Tim led us to a conference championship. He's the heart of our team. Please call if you're are interested in learning more.
- GPA: 4.0
- UPCOMING TOURNAMENTS:
  - i.e. Tournament/Team name/Jersey #
  - _ _ _ _ _ _ _ _ _ _ _ _ _ _
  - _ _ _ _ _ _ _ _ _ _ _ _ _ _

Thank you for your consideration.
Sincerely,
Name

When to follow up?

Consider reaching out before your tournaments to remind the coach of where and when you will be playing. You can also reach out with updated film and accolades.

What if you don't hear back? How much communication is too much?

Keep in mind DI coaches can't respond until September 1st of your junior year. If a coach wants you, they will be happy to receive your email.
If they aren't currently interested, they may not initially respond. However, continue to check in periodically. You don't want to annoy them, but it's their responsibility to let you know if an opportunity doesn't exist.

Short and simple. Your goal is to get the coach to watch you play!

Go to dojodecision.com for updates!

Tactical Recruiting Advice (+1's)

Visit DojoDecision.com, scan the QR code below, or search the keywords in the *Heroic App* to learn the origins of the lessons introduced in this chapter!

214. +1: So Good They Can't Ignore You | So Good They Can't Ignore You by Cal Newport

215. +1: Want to Improve? Measure! | Eat Move Sleep by Tom Rath

216. +1: The Audience Effect | How Bad Do You Want It? by Matt Fitzgerald

— How to Train Like a Pro and Learn Any Skill[217] —

Back in the Dojo with Coach Brian

The Summer Before Jordan's Freshman Year in High School

The First Day of Training After Hearing The Dojo Decision Speech

Jordan and Coach Brian parked their car and began walking down a path through the trees that led to an isolated lacrosse field. It was a secret spot, one few people knew about. It had a concrete wall directly next to the field, making it ideal for both field and wall-ball training. But Coach hadn't asked Jordan to bring his lacrosse equipment, so he was curious why they were going there today. "Jordan," Coach began as they were walking, "You want to develop a Black Belt Mentality, right?"

"I do."

"Well, like learning anything, whether it be a lesson in school or a new tactic on the field, there are proven tactics of how to learn."

"So, you're saying before I can learn my Black Belt Mentality, first I need to learn how to learn? Why don't my teachers teach this to us in school? Seems like a pretty important lesson!"

Coach threw up his hands and grinned. "I know, right? I'm sure they try. However, they don't teach you how to develop a Black Belt

217 101 Course: Learning 101 | Brian Johnson

Mentality in school either—and I believe that's the most important thing you *must* learn!"

"Alright," Jordan said. "But why do you think they don't? What's going on?"

"It baffles me, but I believe they don't teach it because they *can't* teach it. You see, you need a subject you're really passionate about in order to make a Dojo Decision. That's why sports are so powerful. If only you could get as excited about math class as you do when you strap on your equipment and compete with your friends, then you'd be really successful!"

Jordan frowned. "Yeah, unfortunately, I never really caught the math bug. It's lacrosse for me. *This* is what I love and think about all the time."

"And that's okay. You're like 99 percent of people in the world who may not be destined to become a nuclear physicist, but can still be very successful. And who knows? Maybe lacrosse will fuel you to develop your Black Belt Mentality, gain a new appreciation and passion for math, and become a nuclear physicist!"

Jordan shook his head and rolled his eyes. "You're dreaming, Coach," he said. "Or maybe I'll just become a pro lacrosse player!"

Coach shrugged and looked into the distance. "You never know where your Black Belt Mentality will lead you." He turned back to Jordan and the task at hand. "So, as I was saying, our goal is to *learn* a Black Belt Mentality and apply it to your lacrosse training as efficiently as possible. We need to optimize our time together, and we need to make these lessons stick. You will be drinking through a virtual firehose of knowledge as we begin our training. Also, from this point on I'm going to address you as an adult, because that's the way I like to be treated, and I know you can handle it. Are you comfortable with that?"

Jordan smiled. "Please. I wish *more* people would ask me that." He thought about how he always hated when adults dumbed things down for him. He always thought this was counterproductive. While he understood he would have to learn the basics first, if he wanted to be the best, he needed to know what the best looked like. It always helped to see the big picture. It just so happened that the best constantly practiced the basic training any kid could replicate. "But I don't get why we're heading to a lacrosse field without my stick. I'm ready to train!"

"Well, Jordan, first, you need to know and remember one thing. You need to know what the best version looks like when you learn any new skill. And this applies to whether that skill is something you learn in school, or through our conversations that you will apply to improve your lacrosse skills. Then you need to begin with the end in mind, and that means knowing what you want to accomplish.

"For instance, if you want to be the best lacrosse player, you need to see what the best training looks like. Once you know that, you can begin to deconstruct it and learn the pieces that make up a great lacrosse player. What do you think those are?"

"Easy," Jordan said, starting to think he already knew the basics and was ready for the more advanced stuff. "I need to know lacrosse IQ, I need to train my individual technique, and I need to improve my mindset and physical performance."

"Good!" Coach said. "Now, as we train those key fundamentals, you also want to optimize your most valuable resource. Any guesses for what that is?

"My time! And you know me Coach, I put in the time. I'm out on the field for hours, way longer than any of my teammates."

"That's good, but don't pat yourself on the back just yet. Before you do that, you need to ask yourself, is your practice *purposeful*?[218] Remember, your time is limited, so it's important to be efficient with it. I wouldn't assume this of you, but I know many players who are constantly practicing yet never seem to improve. If that's the case, your teammates who aren't practicing as long might just be prac-ticing smarter!"

---

218 +1: The Science of Being Awesome | Peak by Anders Ericsson and Robert Pool

Jordan sighed, sheepishly realizing that just putting in more time wasn't going to impress Coach Brian.

"To get the most out of your training," Coach continued, "you need to remember that quality practice equals time training multiplied by the intensity you train at.[219] Their problem is they are ignoring a variable of that equation—intensity!"

"Well, that's not a problem with me, you can call me Mr. Intensity," Jordan said, believing he practiced harder than his teammates.

"Good. If you don't bring intensity and focus to your workout, you'll be wasting your time. And this is why I brought you here, for you to take a second look at the intensity of your practice. Jordan, do you think you're practicing at the same intensity as a pro?"

As the two rounded a corner, they saw a large training field ahead of them. They followed the grunts of a man pushing himself to exertion, along with the thuds of a ball repeatedly bouncing against a wall. Soon they saw a lone player going through his practice routine. He was practicing each rep so hard! And although the pace looked grueling, he also looked like he was having a blast! They watched as he meticulously honed his stick skills through each iteration of his routine.

Right hand for ten reps, then switching to his left for another ten reps. He would then change to release the ball underhand, followed by releasing the ball behind his back for ten reps. Cross-handed. Shovel passes. He even practiced passing the ball one-handed!

Although Jordan knew these variations were seldom used in a game, he could tell this player thought it was important to have a plan in his arsenal for any situation he might face during a game. Jordan's eyes widened as he studied the player's focus. Not only was his intensity at a different level, but the man was executing each rep to perfection. He had taped square targets on the wall and seemed to hit them the vast majority of the time.

---

219 +1: Deep Work | Deep Work by Cal Newport

"So tell me," Coach Brian said, gesturing to the man. "Is this what your practice looks like, Mr. Intensity?"

Jordan shook his head, still gazing at the player practicing his routine. "Uhhhh ... not exactly," he muttered. "To be honest, Coach, I've never seen *anyone* practice like this."

"You see, Jordan, many people *think* they are practicing at the intensity level of a ten when they are *really* practicing at a three. This is why I brought you here, so you could see and experience an example of what is possible."

"I get it. I mean, look at him." Jordan gestured at the player. "Even when he's taking a break, the guy still has the intensity and focus of a machine. Who *is* this guy?"

The two now looked at the player as he slowed down his routine for a few reps, relaxing his physical intensity, giving his body time to rest, but didn't let down his focus for a single second. For this segment of his routine, he wasn't even releasing the ball! Instead, he focused on every tiny detail of his shooting form, stopping just before the moment that he would release the ball.

Regrouping, he reset his feet and repeated the motion with 100 percent focus and purpose for ten more reps with each hand. With each rep he made sure his hands were open, facing the sky, reaching his hands back as far as they could be stretched. Then he'd place his chin on his shoulder, bring his arms, hands, and stick over like he was chopping wood before following right over his front leg as he focused on his footwork, stepping towards the goal.

Coach leaned over again. "You see how he slows down and focuses on the basics? Can you imagine how many micro-habits he has grooved into perfecting that form? The man has drilled this so many times he now trusts his body to perform it to perfection without even having to think of the dozens of prompts that must have once gone through his head."

"Wow. I need practice like that," Jordan said. "It's like he's training his focus. Every tiny habit seems important. *Everything.* Even his self-talk and body language after each rep. Coach, do you hear him? He's saying, 'That's like me!' and 'Needs work' after each rep. And before, it seemed like he was mumbling something to himself, to prompt him to practice a certain way." Jordan looked over at Coach and smirked. "Hold up. Have you taught this guy your Black Belt Mentality?"

Coach winked. "Maybe a little. I'm guessing that's his best-self identity he's mumbling before each shot, as a single prompt to remind him to incorporate all his tiny habits. And the 'Needs work!' and 'That's like me!' part, well, that's him reinforcing the good while noting what needs improvement. But don't worry about that right now, we will get to that eventually."

"Gotcha. Yeah, that's a pretty neat idea. To have a single word reminding him to reset and instantly remember to practice all of his tiny habits at that intensity, then trusting himself to let it rip!"[220] He paused and gestured toward the field. "When can we learn about that?" he asked.

Coach Brian patted Jordan on the back and leaned over. "You'll get there in good time. But stay present. We can only get better in the current moment."

"Sure. Makes sense."

They turned back to watch the player finish his routine, focusing on the basics. He then bent down to pick up his water bottle, took a sip along with a few, deep, refocusing breaths, before going right back to it. Only this time he pulled out a stopwatch, pressed start and began the same routine at a rapid pace, even faster than before!

"Now, take note of how he added constraints to make his training a game. By timing his routine and only counting the reps where he hit the exact brick he was aiming for, he's able to compete with himself and make his training more fun and purposeful."

---

220 +1: Squirrels, Einstein, and YOU. Two Mindsets: Training Vs. Trusting | How Champions Think by Bob Rotella

The two watched for twenty minutes before the player took his first two-minute break. He tilted his helmet up, took a sip of water, looked up and acknowledged Coach Brian with a wave. Then he headed to the field where piles of balls and cones had been previously set up to continue his training.

Even that brief pit stop was impressive. Jordan realized if it were he and his teammates, they would have taken all their equipment off. Alternatively, it was as if this player had planned for his heart rate to only drop to a specific level before jogging back out to his next drill.

"You're in for a treat now, Jordan," Coach Brian said, grinning wide.

The player began his training, perfecting a specific skill for several minutes. In the first station, he dodged upfield from behind the goal to get to a predetermined spot roughly five yards above and five yards to the side of the goal. When he arrived at that spot, he performed a variety of moves designed to get his hands free for a shot. He'd roll back, use a rocker move, or just step back to create space and shoot a rifle, changing planes from his underhand release that he delivered to the top corner of the goal.

Jordan noticed he didn't repeat and perfect the exact sequence of moves twice in a row. Instead, he changed things up. He alternated the range of his shot and his release points to not create a false sense of fluency that comes from repeating the exact repetition again and again.[221] After several minutes of this, he quickly transitioned to the next station that he had already set up. Here, he worked to perfect another important skill—his time and release shooting off a catch.

The drill was simple, he passed the ball against the wall, caught it, and then quickly shot the ball at the goal. Most of the goals appeared to hit his target, but when Jordan looked closely, he saw that he wasn't working on the accuracy of his shot. He was working on his footwork and lightning-fast release immediately after he caught the ball. True to form, he didn't take the exact same shot

221 +1: Interleaving, A Key Way to Learn | Make it Stick by Peter C. Brown, Henry L. Roediger and Mark A. McDaniel

twice. He alternated his shots, playing with different release points, placing his shots in different areas of the goal, and alternating the type of shot.

First, he stepped into the pass, simulating a short cut towards the ball. Then, he stretched away from the pass, simulating giving himself more time and room to catch and shoot the ball when the opponent covering left him to slide to cover his teammate passing to him. However, whatever the variation, the man concentrated on getting his hands and feet in position to shoot before the ball arrived to his stick.

To Jordan, the exactness of the training was a work of art. "This is amazing. During every rep he seems to be training with the intensity of playing in the National Championship game."

Coach grinned and couldn't help but chuckle. "So, be honest with yourself, is this what your practice looks like?"

"Oh, no. No way. Definitely not," Jordan said, thinking of how, in comparison, he lolly-gagged through his training. "I mean, if I thought I was practicing at a 10, this intensity is 100!"

"Good. That fluency illusion is the number one obstacle you need to master. Experts never feel they've arrived at the top of their field and are always looking for ways to improve. I know this guy, and even after this practice, I guarantee he'll have brainstormed another handful of new micro IF / THEN habits he will want to experiment with. So, my next question is simple: do you believe you could get here? Do you truly believe you could bring this same mindset to your practice? Confident, gritty, focused?"

Jordan looked back at the player and studied his every move. Every rep, he seemed to go harder than the one before. "I want to," he admitted. "I mean, sure, I'm committed. And I do believe I'll get there eventually. I'm just a kid, so it makes sense I'm not there yet, right?"

"That's only fair."

"This pro looks like he's been at this routine for twenty years, so it wouldn't make sense if I got frustrated that I'm not there yet. Plus, he had to have been in my shoes at one time, just starting out and equally overwhelmed at how much work he had before him."

"You can bet on that," Coach said. "And may I just say I'm impressed with your response. Hearing such an honest self-assessment from someone of your age is ... rare. It's refreshing."

They continued to watch for another twenty minutes until the player ended his training. He walked around, hands back behind his head, concentrating on his breathing as he recovered from the most intense training session Jordan had ever witnessed. As the man made his way to the sidelines to greet them, Jordan's eyes widened in recognition. "Oh my god. Is that ... Marcus Holman?"

Jordan was speechless, realizing he had just watched one of the best shooters *ever* go through his training routine. Holman was fifteen years into his pro career and here he was, still training like a champion. Jordan was amazed.

"What's up, Coach!" Marcus shouted as he closed the gap between them. He gave Coach Brian a high five and, ignoring his sweaty state, brought him in for a hug.

Coach smiled and laughed as the two embraced. "Marcus, you're just lucky I forgive badasses who train hard, hugging me before you shower..."

"Ha. Sorry, Coach. I'm just excited to see you!" Marcus said, releasing him and grinning.

"Thanks for putting on that clinic for us," Coach said. "You still got it! That was a long session! What, were you out here for an hour?"

"Yeah, I wish I could have pushed myself even harder so I could have gotten off the field even sooner, but you know I'm getting older and slowing down. But you know me, I don't have time to waste practicing at a pace that's unrealistic. If I'm going to train, might as well go all in!"[222]

"As it should be."

"So, I'm out there a bit longer than usual 'cause my old body needs breaks," Marcus continued. "But yeah, that's about as long as I can train at that pace in any given time slot."

"You're ... you're Marcus Holman," Jordan blurted out.

"I am," Marcus said casually, before turning back to Coach Brian. "But yeah, I'll probably be out here for another half hour or so, stretching before getting treatment and hitting the ice bath. Us old guys have to train our recovery just as hard, so I can be out here later this afternoon for another session."[223]

"What?!" Jordan stared at him in disbelief. "A second session?! That's ... that's amazing."

Marcus looked back at Jordan. "Yeah, I like to space out my training segments to allow a little forgetting to occur. It kind of gives my body and mind time to digest what I learned, remember how to recreate it, you know?" He looked at Coach and nodded toward Jordan. "Who you got with you, Coach?"

"This is Jordan, and let's just say that someday he wants to achieve what you have accomplished. I think he's got the passion, but before we begin, I wanted him to see what it takes."

Marcus chuckled. "Good call," he said.

"Again, Thanks for putting on that show. I needed to show him the power of having a role model, to show him what's possible. Jordan was thinking he had been practicing about as hard as possible, but as you know, it's almost impossible to practice at that intensity if you've never seen it before."

222 Areté +1: How To Be Like Mike. Go All In! | Relentless by Tim S. Grover

223 +1: Training Your Recovery | The Endurance Handbook by Dr. Philip Maffetone

"Hopefully I didn't scare you off," Marcus said to Jordan, grinning.

Jordan shook his head. "Scared? No way. Inspired is more like it. But I gotta ask, do you always practice that hard?"

Marcus laughed. "That's not hard! That's just the pace of lacrosse. Honestly, I'm having so much fun out there I don't see it as work. I enjoy the feeling of pushing myself to exhaustion, the feeling I get when I'm so immersed in my training that time just slows down. When I can't keep up that intensity, that's when I know it's time to take a break."

"The flow state," Jordan said, nodding.

"Look at you!" Marcus exclaimed." Keep listening to Coach Brian, kid. Following his advice will take you far. He actually took me to watch a pro when I was your age, just making my first Dojo Decision."

"He did?" Jordan asked, suddenly realizing he could be on the same trajectory to success as Marcus Holman had been at his age.

"Oh yeah! We watched Paul Rabil. And I was blown away just watching him, kinda like you are with me."

"That's ... awkwardly accurate," Jordan said, blushing.

"But once I knew what was possible, just reminding myself of that truth was enough for me to increase the intensity of my practice. That's why I rehearse my best-self identity multiple times—at practice, during a PLL game or whenever. Heck, I rehearse it anytime I need a reset to snap back to acting like my best self. Within that practice segment you just watched, I probably *flipped that switch* over a hundred times. From lolly-gagging through a workout to practicing with the intensity of a pro as quickly as flipping on a light switch."

Jordan nodded.

"Want some advice?" Marcus asked. He usually wouldn't give advice unless asked, but he could tell Jordan was just looking for the perfect question to ask.

"Of course!"

"The way I practice out on the field is the same way I practice learning the lessons Coach taught me. I began by going all in. I made that Dojo Decision thing he's always talking about. Deciding to train like a Black Belt, right?"

"Sure!"

"When I was your age, I was at that same camp and heard that same speech!"

"You did?" Jordan asked.

"You know it. So, once I committed, I decided to make my training a game. As I pushed outside my comfort zone, I knew I would inevitably lose my focus, my drive, my equanimity. I would get frustrated, down on myself, and lose my confidence."

"Wait," Jordan interrupted. "You? Marcus Holman? No way."

"It's true," Marcus said. "Turns out I'm human, you know? But I planned for these setbacks. When these things happened, I made it a game to see just how quickly I could get back on track!"[224]

"Make it a game. I like that! Make setbacks fun."

"You got it. Truth is, you can make almost any activity fun. Take school, for instance. Going to class wasn't always my favorite activity when I was your age, but when I lost my focus I would rehearse my World's Best Student identity and get back on track as quickly as possible.[225]

---

224 +1: The Equanimity Game | Meditations by Marcus Aurelius

225 +1: Collecting Turn-Arounds | The Tools by Phil Stutz and Barry Michels

"My game would even continue after the class concluded. Champions always do more, right? I wouldn't get up and leave like most kids. I'd try to recall three things I learned and identify one concept I was learning that needed some extra attention."

"That ... sounds strange. And simultaneously inspiring," Jordan admitted, having never thought about this.

"Yup. Then, when I was walking to the next class, I'd try to teach it to whoever I was walking with, but really dumbing it down, like I was teaching it to a five-year-old, so anyone could understand it. I figured if I could do that, I'd really command the material and hope-fully recall it when I needed it later."[226]

"And did you?"

"Eventually," Marcus said. "I'd repeat it throughout my day, teaching it to anyone who would listen, you know, like my parents when I got home from school. Even my dog, but I guess he really didn't have a choice."[227]

Jordan laughed, picturing Marcus Holman teaching his dog math. "You teach your pup how to shoot, too?"

"Ha-ha, darn right I did! Granted, Biscuit lacks my opposable thumb so he's kind of at a disadvantage trying to hold a stick."

"Just a bit," Jordan said, smiling.

"Plus, he's only interested in food, playing, and getting love, so there's that." Marcus mirrored Jordan's smile. "But Biscuit aside, I'll be doing the same recall routine for this training session in a minute when I start stretching. Brainstorming three things that went well and one thing that needs a little improvement—the process stays the same."

226 +1: Want to Make it Stick? Explain Like I'm 5 | A Mind for Numbers by Barbara Oakley, Ph.D.

227 +1: How to Learn Faster | Limitless by Jim Quik

Interesting. Jordan thought, recalling three things he liked about Marcus's training session that he had just watched. He really appreciated the fact that Marcus never seemed to procrastinate during any part of his training—especially the tough parts.[228]

He also really liked how Marcus worked in twenty-minute bursts, pushing himself to exhaustion, resting, and then getting right back to it for another twenty minutes once refreshed. He practiced at an even more intense pace than he would see in a game so he could be confidently assured he was prepared, and therefore wouldn't choke when he faced a stressful moment in a game.[229]

Finally, Jordan liked how Marcus always looked for new, subtle ways to improve. Even though he was already one of the best to ever play, he was always competing with himself to get just a little better.

"Oh, wow," Jordan said, recalling his lessons and recognizing the patterns "You really do approach training and school the same, don't you?"

"Absolutely," Marcus said. "Plus learning my Black Belt Mentality! The thing is, Jordan, whatever you choose to pursue in your life, choose to make it fun! If that's lacrosse? Great. Then seek out mentors and read whatever books they share with you. But don't just read them—compete with yourself to see just how much you can retain. Measure when you lose focus. To be honest, whenever I read a book I actually note in the margin each time I lose focus or start daydreaming. Then I later compete to see which chapter I lost focus on the least."

"I imagine you do the same thing on the lacrosse field?"

"Yep, that's how you learn any skill, you compete with yourself. I competed to see which drill I went the hardest in. I made it fun!"

"Got it," said Jordan. "This is awesome. Thanks for your advice! This was really cool!"

---

228 +1: Just Get Started | Solving the Procrastination Puzzle by Timothy A. Pychyl

229 PN: Choke by Sian Beilock

"Agreed," Marcus said, extending a hand. "Nice to meet you, Jordan. I look forward to seeing you and how your career develops!" Then he looked at Coach Brian, grinned, and launched forward to give him a final hug.

"It was good to see you," Coach grunted with a grin. "Much better than smelling you..."

"Uh-huh. Love you too, Coach," Marcus said before releasing him.

Jordan and Coach Brian started walking back to the car as Marcus began his cool-down and stretching routines.

"Hey Jordan!" Marcus called after them.

"Yeah?" Jordan asked, spinning around to face him.

"Good luck. Always push yourself outside your comfort zone. That's where you will find your joy. The juice is worth the squeeze," he said, giving Jordan a thumbs up.

Jordan grinned, returning the thumbs up. He turned back around and looked at Coach Brian. "That was Marcus Holman," he said, shaking his head. "This day is just ... awesome."

"And we've only just begun," Coach Brian said, slapping him on the back. "Just wait for what's in store for you, Jordan. I have a feeling you're really going to like what's next."

How To Train Like a Pro & Learn Any Skill (+1's)

Visit DojoDecision.com, scan the QR code below, or search the keywords in the *Heroic App* to learn the origins of the lessons introduced in this chapter!

217. 101 Course: Learning 101 | Brian Johnson

218. +1: The Science of Being Awesome | Peak by Anders Ericsson and Robert Pool

219. +1: Deep Work | Deep Work by Cal Newport

220. +1: Squirrels, Einstein, and YOU. Two Mindsets: Training Vs. Trusting | How Champions Think by Bob Rotella

221. +1: Interleaving, A Key Way to Learn | Make it Stick by Peter C. Brown, Henry L. Roediger and Mark A. McDaniel

222. Areté +1: How To Be Like Mike. Go All In! | Relentless by Tim S. Grover

223. +1: Training Your Recovery | The Endurance Handbook by Dr. Philip Maffetone

224. +1: The Equanimity Game | Meditations by Marcus Aurelius

225. +1: Collecting Turn-Arounds | The Tools by Phil Stutz & Barry Michels

226. +1: Want to Make it Stick? Explain Like I'm 5 | A Mind for Numbers by Barbara Oakley, Ph.D.

227. +1: How to Learn Faster | Limitless by Jim Quik

228. +1: Just Get Started | Solving the Procrastination Puzzle by Timothy A. Pychyl

229. PN: Choke by Sian Beilock

Want to see the big picture and start practicing your Black Belt Mindset now? Stephen Covey, in The 7 Habits of Highly Effective People, tells us how successful people 'Begin with the end in mind.' They know exactly what they want to create before they manifest it in reality.

Begin With The End In Mind
30-Second Journaling Exercise

0. COMMIT – To Journal and Boost Your Probability of Success by 42%

Don't have time to journal? No problem! You can draw this picture to remind you to practice all the lessons you have learned in this book!

Directions: You must be present to maximize the benefits of this journaling exercise. As you draw, recall each lesson, while you envision yourself living each principle today!

1. WISDOM – Remind yourself of the game all humans are playing!

1. Start, by drawing yourself as a 'smiling stick-figure'.

2. Above the stick figure's head, Write the word 'WISDOM' (leave an inch of space between the word and your stick-figure)

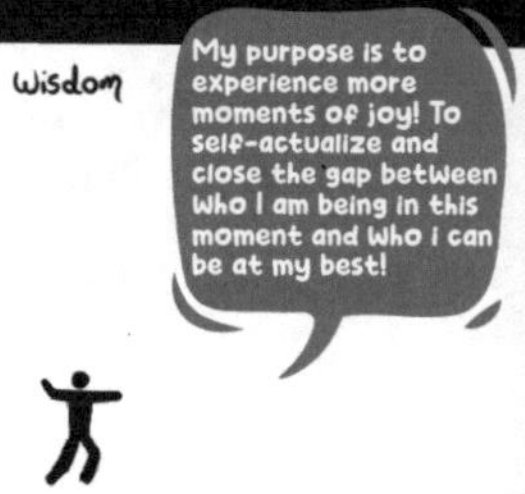

wisdom
My purpose is to experience more moments of joy! To self-actualize and close the gap between who I am being in this moment and who I can be at my best!

- We all want to be happy. Striving to achieve happiness is the 'universal game of life' all humans are playing. You take your turn playing when you spend your limited time. You must decide what activities to spend it on.
- When you spend your time you will always be training your mind for the better or for worse. It's easy to forget you're even playing this game called life, let alone the rules you must follow to 'win' at it. You actively practice wisdom when you remind yourself that your ultimate goal is happiness, and you win by honoring your fundamental habits and living with integrity, living out the virtues that are important to you (self-mastery, energy, courage, hope, gratitude, teamwork, and passion).

3. Draw Maslow's Hierarchy of Needs pyramid around your 'smiling stick-figure' with a sun at the pyramid's peak.

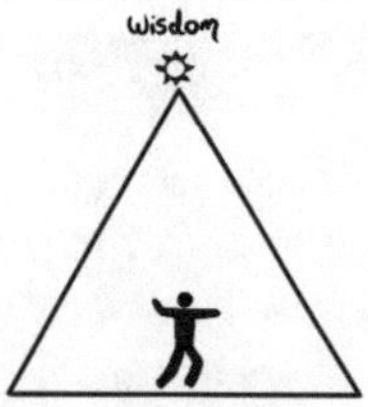

- Abraham Maslow, the father of positive psychology, studied what makes people happy. His pyramid shows you how, as you meet your basic needs, you climb the levels of the pyramid to discover new needs you must meet to experience happiness.
- At the top of the pyramid you find the need to self-actualize. Which means "to be your best self." When your lower needs are met, this need becomes just as important as breathing (if you want to experience happiness). To self-actualize, you must have a clear idea of 'who' that looks like so you can take action to practice the virtues and habits of that person.

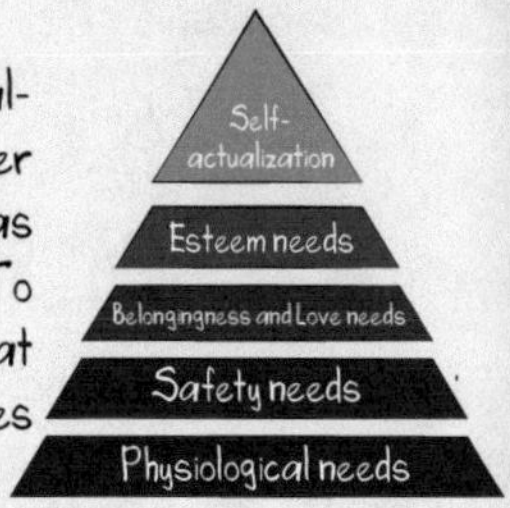

4. Draw a line from your 'stick-figure' straight up towards the peak of the pyramid

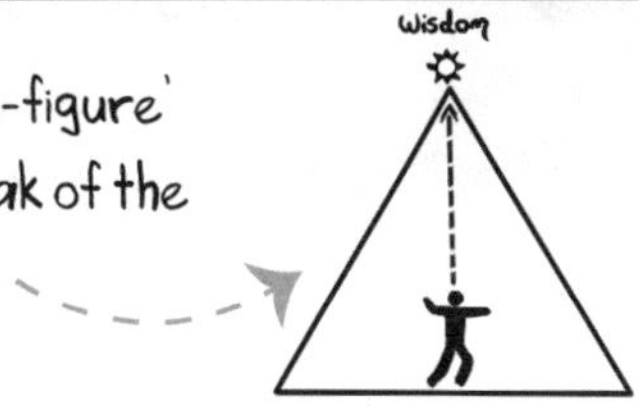

- This represents how you will close the gap between who you are capable of being in this moment and who you can be at your best!

5. To the upper-right of your 'stick figure, pyramid,' draw your 'guiding star.' Your smiling stick-figure should always be looking at this star.

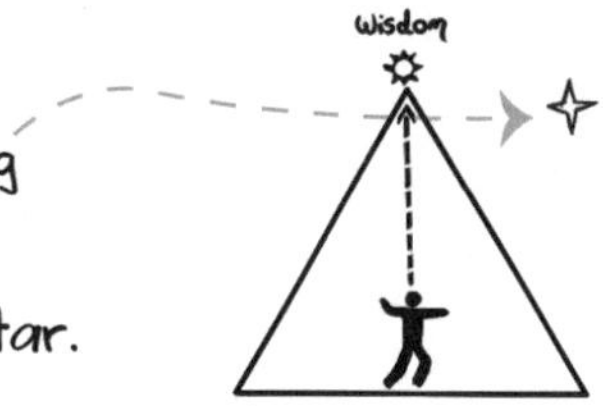

- This will represent your 'identity goal', something you can always look towards to guide you to 'who' you want to be at your best!
- Following that star is your ultimate purpose. You will always be a work-in-progress, trying every day to self-actualize your potential. Keeping that star at the front of your mind will guide you.

SUMMARY

- Every day you must remind yourself of your purpose, which is represented by your 'guiding star.' You practice wisdom when you remember this throughout the day. Here, we depict our universal purpose as climbing the levels of Maslow's Hierarchy of Needs.
- As you climb, you experience happiness when you close the gap between how you are currently behaving and how you can behave at your best. Maslow called this, "self-actualizing".
- Your best is represented by your guiding star.
- When you have fulfilled all of your basic needs, you move up the levels of Maslow's pyramid. If you're reading this, you have been blessed to have already climbed the base levels of the pyramid. However, as you climb each level, your needs at the top level of the pyramid (connection, respect, being your best self), will become just as important as the needs at the bottom level (food and shelter).

2. Self-Mastery

6. Write 'Self-Mastery' under your pyramid

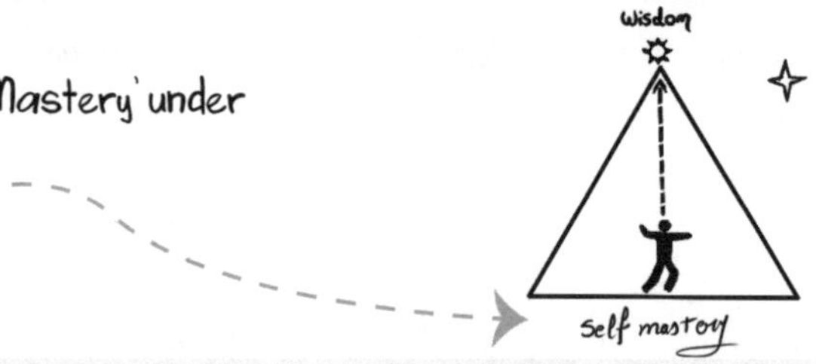

- You win the game of life when you practice the habits the best version of yourself, 'your guiding star,' would practice.

7. Now, 'Draw a mountain with a flag at the peak', directly underneath your 'guiding star', to the right of your 'pyramid.'

- This symbolizes the current goal you're trying to achieve. It's the arena you have chosen to practice your self-mastery. You will enjoy the journey of climbing this mountain every day!

8. Next, draw your 'first hashed arc' behind the 'base of your pyramid.'

- Throughout each day you can close the gap between your current and best self by practicing your chosen habits.
- Recommit to this first thing each morning (write the time you plan to set your intention).
- This indicates your commitment to practice your AM routine, where you will recommit to your intention and energize yourself to practice your pre-set throughout the day.

9. Draw a 'second hashed arc' above the first, to commit to reflecting on your mid-day or when you start your p.m. time block. Most people know who they want to be, but they are distracted by their daily distractions. To combat this, this will be your cue to recommit to 'who' you want to be throughout the day.

SUMMARY

- If you want to be happy and feel in control of your life, you must first master your mind. You do this by defining clear targets you are working toward each day. These targets are the habits and routines your best self would practice as you strive for a goal you want to accomplish.

3. ENERGY

10. Write the word "Energy" under the bottom-left corner of the base of your pyramid.

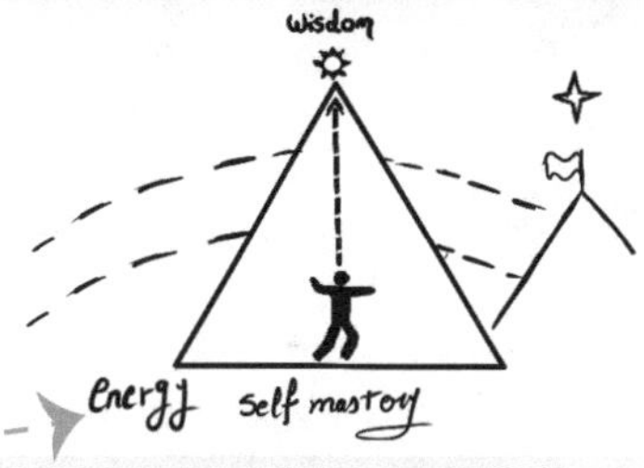

- You will need this consistent energy throughout the day to show up as your best at your hobby/work/exercise and in your relationships!

11. Draw four lines within the lower base of the pyramid. Write: E, M, S, B above each line to remind yourself of each fundamental habit you need to address to build your energy reserve.

- These lines symbolize your commitment to your fundamental habits (Eat! Sleep! Move! Breath!)

12. Retrace the line straight up towards the peak of the pyramid, representing you're honoring your base fundamental habits. This will give you the energy you need to climb your personal mountain and rise up the pyramid (be your best self).

4. COURAGE

13. Write the word "Courage" on the left side of the pyramid.

> Remind yourself to show up in each Moment with courage and confidence!

14. Draw an "x" halfway up the slope of your mountain to represent when you will undoubtedly face obstacles and set backs on your journey up to your mountain peak. "Expect them! Scream, "Bring it on!" whenever you face an obstacle!

15. Draw brackets around the smiling stick-figure you. This represents your comfort zone!

16. Draw two addition brackets to the left side of your stick figure. This represents your stepping outside of your comfort zone. The three brackets remind you to look for three opportunities to step outside your comfort zone each day. By definition, these moments will be uncomfortable. But these will be the times you'll remember, the moments that gave you the greatest fulfillment. You must remind yourself to look for opportunities to enter your growth zone every day!

17. Now, draw a lacrosse stick in the hands of the smiling, stick-figure you. This signifies how, in the heat of competition you will trust your preparation. In that moment, you aim at your target, and "Let it rip!" The time for second guessing yourself is over!

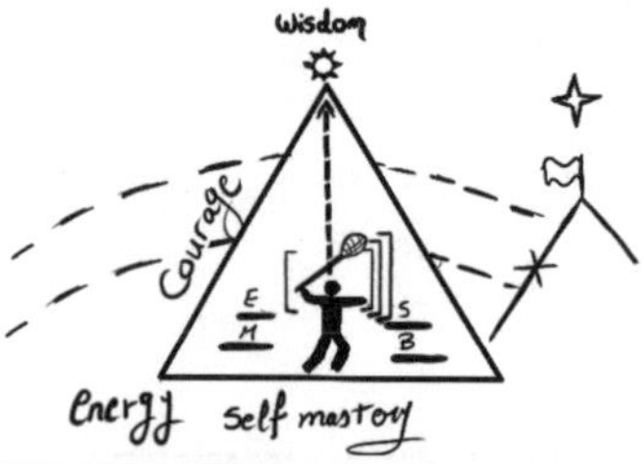

SUMMARY

>> You will need the courage to climb the peak and see obstacles as opportunities for growth!

5. HOPE

18. Write the word "HOPE" on the upper-left corner of your pyramid. Directly underneath, write H = C + P + G to remind yourself that hope = Having a bold goal, confidence that you will achieve your goal, + many pathways to achieve it.

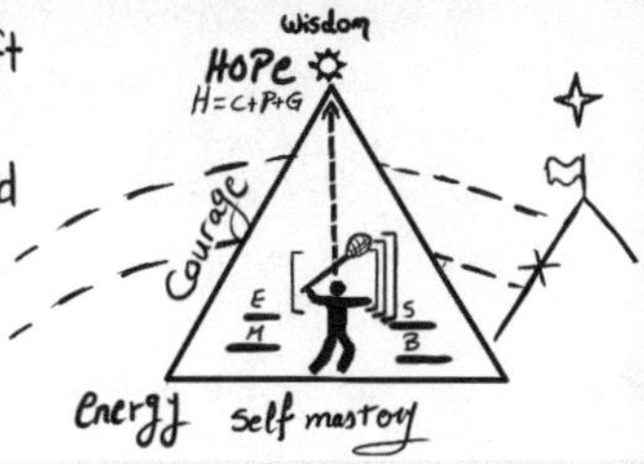

>> On your journey up your 'goal' mountain, it's important to check in to make sure your goals still fire you up, and you're confident you can achieve them.

19. Draw multiple arrows (pathways) around your obstacle 'X' to represent how you have 'IF: THEN' planned your reaction for when adversity strikes. (And make no mistake, it will strike!)

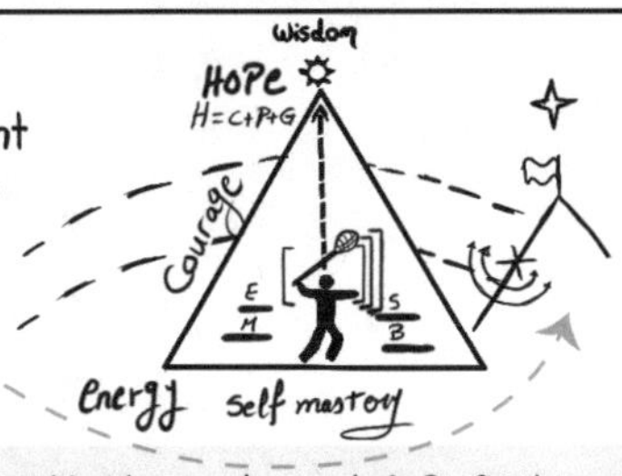

>> This also represents your backup plans: You have planned: A, B, C...through Z for the times your plans fail. You will reach your mountain peak one way or another. You will continue to take action and never quit halfway towards your goal. You will be great, you will not be mediocre (Did you know the origins of the word 'mediocre' means 'stopping halfway up a mountain'?)

>> Review your picture. You have a flag at the top of your mountain which represents your goal. Your smiling stick-figure self is confident, and you have many pathways around your obstacles to climb your mountain!

6. GRATITUDE

20. Retrace your stick-figure (best-self's) smiling face.

>> If you want to be happy and enjoy life's journey, you must practice gratitude!

>> As you draw, reflect on your favorite gratitude practice you will execute today. (Grateful flow / "What if this is the last time?" / Negative visualization / Active love, etc.)

7. TEAMWORK

21. Draw '4' smiling stick figure friends, joining you on top of your mountain.

> This represents how you work towards your goal to share more moments of joy with the people you care about. Serving others is your 'why.' Without meaningful relationships, what is the point of the journey? Remind yourself of the story of Hercules or any hero from any movie. Did they improve their physique and mind only to 'look good and snap selfies'? Heck No!! They developed their talents to serve their teammates, friends, families, and communities.

22. Label each of your four friends: C. | A. | R. | E.

> This will remind you to practice Alden Mill's principles of C.A.R.E (connect, Achieve, Respect, Empower with your teammates, coaches, family, and friends. This is how you will build and maintain amazing relationships with the people you love and care about.

8. PASSION

23. Draw a distant mountain range beyond the mountain where you have planted your 'goal' flag.

> When a Black Belt Athlete reaches their goals, they don't stop! They look for the next challenge! Their next goal! A champion knows they are, and will always be, a work in progress. They're always passionately writing the next chapter of their story. Following their guiding star, always enjoying the process of being their best self. That's how Champions live!

Active Recall

Draw this picture in your "Black Belt Mentality Journal Template" now! Can you recite the story while you draw it? Practice here:

Bibliography

Adams, Scott. *How to Fail at Almost Everything and Still Win Big.* Penguin, 22 Oct. 2013.

Afremow, James A. *The Champion's Mind: How Great Athletes Think, Train, and Thrive.* New York, NY: Rodale, 2014.

Afremow, Jim. *The Champion's Mind.* Rodale Books, 15 May 2015.

Aïvanhov, Omraam Mikhaël. *Golden Rules for Everyday Life.* Editions Prosveta, 14 June 2012.

Allen, James. *As a Man Thinketh.* 1903. Sristhi Publishers & Distributors, 1 May 2021.

Allen, James. *As a Man Thinketh.* Philosopher's Notes, 2008.

Alter, Adam. *Irresistible: Why You Are Addicted to Technology and How to Set Yourself Free.* London: Vintage, 2017.

Balchan, Michael. "Hit the Focus Gym." Heroic, 2020, www.heroic.us/coach-practices/hit-the-focus-gym?fpr=dojodecision. Accessed 11 Jan. 2023.

Barker, Eric. *Barking Up the Wrong Tree.* HarperCollins, 16 May 2017.

Bassham, Lanny R. *With Winning in Mind: The Mental Management System – An Olympic Champion's Success System.* Flower Mound, TX: Mental Management Systems, 2011.

Baumeister, Roy F, and John Tierney. *Willpower.* Penguin, 1 Sept. 2011.

Baumeister, Roy F., and John Tierney. *Willpower: Rediscovering the Greatest Human Strength.* Penguin Press, 2012.

Bergeron, Ben, and Katrin Davidsdottir. *Chasing Excellence: A Story about Building the World's Fittest Athletes.* Austen, TX: Lioncrest Publishers, 2017.

Biswas-Diener, Robert, and Proquest (Firm). *The Courage Quotient: How Science Can Make You Braver.* San Francisco: Jossey-Bass, 2012.

Brown, Brene. *Daring Greatly: How the Courage to Be Vulnerable Transforms the Way We Live, Love, Parent, and Lead.* Penguin Random House Audio Publishing Group, 2017.

Butterworth, Eric. *Spiritual Economics.* Unity Books (Unity School of Christianity), 1 Feb. 2001.

Cabane, Olivia Fox. *The Charisma Myth: How Anyone Can Master the Art and Science of Personal Magnetism.* New York: Portfolio/Penguin, 2013.

Cain, Brian M. *One Percent Better.* Independently Published, 2023.

Cain, Brian. *The 10 Pillars of Mental Performance Mastery.* Createspace Independent Publishing Platform, 8 Dec. 2018.

Campbell, Joseph, and Diane K. Osbon. *Reflections on the Art of Living: A Joseph Campbell Companion.* New York, NY: Harper Collins, 1991.

Cardone, Grant. *The 10X Rule: The Only Difference between Success and Failure.* Hoboken, NJ: John Wiley & Sons, Inc, 2011.

Carnegie, Dale. *How to Win Friends and Influence People.* Simon & Schuster, 1936.

Carnegie, Dale. *How to Stop Worrying and Start Living.* S.L., Jaico Publishing House, 2019.

Carroll, Pete, et al. *Win Forever: Live, Work, and Play like a Champion.* London: Portfolio Penguin, 2011.

Cialdini, Robert B. *Influence: The Psychology of Persuasion.* 1984. Collins, 1 Feb. 2007.

Clear, James. *Atomic Habits: An Easy & Proven Way to Build Good Habits & Break Bad Ones.* Avery, 2018.

Cohen, Alan. *Why Your Life Sucks.* Bantam, 18 Dec. 2007.

Collins, James C. *Good to Great: Why Some Companies Make the Leap ... And Others Don't.* New York, NY: Harper Business, 16 Oct. 2001.

Covey, Stephen R. *Primary Greatness: The 12 Levels of Success.* New York: Simon & Schuster Paperbacks, 2016.

Covey, Stephen R. *The 7 Habits of Highly Effective People: Powerful Lessons in Personal Change.* London: Simon and Schuster, 15 Aug. 1989.

Csikszentmihalyi, Mihaly. *Flow: The Psychology of Optimal Experience.* New York: Harper and Row, 1990.

Cuddy, Amy. *Presence: Bringing Your Boldest Self to Your Biggest Challenges.* New York: Back Bay Books, 2018.

Dalio, Ray. *Principles.* Simon and Schuster, 7 Aug. 2018.

De Sena, Joe, and Jeff O'Connell. *Spartan Up! A Take-No-Prisoners Guide to Overcoming Obstacles and Achieving Peak Performance in Life.* Boston: Houghton Mifflin Harcourt, 2014.

De Sena, Joe, and John Durant. *Spartan Fit! 30 Days. Transform Your Mind. Transform Your Body. Commit to Grit. No Gym Required.* Houghton Mifflin Harcourt, 2016.

Divine, Mark, and Allyson Edelhertz Machate. *The Way of the SEAL: Think like an Elite Warrior to Lead and Succeed.* New York, NY: The Reader's Digest Association, Inc, 2018.

Donnelly, Darrin. *Think like a Warrior: The Five Inner Beliefs That Make You Unstoppable.* Lenexa, Kansas: Shamrock New Media, Inc, 2016.

Dorfman, H A. *Coaching the Mental Game.* Taylor Trade Pub, 2016.

Drucker, Péter. *The Effective Executive.* Routledge, 2018.

Duckworth, Angela. *Grit: The Power of Passion and Perseverance.* New York: Scribner, 2016.

Dweck, Carol S. *Mindset: The New Psychology of Success.* New York: Ballantine Books, 2008.

EDS / Hewlett Packard: Cat Herders (Super Bowl Ad). www.youtube.com/watch?v=G8SdsQjdHnM. Accessed 16 Jan. 2024.

Eknath, Easwaran. *Words to Live by: Inspiration for Every Day.* Nilgiri Press, 1996.

Eknath, Easwaran. *Words to Live by: Short Readings of Daily Wisdom.* Tomales, CA: Nilgiri Press, 2010.

Emerald, David. *The Power of TED: The Empowerment Dynamic.* Bainbridge Island, WA: Polaris Publishing, 2016.

Emerson, Ralph Waldo, et al. *Selected Writings of Ralph Waldo Emerson.* New York: Simon And Schuster Paperbacks, 2010.

Emmons, Robert A. *Gratitude Works! A Twenty-One-Day Program for Creating Emotional Prosperity.* Jossey-Bass, 2013.

Emmons, Robert A. *Thanks! How the New Science of Gratitude Can Make You Happier.* Houghton Mifflin Co., 2007.

Ericsson, Anders and Pool, Robert. *Peak: Secrets from the New Science of Expertise.* Boston: Mariner Books/Houghton Mifflin Harcourt, 2017.

Fitzgerald, Matt. *How Bad Do You Want It? Mastering the Psychology of Mind over Muscle.* VeloPress, 2015.

Fogg, B. J. *Tiny Habits: The Small Changes That Change Everything.* S. L., Houghton Mifflin Harcourt, 2020.

Ford, Debbie. *The Dark Side of the Light Chasers.* Riverhead Books, 1998.

Frankel, Viktor. *Man's Search for Meaning.* 1946. London: Pocket Books edition, 1997.

Gelb, Michael J. *The Art of Connection: 7 Relationship-Building Skills Every Leader Needs Now.* Novato, CA: New World Library, 2017.

Glei, Jocelyn K. *Manage Your Day-to-Day.* Amazon Publishing, 2013.

Goodwin, Doris Kearns. *Leadership in Turbulent Times.* New York: Simon & Schuster, 2018.

Gordon, Jon. *The Energy Bus.* John Wiley & Sons, 26 May 2015.

Green, Robert, and Joost Elffers. *The 48 Laws of Power.* London: Profile Books, 1998.

Greitens, Eric. *Resilience.* Houghton Mifflin, 2016.

Greitens, Eric. *Resilience: Hard-Won Wisdom for Living a Better Life.* Boston: Houghton Mifflin Harcourt, 2015.

Grover, Tim, and Shari Lesser Wenk. *Relentless: From Good to Great to Unstoppable.* Simon & Schuster, 2014.

Guise, Stephen. *How to Be an Imperfectionist: The New Way to Self-Acceptance, Fearless Living, and Freedom from Perfectionism.* Selective Entertainment, 2021.

Guise, Stephen. *Mini Habits.* CreateSpace, 22 Dec. 2013.

Hadfield, Chris. *An Astronaut's Guide to Life on Earth.* Toronto: Vintage Canada, 2015.

Haidt, Jonathan. *The Happiness Hypothesis.* Basic Books, 2006.

Hardy, Darren. *The Compound Effect: Multiplying Your Success, One Simple Step at a Time.* Da Capo Press, 2013.

Harris, Sam . "Gratitude | Waking Up." Https://Dynamic.wakingup.com/Course/CO12EEC99?Source=Content%20share&Share_id=A00DD7D2&Pack=PKWAVC&Code=SC3CD0697." Wakingup.com, dynamic.wakingup.com/course/CO12EEC99. Accessed 16 Jan. 2024.

Harris, Sam. "Start Here | Waking Up." Wakingup.com, dynamic.wakingup.com/course/CO6C3B2BQ?source=content%20share&share_id=22418087&pack=PFCE0B&code=SC3CD0697. Accessed 17 Jan. 2024.

Harris, Sam. "The Last Time | Waking Up." Wakingup.com, dynamic.wakingup.com/course/CO9D9C921?source=content%20share&share_id=BDF4BD4C&pack=PKWAVC&code=SC3CD0697. Accessed 16 Jan. 2024.

Harris, Sam. *Waking Up.* Simon and Schuster, 2014.

Helmstetter, Shad. *What to Say When You Talk to Your Self.* Simon and Schuster, 2017.

Henry, Todd. *Die Empty: Unleash Your Best Work Every Day.* New York: Portfolio/Penguin, 2015.

Herman, Todd. *The Alter Ego Effect: The Power of Secret Identities to Transform Your Life.* Harper Business, 2019.

Holiday, Ryan. *Ego Is the Enemy.* London: Profile Books, 2016.

Holiday, Ryan. *Stillness Is the Key.* Penguin, 1 Oct. 2019.

Holmes, Ernest. *The Art of Life.* New York, NY: Jeremy P. Tarcher/Penguin, 2004.

Irvine, William Braxton. *A Guide to the Good Life: The Ancient Art of Stoic Joy.* Oxford, NY: Oxford University Press, 2009.

Johnson, Brian. *Arete: Activate Your Heroic Potential.* Heroic Blackstone, 2023.

Kethledge, Raymond Michael, and Michael S. Erwin. *Lead Yourself First: Inspiring Leadership through Solitude.* New York, NY: Bloomsbury Publishing, 2018.

Kerr, James M. *Legacy*. London: Constable, 2013.

Kotler, Steven. *The Rise of Superman*. Houghton Mifflin Harcourt, 2014.

Kouzes, James, and Barry Posner. *The Leadership Challenge*. San Francisco, CA: Jossey-Bass, 2012.

Kwik, Jim. *Limitless: Upgrade Your Brain, Learn Anything Faster, and Unlock Your Exceptional Life*. Hay House Inc., 2020.

Leonard, George. *Mastery*. Plume, 1992.

Lopez, Shane J. *Making Hope Happen: Create the Future You Want for Yourself and Others*. New York: Atria Paperback, 2014.

Maslow, Abraham H. *Toward a Psychology of Being*. New York: Van Nostrand Reinhold Co, 1968.

Maslow, Abraham H., and Robert Frager. *Motivation and Personality*. Pearson Education, 1987.

McDougall, Christopher. *Natural Born Heroes: The Lost Secrets of Strength and Endurance*. London: Profile Books, 2016.

McGonigal, Kelly. *The Upside of Stress: Why Stress Is Good for You, and How to Get Good at It*. New York, NY: Avery, 2016.

McRaven, William H. *Make Your Bed: Little Things That Can Change Your Life ... And Maybe the World*. New York: Grand Central Publishing, 4 Apr. 2017.

McRaven, William H. *The Hero Code*. Grand Central Publishing, 13 Apr. 2021.

Michels, Barry, and Phil Stutz. *Coming Alive*. Random House, 22 Aug. 2017.

Miller, Donald. *Hero on a Mission*. HarperCollins Leadership, 11 Jan. 2022.

Mills, Alden. *Be Unstoppable*. Tilbury House, 2013.

Mills, Alden. "Unstoppable Teams 101." Heroic, www.heroic.us/101/unstoppable-teams?fpr=dojodecision. Accessed 16 Jan. 2024.

Mills, Alden M. *Unstoppable Teams: The Four Essential Actions of High-Performance Leadership*. HarperBusiness, 2019.

Morris, Thomas V. *The Stoic Art of Living: Inner Resilience and Outer Results*. Chicago: Open Court, 2004.

Napper, Dr. Paul, and Anthony Rao. *The Power of Agency*. St. Martin's Press, 5 Mar. 2019.

NCAA. "Estimated Probability of Competing in College Athletics." NCAA.org, 8 Apr. 2020, www.ncaa.org/sports/2015/3/2/estimated-probability-of-competing-in-college-athletics.aspx.

Neff, Kristin. *Self-Compassion: The Proven Power of Being Kind to Yourself*. New York: HarperCollins Publishers, 2011.

Newport, Cal. *How to Become a Straight-A Student: The Unconventional Strategies Real College Students Use to Score High While Studying Less.* New York: Broadway Books, 2007.

Newport, Cal. *So Good They Can't Ignore You: Why Skills Trump Passion in the Quest for Work You Love.* New York: Grand Central Publishing, 2012.

Oakley, Barbara. *A Mind for Numbers.* Penguin Publishing Group, 2014.

Oettingen, Gabriele. *Rethinking Positive Thinking.* Current, 2014.

Pang, Alex Soojung-Kim. *Rest: Why You Get More Done When You Work Less.* New York: Basic Books, 2016.

Pasricha, Neil. *The Happiness Equation: Want Nothing + Do Anything = Have Everything.* New York: G.P. Putnam's Sons, 2016.

Pryor, Karen. *Don't Shoot the Dog! The New Art of Teaching and Training.* Dorking, Surrey: Ringpress Books Ltd, 2018.

Rand, Ayn. *The Fountainhead.* Plume, 2005.

Rath, Tom. *Eat Move Sleep.* Missionday, LLC, 8 Oct. 2013.

Rice, Jerry, and Brian Curtis. *Go Long!* Ballantine Books, 29 Jan. 2008.

Robbins, Mel. *The 5 Second Rule: Transform Your Life, Work, and Confidence with Everyday Courage.* United States of America: Savio Republic, 2017.

Robertson, Donald J. *How to Think like a Roman Emperor.* St. Martin's Press, 2 Apr. 2019.

Robertson, Donald. *The Philosophy of Cognitive-Behavioural Therapy (CBT): Stoic Philosophy as Rational and Cognitive Psychotherapy.* London: Karnac, 2010.

Rohn, E. James. *Leading an Inspired Life.* Niles, IL: Nightingale Conant, 2010.

Rohr, Richard. *Falling Upward: A Spirituality for the Two Halves of Life.* San Francisco: Jossey-Bass, 2013.

Rosenberg, Merrick. *The Chameleon.* Take Flight Learning, 2016.

Rowling, J K. *Harry Potter #1: Harry Potter and the Sorcerer's Stone.* New York, NY: Scholastic, 1999.

Segar, Michelle. *No Sweat: How the Simple Science of Motivation Can Bring You a Lifetime of Fitness.* AMACOM, 2015.

Selk, Jason. *10-Minute Toughness: The Mental Exercise Program for Winning before the Game Begins.* New York: McGraw-Hill, 2009.

Siegel, Daniel J. *Mindsight: The New Science of Personal Transformation.* Bantam Books Trade Paperbacks, 2011.

St-Pierre, Georges. *GSP.* HarperCollins Publishers, 12 Nov. 2013.

St-Pierre, Georges, and Justin Kingsley. *GSP/The Way of the Fight.* HarperCollins, 2013.

Stevenson, Shawn. *Sleep Smarter: 21 Essential Strategies to Sleep Your Way to a Better Body, Better Health, and Bigger Success*. New York, NY: Rodale Books, 2016.

Stone, W. Clement. *The Success System That Never Fails*. HarperCollins Publishers, 2009.

Stutz, Phil, and Barry Michels. *The Tools*. Random House, 2 Jan. 2013.

Stutz, Phil, and Barry Michels. *The Tools: 5 Tools to Help You Find Courage, Creativity, and Willpower--and Inspire You to Live Life in Forward Motion*. Random House, 2023.

Syed, Matthew. *Black Box Thinking: Why Most People Never Learn from Their Mistakes—but Some Do*. Portfolio Penguin, 2016.

Tal Ben-Shahar. *The Pursuit of Perfect: How to Stop Chasing Perfection and Start Living a Richer, Happier Life*. McGraw Hill Professional, 3 Apr. 2009.

Troutwine Athletic Profile (TAP) | https://dojodecision.com/tap.

Waitzkin, Josh. *The Art of Learning: An Inner Journey to Optimal Performance*. New York: Free Press, 2008.

Walker, Matthew P. *Why We Sleep: Unlocking the Power of Sleep and Dreams*. New York, NY: Scribner, An Imprint of Simon & Schuster, Inc, 2017.

Williams, Mark G, et al. *Mindfulness: An Eight-Week Plan for Finding Peace in a Frantic World*. Emmaus, PA: Rodale Books, 2012.

Willink, Jocko. *Discipline Equals Freedom: Field Manual*. New York: St. Martin's Press, 2017.

Willink, Jocko, and Leif Babin. *The Dichotomy of Leadership: Balancing the Challenges of Extreme Ownership to Lead and Win*. New York: St. Martin's Press, 2018.

Wim Hof. *The Wim Hof Method: Activate Your Full Human Potential*. Boulder, CO: Sounds True, 2020.

Wooden, John, and Steve Jamison. *Wooden: A Lifetime of Observations and Reflections on and off the Court*. New York: Mcgraw-Hill, 1997.

Zander, Benjamin, and Rosamund Stone Zander. *The Art of Possibility*. London, Penguin Books, 2002.

About the Author

Tim McDermott is a college and youth lacrosse coach as well as a striving practitioner of the lesson he shares in this book.

Coach McDermott began developing these strategies to make his own Dojo Decision and develop his Black Belt Mentality as an All-American athlete at DIII Geneseo State, where he graduated early to accelerate his academic and athletic pursuits, finishing his college career and receiving his MBA at Loyola University.

Post college, he briefly played in Major League Lacrosse (MLL), before beginning his coaching career at the University of Virginia. Fueled by his passion for personal development, he took a brief hiatus from college coaching to explore his interest in peak performance, venturing into the realm of sports performance entrepreneurship while working for a sports psychology assessment company. At this time, he completed the inaugural Heroic Coaching program and became a certified Heroic Optimal Living Coach.

This eventually led him back into coaching the University of Utah MCLA club lacrosse program. There he served as the director of operations and an assistant coach, helping transition the team to the Division 1 ranks, which culminated in their first NCAA tournament appearance in 2023. Alongside building a Division 1 lacrosse program, Tim was instrumental in establishing a youth club program in Salt Lake City.

Presently, Tim coaches and leads his youth club's personal development program. His influence extends far beyond the playing field, collaborating with individuals, schools, and local businesses to help them unlock the full potential of their teams.

If you would like to work with Tim, he can be contacted at: https://dojodecision.com.

Made in the USA
Thornton, CO
01/01/25 08:17:46

bfc38ceb-99b9-4bf4-ac9a-678ecd6af6bdR01